THE MYTHOLOGY OF TRANSGRESSION

BOOKS BY JAMAKE HIGHWATER

FICTION

Mick Jagger: The Singer Not the Song

Anpao

Journey to the Sky

The Sun, He Dies

Legend Days

The Ceremony of Innocence

I Wear the Morning Star

Eyes of Darkness

Kill Hole

Dark Legend

Rama

POETRY

Moonsong Lullaby

Songs for the Seasons

NONFICTION

Rock and Other Four Letter Words

Indian America (A Fodor Guide)

Songs from the Earth: Native American Painting

Ritual of the Wind: Indian Ceremonies and Music

Dance: Rituals of Experience

Many Smokes, Many Moons: Indian History Through Indian Art

The Sweet Grass Lives On: Fifty Contemporary Indian Artists

The Primal Mind

Arts of the Indian Americas

Native Land: Sagas of American Civilizations

Shadow Show: An Autobiographical Insinuation

Words in the Blood: Anthology of Modern Indian Literature

Myth and Sexuality

The Language of Vision: Myth and Metaphor in the Arts

Athletes of the Gods: The Ritual Life of Sports

A Myth of Our Own: Studies of World Religions

THE MYTHOLOGY OF TRANSGRESSION

HOMOSEXUALITY

AS METAPHOR

JAMAKE

HIGHWATER

OXFORD UNIVERSITY PRESS

New York   Oxford

1997

Oxford University Press

Oxford   New York
Athens   Auckland   Bangkok   Bogotá   Bombay
Buenos Aires   Calcutta   Cape Town   Dar es Salaam   Delhi
Florence   Hong Kong   Istanbul   Karachi
Kuala Lumpur   Madras   Madrid   Melbourne
Mexico City   Nairobi   Paris   Singapore
Taipei   Tokyo   Toronto

and associated companies in
Berlin   Ibadan

Published by Oxford University Press, Inc.
198 Madison Avenue, New York, New York 10016

Oxford is a registered trademark of Oxford University Press

Library of Congress Cataloging-in-Publication Data
Highwater, Jamake.
The mythology of transgression : homosexuality as metaphor /
Jamake Highwater.
p.   cm.   Includes bibliographical references and index.
ISBN 0-19-510180-4
1. Homosexuality—Philosophy.   2. Homosexuality—Mythology.
3. Homosexuality—Religious aspects.   4. Social values.   5. Social
psychology.   I. Title.
HQ76.2.H54   1997
306.76'6'01—dc20   96-20576

9 8 7 6 5 4 3 2 1

Printed in the United States of America
on acid-free paper

FOR THOSE WHO PERISHED
AND FOR THE WITNESSES OF THE DYING

ALAN ALBERT

RICHARD BARR

JAMES LEO HERLIHY

PAUL JABARA

JOHN KUHNER

SHIPEN LEBZELTER

PAUL MONETTE

RICHARD THURN

JOHN WILLIAMSON

CONTENTS

THE MYTHOLOGY OF TRANSGRESSION

In astronomy, vast distance, but we never go into a foreign system. In geology, vast duration, but we are never strangers. Our metaphysic should be able to follow the flying force through all its transformation.
Ralph Waldo Emerson, "Nature," Essays, Second Series

Man's quest for certainty is, in the last analysis, a quest for meaning. But the meaning lies buried within himself rather than in the void he has vainly searched for portents since antiquity.
Loren Eiseley, The Man Who Saw Through Time

OUTSIDE

1 THE WALLS

Our most stubborn and pertinacious assumptions are precisely those which remain unconscious and therefore uncritical . . . concepts we take for granted without realizing that we do so at our peril. . . . The best and perhaps the only sure way of bringing to light and revivifying our fossilized assumptions, and of destroying their power to cramp and confine us, is by subjecting ourselves to the shock of contact with a very alien tradition.

Harold Osborne, Aesthetics and Art Theory

I am an outsider.

When I was about five or six years old, I didn't live in the "real" world. Instead, I lived on the "outside." I was an orphan.

I was taught only two rules at the orphanage: to conform and to obey.

Despite the Dickensian images of foundlings in books and musicals, children who live in orphanages are not jolly little waifs, strongly bonded to one another by their mutual adversity. To the contrary, they do not easily form trusting relationships. Abandonment drains children of the capacity for trust. Like prison inmates, alliances among orphans are not based on compassion and fraternity, but on political expediency, like military alliances.

In youth, most of us must run the gauntlet occasionally, but in order to survive in an orphanage a person must run the gauntlet almost every day. In the world of the dispossessed, every emotional predicament becomes a polarity of power or abuse. There are bullies and there are their victims on every playground, but in an orphanage, where even the ideal of familial love is absent, empathy does not exist. The authority of the strong is monolithic. The older boys dominate, and the younger boys submit to their domination. That's how it was for me in the two years I spent in an orphanage.

One of the older boys often invited me upstairs to wrestle. I didn't understand the implications of our game, but I urgently wanted to be liked, so I went along with the older boy's strategy. Not until a dozen years later did I become aware that the "wrestling" was not a game but a sexual act. I had no sense of molestation because I had no awareness of my own sexuality. For me the fondling was an enigmatic form of kindness that I accepted gratefully, because I had few memories and no understanding of parental love and affection. But I also had no memories or understanding of the rules that coerce us to feel shame and guilt about our bodies.

Only now, when I look back on that experience, do I realize, with a bit of anger, that the young man was exploiting me without my knowledge or consent. At the same time, I have come to understand that, in my own childish way, I was exploiting him.

We were both abandoned children. Refugees from family life, living in an institution where tenderness and generosity were so rare that the children quickly understood they were no longer special, that—for some unknown reason—they no longer deserved or received the love they imagined existed in the happy lives of children who were not abandoned. We were so desperate for tenderness that we armed ourselves against it by pretending we didn't want the approval and affection of adults.

So it is not surprising that, whatever the boy's purpose, I was grateful to him for his attention. I cannot easily speculate about the young man's motives. Was he starved for intimacy and searching for it in the only way he could, or was he indiscriminately acting on the visceral needs of a seventeen-year-old adolescent?

Though I was far too young to grasp his purpose, I was aware that he was providing something vaguely resembling the *intimacy* that is rarely experienced in orphanages, where children are not touched or hugged or held.

When the young man turned eighteen, he left the orphanage without saying good-bye. I remember nothing about him. Not his name. Not his face. I simply recall the distinctive odor of his body.

He joined the world of ordinary people. He got married. He had a child. Then one summer day, word came that the young man had gone off to the war in Korea, where he was killed. And that was the end of him.

As for me, I did not join the world. I stayed on in my island universe, unaware that I was not an ordinary person. I had no idea what "ordinary" meant. In the orphanage, none of us could possibly be ordinary children. We had none of the credentials and little of the experience of kids with neighborhoods, with mothers and fathers and grandparents; kids with a porch or a room or anywhere else called home. We were sheltered—thank goodness for that—but our shelter was an entirely different world from the homes of other children. We began as outsiders, and many of us would remain outsiders for a lifetime.

We often take for granted the notion that some people are insiders, while others are outsiders. But such a notion is a social contrivance, that, like virtually every public construct, is a legacy of a primordial and tribal mentality. If we doubt the existence of such tribalism, we need only recall the endless Balkan battles fought by various "ethnic outsiders." The wall that separates insiders from outsiders is not born of human nature but methodically built, brick by brick, by tribal convention. The "wall" about which I will often speak in this book is not an organism or a membranous extension of some inborn aspect of "human nature." It is a mechanistic process—a barrier meticulously constructed by erratic community decrees as a means of identifying those who are part of the group and marking those who are not. It is not difficult to imagine the chauvinism that requires a community to mark its territories and distinguish its members from its enemies. It is far more difficult to understand the kind of "outsiders" who are the subjects of this book—those who are part of the group and yet are rejected by their peers and cast into a terrible, internal exile. It is an exile called "alienation."

A few years after I was left at the orphanage by my mother, I was adopted and taken into a new world. It was only in that curious outside world that I came to understand the extent of my alienation. Whereas the young man who molested me had quite easily entered the world to become a "normal" person, I remained an outsider because of a multiplicity of cultural problems, which had little to do with sexuality. Gradually I realized that "alienation" suited me. Because of a few extraordinary teachers and elders who befriended me and praised my idiosyncracies, I was encouraged to speak my mind—to find a voice that could be heard *through the wall*. As a result, I eventually came to cherish my "alienation" as a gift.

I have spent most of my adult life in a ghetto among countless other outsiders who have also learned how to talk through the wall. We revel in each other's voices, but the people within the walled city are often offended by the sounds of outsiders that penetrate the sturdy barriers of conformity. They attempt to silence the voices, but occasionally the valiant utterances of outsiders manage to loosen a bit of mortar, perhaps even dislodge a few bricks, opening the wall to a strong, new light that has never before been seen by those who are safely walled up.

Not everyone has a voice. Many outsiders cannot speak through walls, and, as a consequence, they become silent and invisible. Some give up their voices willingly. Others cannot face the ferocious silence of their lives; so they replace their genuine voices with incomprehensible shrieks of rage. They bombard the wall with wrath or batter it with explosives. The silence is broken by their rage, but nothing changes. They remain outsiders who are desperate to be allowed into the world.

There are, however, those who will not be silenced or driven into self-destructive violence. There are always those who must speak or die. It was the African-American author James Baldwin who said: "The victim who is able to articulate the situation of the victim has ceased to be a victim—he or she has become a threat."

Most of us regard alienation as a tragic estrangement from the group, a terrible situation that deprives us of all the bounties of social privilege. We believe that alienation means that we don't measure up, that we don't fit, that we can never be members of the "A Team." We see ourselves as outsiders who ardently want to be insiders. Our sense of isolation is so profound that we often accept our socially mandated role as aliens without questioning if the social attitude that makes us outsiders is a malady we harbor or if, perhaps, it is the malady of the group that designates us as aliens: as niggers, queers, kikes, chinks, and the dozens of other marginal persons whose very existence is denigrated by words intended to hurt.

In much the way that I will attempt to redefine the core meaning of a term like "transgression," I also want to modify what we usually mean when we speak of alienation. These definitions are essential, because words are so often loaded by social manipulation, often attaining a significance in one social system that is quite different from their meanings in other systems. I don't use the term "alienation" to describe simply a sense of castigation or the feeling people have if they are ostracized; nor do I mean a condition of being emotionally isolated or socially estranged, though such conditions and feelings can have an impact on an "outsider." In this book, I want to reexamine the basic meaning of the term "alien," which is derived from the Old French *allien* and the Latin *alienus*: "a person of another place." I also want to examine the equally significant Old French term *alius*—referring to the "other" or "another," which does not necessarily signify a person from a foreign land.

It is widely believed that alienation disempowers people. Some of our most vivid social and political rhetoric is built on this particular notion of the injustice of alienation. But there are also elements of alienation we rarely discuss. What interests me is the empowering aspects of alienation suggested by Arthur Miller when he said, "Without alienation, there can be no politics." So I am interested in the alienation of the aliens who stand at the center of their own worlds and are regarded as "outsiders" only because alienation is so endemic in twentieth-century Western societies that it is regarded as the "norm" against which the "other" is judged to be "another." Clearly, I am reiterating a concept of R. D. Laing: "I'm okay, but everybody else is nuts."

In *The Sane Society*, his popular study of social psychology, Erich Fromm described an attitude of the West that has managed to normalize the process by which the group disempowers and stigmatizes the idiosyncratic behavior of the individual. Fromm spoke of a widespread social mentality that confuses the experience of the self with the experience of the group. When such a psychological distortion occurs, the group becomes not an amplification of individuals but a substitute for the individual, which is a subject I will return to several times in the course of this book.

From the time of the Industrial Revolution, the alienation of self in response to the conformist pressure of the group became such a common social experience that it resulted in a society largely composed of those who have no awareness of the difference between the idiosyncratic self and the conformity of the group. This process has become a quirky result of that "democratic" attitude that confuses equality with conformity. The pandemic alienation described by Fromm became a social malady, resulting in people who are not the masters of their own decisions or their own acts. On the contrary, they became slaves to the socially determined expectations of their acts. As Fromm pointed out, when depersonalization becomes the norm, individualists are experienced in the same way that objects are experienced: with the senses and with common sense, but without empathy or the realization that there is a crucial relationship in human society between one's self and the limitless possibilities of others. The community ceases to be a collection of individuals and begins to look like an alliance of clones.

Writing in 1955, Erich Fromm pictured Western society as a vast population of dissociated, unrealized persons who are largely estranged from themselves as individuals. That estrangement is so extensive that "normal" people have somehow turned those who are visibly individualistic into outcasts or aliens. In this curious way, those who are not alienated from themselves are regarded as aliens. As we will see, in the nineteenth century, the mad were regarded as "aliens" and their physicians were called "alienists." The French word *alieniste*, from *aliene*, means "'insane" and is derived from the Latin *alienatus*, the past participle of *alienare*, "to deprive of reason." In this way, alienation insinuates madness.

Lewis Carroll understood this dilemma.

"But I don't want to go among mad people," Alice remarked.

"Oh, you can't help it," said the Cheshire Cat, "we're all mad here. I'm mad. You're mad."

"How do you know I'm mad?" said Alice.

"You must be," said the Cat, "or you wouldn't have come here."

As I see it, alienation is not estrangement from the community—nor is it estrangement from the communal madness of what Carroll calls "here" in Alice's Wonderland. Alienation is estrangement from the self. Fromm would tell us that we have confused the "here" (the community) with the self. He would say that we have substituted our essential relationship to ourselves with a highly socialized kinship to the group. He would say that estrangement from one's self is madness, and such madness is so pandemic in the West that normalcy is now built on the assumption that a person's ultimate relationship is to others—rather than to *one's self*.

"You must be mad," the wise Cat might tell us, "or you can't be one of us."

In a curious twist of social attitudes, those who are in touch with the community, but out of touch with themselves, have somehow decided that those who seem to be out of touch with the community are alienated, even if they are fully in touch with themselves.

What is most curious about this social deception is that those who experience themselves an individuals rather than as mere aspects of a group are often convinced that their critics are right—they believe that they somehow fall short of the standards set by the community. Defeated by consensus, they internalize the contempt the group feels for them, and, consequently, they fulfill their role as self-denigrating aliens and outsiders. To be hated by others is far less destructive than to loathe one's self. Yet the one inevitably turns into the other.

Outsiders find it very difficult to slip past the sentries who guard the ordinary, the normal, even when what passes as "normalcy" seems quite arbitrary. It sometimes appears to me that members of the group can actually *smell* outsiders, in much the way creatures sniff one another for tell-tale scents that determine friends and foes. It is as if the status of outsiders leaves a palpable and indelible trace on some people. As an adult, I eventually came to regard that trace as a mark of honor.

Outsiders don't act like "ordinary" people. Many outsiders don't look like the people in movies and magazines and advertisements. They are the wrong color or the wrong shape. They have the wrong way of moving, and they have the wrong light in their eyes. Some of them don't make love the way other people make love.

In our world, outsiders are not honored or venerated. They are castigated. As we will see, they are often regarded as freaks of nature. They are avoided and ostracized. To be left on the bench is a familiar trauma of childhood. To be left on the bench for an entire lifetime is for many people a catastrophe. What causes such a fate? Is it something inherent in the rejected outsider or something intrinsic in the society that rejects the unfamiliar and, through rejection, turns the remarkable or the unfamiliar into the abnormal? When speaking of her freakishly large thumbs, the main character of Tom Robbins's novel *Even Cowgirls Get the Blues* says that her deformed thumbs are not her problem. "It's the people who are deformed by society that I pity."

It seems to me that we live in a society in which science, religion, and government have consistently conspired to keep many exceptional people on the bench. Yet, for me, being "left out" has always been a luxury, because it allowed me to evade the rules governing conformity. For me, to be left out was to be forced into a personal quest I may not have dared if I had other, less arduous options. For as long as I can recall, I have always seen my separateness as the basis of a cherished freedom from constraints, preconceptions, and social expectations. Not everyone is so fortunate. Many people internalize the mentality that disempowers them. My awareness of such misfortunate people is one of my motives for writing this book.

I owe much of my ability to celebrate differences to my biological mother. Before she abandoned me, she taught me some important lessons. When I was ridiculed by children because I looked different from them, she told me: "Chocolate ice cream doesn't run off and kill itself just because somebody orders a vanilla cone." And when I was to be adopted she warned me: "You are going into a world where the men give up everything that's best about being a human being to women and children. Don't let them take it away from you!"

Children are often warned that they will not be loved if they do not behave. In other words, children are told that if they act like outsiders, they will become outsiders. But for me it was quite different. How could it have been otherwise? When your family and your society have already abandoned you, there remains little reason to worry about censure, rejection, and abandonment. In an orphanage, you are your own person and your own family, whether you like it or not. Abandonment becomes a way of life. Either you become the center of your own world or you don't survive.

I don't dispute the current wisdom that views *Homo sapiens* as having a biological predisposition to form familial relationships. Nor do I dispute that we are wired in such a way that we want to be held and protected and loved. We may even be biologically programmed to adhere to the rules of our particular group and respond with shame and guilt when we break those rules. But, by and large, I think we know nothing about the rules until someone teaches them to us. And that's the point I intend to make with the story of the young man who sexually molested me.

How can I be so blasé about an abuse that is regarded in our society as an appalling crime against nature? Is it possible that I came away undamaged from two years of a "loathsome" experience because I didn't know it was "loathsome"?

The evidence of decades of transcultural studies indicates that social codes and moral strictures are socially constructed, but based on nonspecific biological elements. Apparently, we have an inborn capacity for the response we call shame. But we are taught which of our actions are shameful. We cannot become victims of shame until we are taught about shame. Yet, despite the evidence, there is still an insistence among both religious fundamentalists and many sociobiologists that our sense of shame is an unalterable part of a specific moral conscience that we are born with. A belief in such "inborn" shame is the basis of the Western mythology of transgression.

The fundamental differences between the cultural values of various societies have been observed for decades.[1] But what still fascinates me are the remarkably different ways (from reverence and worship to rejection and punishment) in which various cultures respond to those who do not conform to mythologically based rules, whether those rules deal with morality, sexuality, or norms of biology and anatomy.

Though many behavioral scientists believe that human beings, like dogs and chimpanzees, are social animals who universally create close-knit, conformist, and familial groups, there is, nonetheless, little doubt that major human achievements have resulted from the efforts of people who have not necessarily been members of the pack. On the contrary, major contributions in almost every field (for better or for worse—whether it be art, homicide, science, religion, warfare, or politics) have been made by mavericks, loners, misfits, oddballs, and nonconformists. And their offbeat contributions have been so remarkably sublime or so appallingly heinous, depending on one's point of view, that romantics invented the notion that true greatness and inventiveness are the result of emotional hardship, financial privation, or a dysfunctional life. In fact, greatness has regularly been viewed as a sublime affliction—the pearl that results from the ailment of the oyster—a malady that provides an amplitude of vision not available to those who conform to society's rules.

Being an outsider among outsiders, I didn't realize in the orphanage how fortunate I was to live in my island universe. It was only later that I discovered my good fortune. And that discovery was largely based on my gradual realization that I had been spared the shame of a "shameful" experience because I had never been taught to feel shame about my body or what had been done to it in the orphanage.

In an era when everyone seems to be a victim with a horrifying story to tell about childhood molestation, I'm in the curious position of knowing that I came away from my own "trauma" with no apparent damage and no sense of shame. No one has ever proved to my satisfaction that my experience of molestation had any impact on my sexual orientation, my social attitudes, my artistic abilities, my political point of view, my emotional health, or my attitudes about men, women, and children.

Why wasn't I damaged by prolonged sexual abuse? Could it be that I had never been taught that such an experience is shameful? Could it be that I felt no shame because the young man didn't tell me that the "game" was *our secret*—something I was not supposed to mention to anyone? Could it be that I had not been taught that "homosexuality" is evil? Could it be that I was spared the expertise of therapists who inadvertently cajole molested children into nightmarish self-recrimination? Could it be, finally, that I could not feel shame until I was methodically and systematically *taught shame* by example, by command, by dictum, by discipline, and by every other available social and psychological mechanism used to shape our most fundamental and intimate attitudes and beliefs?

What are we before we are taught the rules of our particular society? Are we examples of those fascinating but troubling freaks of nature called "wild children"—raised in the wilderness by wolves or apes? Are we deformities, semihuman monstrosities who still possess that mysterious state of mind that mythologies tell us existed before the incursion of morality? Are we creatures in possession of an elusive heritage to which we so often allude, when we speak with remorse of lost innocence and with longing for that paradisiacal state of mind called Eden?

Such questions raise issues that may make some of us exceptionally uncomfortable. Though religious fundamentalists and sociobiologists would like us to believe that morality is an inborn knowledge based on either "divine law" or "natural law" or on some other fixed and eternal order, there is an overwhelming amount of transcultural evidence suggesting that morality is nothing more or less than a set of social agreements and arbitrary conventions about what is good and what is normal as distinct from what is evil and abnormal.

Such relativism suggests that if we do not know the rules, we don't know we are breaking them. If we don't know about "heterosexuality," we don't know about "homosexuality." The predisposition to create gender roles and social rules may be intrinsic, but it seems to me that the roles and the rules themselves are highly capricious.

If, in the judgment of our Western societies, we are different in appearance or behavior, we are too often in danger of being rejected because we seem to offend community expectations and standards. The rejection of those who do not conform to social expectation is built on one of our most pertinacious assumptions, which presumes that our community standards are the result of some kind of revealed and eternal *truth*, whether that truth happens to be scientific or religious. It is the inflexibility of that kind of truth that has been the basis of both social achievements as well as every form of bigotry.

There are many ways in which various people have offended community standards. At one time, African Americans did so when they used public restrooms or fraternized with whites. They were castigated for these violations because many community leaders believed that their rules about "race" were infallible. How could they think otherwise? After all, theologians had explained that "Negroes" were the offsprings of Ham—that unsavory biblical character who was cursed to be the servant of his brothers because he looked on his naked (drunken) father, Noah. What is more, several famous nineteenth-century craniometricians, like neurologist Paul Broca, devised a complex set of cephalic indexes based on measurements of the human skull, and they concluded on the basis of such studies that Africans were mentally inferior to white Europeans and Americans.

How could both science and religion be wrong about the rules?

Women also offended social standards when they expressed the desire to be doctors instead of housewives, particularly since it was presumed by the best scientific minds of the early twentieth century that females were impervious to the enrichment of education. In religion, the disempowerment of women had supposedly been announced by an authority no less impressive than God Himself. According to Genesis (3:16), the Lord said to Eve: "I will greatly multiply your pains in childbearing. In sorrow you will bring forth children. And your desire shall be for your husband, and he shall rule over you."

Even Jews, whose God is often interpreted as having demonized women, were themselves demonized by anti-Semites who accused them of breaking the irrefutable rules governing physical normalcy, when anti-Semites created the witless notion that Jews were freaks with horns hidden in their curly hair.

Generation after generation, judges, politicians, clergy, and scientists justified the punishment of outsiders because they claimed to possess a truth and a righteousness that others did not possess. And, yet, those religious doctrines, those family values, those community standards, and those scientific truths that long vindicated the harassment of mavericks have faltered and failed, and they have been relentlessly changed, time and again, slowly and imperfectly. Yet, as fundamentalism makes clear, the more imperfect the truth the more vicious its punishment of nonconformists.

Today the "truths" have changed to such an extent that we begin to suspect that perhaps our avowed rules of conduct may have no basis in either science or heaven. As Oxford professor J. M. Roberts reports in his *History of the World*:*

> By 1914, science obviously was contributing to an ill-defined sense of strain in European civilization. The most apparent manifestation of this was the problems it posed to traditional religious values. The determinism derived from evolutionary theories and the relativism suggested by anthropology and physics sapped confidence in the values of objectivity and rationality, which had been central to European civilization. . . . As the twentieth century went on, science seemed increasingly difficult to reconcile with any fixed form of belief. It appeared to stress the relativism of points of view and the pressure of circumstances in the establishment of truth up to a point at which any unchallengeable assumption or truth or viewpoint seemed ruled out.

Clearly, the majority of our problems at the end of the twentieth century have resulted from the decline of the most rudimentary concepts and beliefs of the Judeo-Christian worldview we collectively call Western civilization. Yale University historian R. R. Palmer and his colleague Joel Colton, of Duke University, put it this way:

> The law of universal gravitation reigned unquestioned, and with it, hardly less so, the geometry of Euclid and a physics that was

---

* In order to retain the uninterrupted flow of this narration, attribution for all materials quoted and paraphrased in this book are placed in the Bibliography under the author's name. If there is more than one book or article listed for a given author, then the date of publication of the work from which a quotation or paraphrase is drawn is listed after the name of the author each time it appears in the text: for example (Campbell, 1986).

basically mechanics. The ultimate nature of the universe was thought to be regular, orderly, predictable, and harmonious with Christian values; it was timeless and unchanging. By 1914, the old conceptions had begun to yield on every side.

And yet, as we will see, the Judeo-Christian mythology that produced traditional Western concepts and beliefs has continued to have a subversive influence on almost every aspect of our lives long after the concepts and beliefs have eroded. The harrowing breakdown of Western values has raised a firestorm of reaction among those who are inclined to turn their convictions into hysterical dogma when their beliefs are challenged. The zealots are not alone. Many good people are deeply frightened because it begins to occur to them that all the rules on which they have built their lives are somewhat less than perfect and far less than eternal. Somehow, this popular realization comes very belatedly, and it is still resisted at the close of the twentieth century. In "Dover Beach," the British poet Matthew Arnold faced that Western predicament almost one hundred years ago, while the rest of us have taken a great deal longer to recognize the cultural calamity that Arnold and many other philosophers and artists saw with great clarity.

> . . . for the world, which seems
> To lie before us like a land of dreams,
> So various, so beautiful, so new,
> Hath really neither joy, nor love, nor light,
> Nor certitude, nor peace, nor help for pain;
> And we are here as on a darkling plain
> Swept with confused alarms of struggle and flight,
> Where ignorant armies clash by night.

For insiders—for "ordinary" people—the world is no longer a safe place, and so they fear that the barbarians have won their battle against Western civilization. Such fear may be fitting. One thing about any civilization seems to be an inescapable historical process: If people wait long enough on the outside of the walled city, they will inevitably survive the collapse of the civilization that excludes them and be among the barbarians who pick up the pieces of broken worlds.

As I see it, all walls—all rules—are obsolescent. So in a disintegrating world of obsolescent rules, what is the predicament of marginal people who did not make the rules in the first place, but always suffered under them? In other words, now that the carefully constructed city's walls are coming down, what is the role of those who had to live outside and beyond the gates?

Today outsiders face an even greater "alienation" because they are perceived as the barbarians who brought down the protective walls of order and civilization. The rhetoric of fundamentalists is filled with anguished contempt for the destroyers of their orderly world. Yet, ironically, it was some of the best and brightest minds produced by Western civilization itself who invented the revolutionary ideas and strategies that have caused the collapse of Western religious and scientific certitude. Though it may seem that deconstructionist philosophers like David Hume and Friedrich Nietzsche, psychological theorists like Sigmund Freud, physicists like Niels Bohr, evolutionists like Charles Darwin, political theorists like Karl Marx, or tonality-defying composers such as Arnold Schoenberg, or realism-debunking painters like Pablo Picasso represent the very epitome of Western civilization, at least in terms of the Judeo-Christian cosmography, they were, on the contrary, the people who brought down the walls of Western civilization, questioning the nature of perception, questioning the religious basis of morality, refuting the mechanistic nature of reality, disputing the story of human genesis, and even rejecting the validity of traditional Western imagery and tonality in painting and music. As a result, religious law has been enormously compromised. A great many American Catholics are in conflict with their church about many issues, including the celibacy of the clergy and the use of birth control by the laity. Darwin's revisions of biblical genesis still draws fire from so-called creationists. Many postquantum physicists have suggested that the cosmos is in a state of chaos rather than the idealized vision of order at the heart of Judeo-Christian-Islamic mythologies. The scientific compromise of religious law has spilled over into civic law, calling into question the nature of good and evil, of justice and injustice. On every front, the Judeo-Christian ethos has been under fire. Yet Darwin, Bohr, and other Western revolutionaries were merely the most recent source of earthquakes in a long succession of cultural jolts. The earth began to shake under the stolid feet of Western civilization at the time of Copernicus, who dared to suggest that the earth is not the center of the universe, and effectively kicked human beings from their imaginary place at center stage. The concepts changed, but the mythology of the West refused to change.

A theme I will often recapitulate in this book is the relationship of a society's mythology to that society's particular definition of reality. Every society begins to draw its intellectual and spiritual boundaries by asking very much the same abstract questions: Where do we go when we die? Who made us? What is good and what is evil? Is there purpose in our lives?

What has been remarkable to me in my cross-cultural studies is the realization that most groups of people have come up with drastically different moral stories as a means of answering their fundamental questions. Taken together, those highly diverse stories compose every society's distinctive mythology. It is on the basis of such a unifying mythology that all the values of the community are founded—political values, attitudes about morality, as well as religious convictions, and even cosmology, mathematics, and science. When people of a society speak of "reality," they are inevitably referring to a particular mythic vision of the cosmos that they believe to be so essential to the survival of their society that they allow little or no dissent from the meaning of the mythic tales they repeat generation after generation. In the West, this unique and entirely invented mythology is often regarded as factual history. Even the Western administration of justice has a mythic resonance through thousands of years of mythic adages: "And if any mischief follow, then thou shalt give life for life, eye for eye, tooth for tooth, hand for hand, foot for foot, burning for burning, wound for wound, stripe for stripe" (Exodus 21:23). A cornerstone of Western retaliatory justice turns out to be nothing more than a rather disquieting remnant of one story from one tribe's mythology.

Faith and philosophy once unified the West. Today various notions of faith, philosophy, and science are at great odds with the mythic beliefs and common wisdom of the great majority of people. But ideas are not the only issues that divide us. Sameness of appearance has always been a device of unity and alliance, and difference has always been the basis of disharmony. People who look the same as one another, who act the same, usually perceive each other as allies. Familiarity and sameness are comforting. Disparity is suspicious and fearsome. For some curious reason, in many societies people tend to see difference as deformity. They seem to experience the same discomfort in the presence of someone who is physically handicapped (someone "deformed") as they do when they find themselves with someone whose sexuality does not meet the community's expectations of humanness. Oddity is seen as perversity. Eccentricity is explained away, at best, as flamboyance or, at worst, as disease and depravity. In this way, the unfamiliar is easily transformed into a social response that equates difference with "deformity" and "abnormality."

This perception of "deformity" is often considered a transgression, as we will see when discussing the transgressive aspects of "deformity" as a mark of distinction or as a symbol of a burden placed on people by God.

For those who are different, that widespread community disdain for difference is so real and so constant that it sometimes causes outsiders to believe that they really must be hateful. One of many possible responses of those who are disdained is the tendency to internalize self-contempt, to regard marginality as a burden instead of a gift. Such people who are burdened by their nonconformity believe that they are the *cause* rather than the *object* of hatred; and so they begin to believe they deserve to be objects of hate, which in turn gives way to self-contempt or an unbridled bigotry toward other outsiders who are perceived as being even more "hateful" than they are. There is probably no bigotry as aggressive and cruel as the bigotry of those who are themselves the victims of bigotry.

R. D. Laing once noted that when you destroy a people's experience of themselves, they become destructive. There is little wonder that so many denigrated people politicized their rage, making a cause of their self-contempt. When people can no longer deal with their profound resentment of the people who have made them feel worthless, it seems to many of them that the only way out of their dilemma is to do harm to those who make them feel worthless or to do harm to themselves because you believe they truly are worthless. In one way or another, people who are perpetually rejected and abused are impelled to act out the destruction of their self-respect by becoming destructive. We are so accustomed to thinking of sociopathic behavior as an expression of "alienation" that we forget that it is also possible to turn the idiosyncratic energy of "alienation" into creative efforts.

Aggression is just one of the many ways in which outsiders deal with their sense of "alienation." There are also people who use "alienation" as a springboard for achievement and invention. At the same time, there are people who capitulate to their abusers because they cannot endure the enormity of their stigma. The destruction of self-respect is often played out as silent rage—becoming, instead of aggression toward others, a brutal form of self-denunciation.

Given the social displacement of being different, it is not surprising that many outsiders have made desperate and even heroic efforts to change their appearances, to alter their identities, and to closet and hide their behavior in an effort to avoid rejection by all the people who would turn them into outcasts if they knew their secrets. How much easier it is to remain silent or to laugh at a bigoted joke, instead of objecting vocally because the joke is made at one's own expense.

If people see themselves as victims who deserve contempt, then they usually regard their "alienation" or their closet or bigoted jokes as warranted abuse. Abuse is completely circular in its impact: the abused believe they are worthy of abuse, and the abusers believe that the passivity of those they attack corroborates their worthlessness.

Despite all this bad news, there are also aspects of "alienation" that are not denigrating. It is possible that being an outcast can provide a person with a unique and powerful vision of the world inaccessible to insiders. But it takes a great deal of experience to deal with hatred without turning it into self-contempt. To achieve freedom from the constraints of someone else's notion of "normalcy" is what turns the victim into a social threat. Articulate victims are a threat precisely because they stand somewhere *outside* the social norms that are the basis of their "alienation." And because they possess the unmistakable advantage of being witnesses to their own calamities, they are able, if they will, to describe their social dilemma from a vantage unregulated and uncensored by the social presumptions that have made them outsiders. In recent decades, many outcasts have so successfully challenged the rules of the dominant society that the rules have come into serious question, allowing the consideration of alternative points of view. Those alternatives have chipped away at the biases and power of those who have long been in control of the lives of marginal people. The result, at least so far, has been a very self-concious *tolerance* that falls short of true respect for people and conduct that is different.

The idea of the insider is itself a myth, for no one, finally, stands entirely as the realistic hero of any community. Everyone's life contains some kind of transgressive behavior. But, for our purposes, the myth of the idealized insider has enormous weight simply because the Western religious model has gone to such great lengths to concoct a myth about an insidious "outsider"—the leper, the unclean, the abomination, the outcast, the alien, the misfit, and the "other"—who is always seen as the cause of disease and disaster. The myth of this abomidable "other" is so pervasive in every aspect of Western social consciousness that those who feel left out usually believe that they were left out because of the unlimited power of a mythic oligarchy of insiders.

In other essays, I have referred to the persona of the insider as the Emperor (*Language of Vision*). He is the quintessential patriarch. He wants to discover "the meaning of life," whereas mythologist Joseph Campbell (1986) would tell him that what he really should be after is "an experience of life." As Oscar Wilde shrewdly observed: If such insiders like the Emperor were given the chance to chose between going to heaven or hearing a lecture about heaven, they would go to the lecture. The Emperor—the mythic insider—believes that facts inform us. Unlike the dauntless, medieval outsider on his fabled quest, who lets the reins lie slack on the horse's neck as he ventures into the very darkest part of the forest, the Emperor anxiously tugs at the reins, fearful of being carried away. The insider in us dreads the impetuousness of the horse, for the mythic horse represents the boundless possibilities of nature. And so the fainthearted Emperor insists on retaining control of the beast.

The outsider is another mythic character in the story of Western civilization. In response to the Emperor's apprehension of the dark forest, the outsider exclaims: "Yield to nature. Experience the astonishment of facing the unknown. Let nature take you on its own journey." But the Emperor of the Western world inevitably counters: "Correct nature! Cage and domesticate it! Do not let it lead you into the fearsome possibilities of the unknown!"

In order for me to explore an alternative story that I believe underlies the mythology that bounds our lives, I must tell stories from an alternative mythology, one that places the insider on the outside. It is through such contrariness, through such a process of turnabout, that innovators, eccentrics, visionaries, and artists have made their voices heard and have, therefore, turned their alienation into an expressive gift.

It is in this alternative and mythic context that I see the insider. So I am speaking metaphorically when I envision the insider standing before a mirror, rarely questioning the universality of the image in the glass. Yet, in another mythic context, an outsider like Lewis Carroll's

Alice stands somewhere on the other side of the glass, looking back at the world with a unique clarity of vision, with the rare ability to see the unexpected that is inaccessible to the insider. By stepping through the looking glass, Alice transcends her world and finds herself "somewhere else." But in order to step through the glass, she has to cross— *to transgress*. That positive and adventurous process of transgression is one of the themes of this book.

People who exist at the margins of society are very much like Alice. They are not required to make the tough decision to risk their lives by embarking on an adventure of self-discovery. They have already been thrust far beyond the city's walls that keep ordinary people at a safe distance from the unknown. For at least some outsiders, "alienation" has destroyed traditional presumptions of identity and opened the mythic hero's path to the possibility of discovery. What outsiders discover in their adventures on the other side of the looking glass is the courage to repudiate self-contempt and recognize their "alienation" as a precious gift of freedom from arbitrary norms that they did not make and did not sanction. At the moment a person questions the validity of the rules, the victim is no longer the victim.

"These are singular people," the remarkable American photographer Diane Arbus once said of her models. They are people

> who appear like metaphors somewhere farther out than we do, beckoned, not driven, invented by belief, author and hero of a real dream by which our own courage and cunning are tested and tried; so that we may wonder all over again what is veritable and inevitable and possible, and what it is to become whoever we may be.

Almost two decades ago, I wrote a book called *The Primal Mind* in which I attempted to consecrate people who are outsiders:

> I intend to celebrate those multitude of things that make us distinctive and unique. I hope to convince those who live within a monopolistic mentality that "alienation" is a precious fact of life that has validity and gives vitality to thoughts born of our failure to be the *one* people we thought and hoped we were. This affirmation of the many ideals of outsiders may serve those for whom "alienation" has been a terrible castigation rather than a gift, for whom it has been a blemish on some impossible Faustian dream of human conformity and spiritual unity. I hope to transform a

generalization into a cultural metaphor. I believe that in the experience of the outsider there is an important lesson to be learned. But the virtues of this lesson are not accessible to those who can only see through one cultural window—one sexuality, one mentality, one reality. It demands more than sight to see. It requires vision. And vision, by the definitions of all the prophets, is the gift of those who stand in an ideal isolation . . . astronomers of those deepest spaces where we flash our desperate messages to one another across the infinite space that separates us.

In *The Primal Mind*, it was my intention to celebrate diversity and cultural "alienation." In *The Mythology of Transgression*, I wish to understand the origins of the ancient, inflexible, and pertinacious assumptions of religion and science that turned millions of unique individuals into freaks of nature, abominations, and aliens in their own lands.

INSIDE

2

THE WALLS

It was like those myths of amazing strangers, who arrive at an island, gods or demons, bringing good and evil to the innocence of the inhabitants . . . words never heard before.

Joseph Conrad, Heart of Darkness

When I was adopted and taken from the isolation of the orphanage, I found myself in a new world that has never ceased to amaze and bewilder me. As an orphan, I had been a detached and solitary child living with other detached and solitary children, who, like me, had muddled histories, derelict families, and little grasp of the bonds of blood and emotion. But in the world outside the orphanage, I discovered that I was no longer just a foundling among foundlings. I had somehow become an oddity among "normal" children. I was a kid with a confused identity, a borrowed family, a borrowed name, and an inability to connect with other children, for whom interpersonal *connections* were the most important function of both family and community life.

Like so many other "different" children, I became an outsider. And like many other young people, I was overwhelmed by a sense of alienation that I could not easily reverse by transforming "alienation" into a precious gift—the kind of *cherished alienation* that is one of the themes of my prior books.

Conversations on the playground were incomprehensible to me. My classmates talked about fathers, summer camps, and cars, about family vacations, toys, and favorite baseball teams. They also talked about God and sex and the Boy Scouts. Most of their conversation was entirely unfamiliar. It dealt with things of which I knew little or nothing. I could not respond or react; so I was driven into an embarrassed silence. And my silence on the playground sent me farther and farther into reclusion.

I knew that the kids had sized me up the way people scrutinize strangers who drift into their neighborhoods. They sensed that I was not one of them. They made a wide circle around me day by day, gazing at me as if I were indecipherable. Something ominous came into their eyes when they looked at me. I realized that they were waiting for me to explain myself, but I was afraid to talk about my predicament because I realized that the truth about me would be scorned.

I dared not admit that I lived with people who were not my parents because I was afraid I would be asked why my real family had given me away to strangers. So I lied. When my classmates bragged about all the activities they shared with their fathers, I lied again. Gradually, I began to believe that lies provided my only possible connection with strangers because they were the only "facts" that gave me something in common with other people. Either I lied in order to appear to be just like other children or I remained silent, turning my life into a dirty little secret. I had never before felt shamed by my identity. But shame had now become my only emotional response to myself and my history.

The language of insiders is aimed at the exclusion of outsiders. I understood all too well that my classmates expressed themselves in vicious terms whenever they talked about things they rejected. It didn't take long for me to understand that they had a great many cruel words for things and people they didn't like. Gradually, as I heard those angry words repeated again and again, I began to realized to what extent I was one of the people they hated.

Faggot. Nigger. Bitch. Cocksucker. Spick. Pussy. Kike. Bastard.

At first, the words had no meaning to me. Even when I was told their meaning, I couldn't easily grasp why they were supposed to be shameful. The only word that instantly stung was the word "bastard," because I found out it meant somebody without "real" parents.

eat Wall of their narrow lives. Eventually, the children grew up and re put in charge. They created ethical codes, religions, and scientific acepts to justify their anxiety about the unknown, the darkness behad the boundaries of the little reality of their looking glass.

I had spent my childhood in that same darkness that so greatly ghtened my classmates and their parents, a darkness somewhere on other side of their reality. I understood it because I had lived in it. the age of eight or nine, I had grown far too familiar with the dark be afraid of it. Not only was I familiar with the unknown, but I had o come to realize that I was an intrinsic part of it. It was the darkness at gave my life significance and power. At the moment of that realtion, my sense of "alienation" became a cherished gift.

Today I have come to understand that my classmates and their rents were not the strangers I thought they were. To the contrary, I as the stranger. I found my way, uninvited, into their bounded world, o their territorial morality and their colonized sexuality and ethnic. It was I who had ventured through the looking glass, who had ened the forbidden box, who had strayed into the darkest part of e woods, and who had picked the forbidden fruit. I had transgressed. ad I fully understood that I had been exiled from paradise. But it was meone else's notion of paradise. It was not mine. And so I felt no nse of loss. Like all outsiders, I learned to carry my paradise with e. That personal paradise is a life-support system that has sustained e when I have found myself in places without air.

Only when I looked into *their* mirror did I recognize myself as an ien, as something unnatural and unclean. But, even as a child, I some-w grasped that the image in their mirror was not "me." It was *them* oking back at *themselves*.

We must be mindful in whose mirror we see our reflection.

It is said that the Mixtec sorcerer Tezcatlipoca beguiled Quetzal-atl, the god-king who brought art and literature to ancient Mexico, ith a lustrous object filled with reflections. When the sorcerer tempted uetzalcoatl to look into the glass, he said: "I have something precious r you. It is here in this glass. Come, take just one look, and I will ve you your body."

When Quetzalcoatl saw himself in the mirror of the sorcerer, he rned away from the monstrous, serpentine image, and groaned, as if e had been wounded by the very sight of himself.

As the story goes, seeing himself in the mirror of the sorcerer

The words were whispered in the classroom
shouted when adults were not around. On the
locker room. In the darkness of the balcony at Sa
nees. Those were the words that filled my childhoc

They were words that aroused a sense o
aggrandizement for those who shouted them; they
humiliation in those at whom they were shouted. W
fired in rapid succession in order to hold back in
ers—the "them"—aliens, deviants, perverts, and
were a psychological Great Wall of China, staunchl
tiers of conformity and an unrelenting notion of th
siders.

Then something remarkable happened. I someh
my "alienation" into a benefit. Of all human effor
mation of estrangement into a realization of indivi
the most difficult, especially for children. But I was
many fortunate young people before and after me,
the gradual transition from outcast to individualist.
the other side of the looking glass, and, at some poin
what abusive words meant about me and started to
words meant about those who shouted them. The "d
were supposed to intimidate me, became, instead, a
humiliation by understanding why some people fee
and empowerment when they succeeded in humiliat

I looked back at the name-callers from my side ol
and what I saw gave me the incentive to explore tl
ignorant and bigoted curses—words spoken by stra
mons, who invaded my unbounded childhood, tryi
barbarism with their mendacious scheme of good an

Where do these cruel words come from? Why are
such gratification, conviction, and self-righteous in
makes people so certain that words like "faggot,"
and "bitch" inevitably invoke humiliated silence? H
been arduously and meticulously *taught* to be malici

I suppose the parents of my classmates had told tl
the darkness that terrifies those who cannot see in th
the children had grown up looking into the darkness
of their parents, and so they were frightened by what t
saw lurking somewhere in the unknown regions tha

brought disgrace to Quetzalcoatl. So he abandoned his throne and went into exile, sailing away on a raft made of entwined serpents, accompanied only by a faithful group of dwarfs, hunchbacks, and other mutants.

This metaphor of self-revelation as humiliation is a fascinating insight into Aztec mentality. It is also a story about confronting the Self—the knowledge of nakedness—that is a pervasive theme in Western mythology. There is, for instance, the story about a man and a woman who lived in a garden.

"Where are you?" God asked Adam.

"I heard the sound of Thee in the garden, and I was afraid, because I was naked, and I hid myself."

"Who told you that you are naked? Have you eaten of the tree of which I commanded you not to eat?"

What is this mythic *nakedness* that is such an abomination? What is this revelation of the physical self—this "dreadful nakedness," this "obscene intimacy"—that seems to be the mythological basis of so many moral, religious, and scientific beliefs?

This subject of our mythic "nakedness" is one of the overriding explorations of this book. I want to know the myth that hides behind the myth. I want to glimpse our nakedness.

My exploration began when I rejected the moral application of something called "natural law." The conviction that drove this rejection of natural law was unclear to me until I read Maurice Merleau-Ponty's book *Phenomenology of Perception*, in which he confirmed a radical concept I had long suspected: "Man is a historical idea and not a natural species." What this rejection of anthropocentric natural law implies to me is that morality, religion, and science—*that truth itself*—are not the same for all peoples at all times. I also have many doubts about the concept of "human nature," since it is apt to imply that some of our socially constructed notions about norms are the result of a transcendent humanness. I don't deny that there are evolutionary elements that define our particular biochemical structure and behavior. But let me admit that I am far less interested in the structure of a piano than in the music the piano makes.

I believe that the ways in which we are fundamentally the same are far fewer and far less interesting than the great multiplicity of ways in which we have invented and reinvented whatever it is we mean when we speak of "human nature."

Naturalist Stephen Jay Gould has resisted the powerful lobbyists of biological determinism who have been trying to resurrect social Darwinism during the 1990s. In his essay "The Nonscience of Human Nature," he said that "human behavior was long attributed to innate biology, we do what we do because we are made that way." I agree with Gould when he concludes that "a movement away from this biological determinism has been a major trend in twentieth-century science and culture." It is a pity that that battle must be refought in the 1990s.

In this book, I am interested in the elusive social mythologies that create the antagonistic attitudes about people who do not fit neatly into the Western standard of norms. Sexologists at the turn of the century, following in the steps of Freud and Kraft-Ebbing, spent years cataloging all the ways in which people are deviant. As Jonathan Katz has pointed out, they created our current value judgments about normalcy by arbitrarily stigmatizing desire and colonizing sexuality. I care little about such deviant categories, but I am deeply interested in why such categories were invented in the first place.

What interests me is the source of the enormous fear that has built the walls around a Judeo-Christian-Islamic mentality, imposing on the world its arbitrary ideas about normality and naturalness. What concerns me are the methods by which the West has assigned both a moral and scientific consequence to private behaviors having little or nothing to do with either morality or science.

I do not mean to suggest that only the West has produced social dogma. To the contrary, I hope to indicate that it is specifically a community's agreement on norms, for better or for worse, that makes a society possible in the first place. But I also hope to demonstrate the vast variations of response to nonconformity in various societies.

This book comes from the vantage of an alien who cannot understand the reasons a brilliant, technologically advanced twentieth-century civilization continues to assume, with little hesitation, that its particular social mirror provides the ultimate image of humanness—of what is right and wrong, what is natural and unnatural, and what is normal and abnormal. I want to explore what becomes of us when we are defined by social boundaries in which we cannot truly exist as ourselves without choosing between self-contempt or self-deception. But, primarily, I want to understand why people create social boundaries that produce bigotry, humiliation, and self-denial.

In the classic comedy *Arsenic and Old Lace* by Russell Crouse and Howard Lindsay, a character believes he is Teddy Roosevelt. Someone asks his sisters: "Have you ever tried to tell him he isn't Teddy Roosevelt?" And they answer: "Once we tried to suggest that he was George Washington, and he just laid under his bed and wouldn't be anybody."

There are a great many people who respond to the demands of their society by climbing under their beds and refusing to be anybody at all. They feel an outright disgust for themselves. They are uncomfortable living in their own bodies and minds. They accept as valid the repulsion they arouse in their families and their communities. In confidential conversation after conversation, they reveal their need to apologize for their identifies and their behaviors. They want to know why they are the way they are. They crave an impossible absolution for imaginary sins they have not committed. They want to find a gene or a unique cluster of brain cells that justifies their existence. They want an explanation—an excuse for existing—while what they should want is a life *lived* and not a life *defended*. Such a state of mind is usually what we mean when we speak of "alienation," but it is not what I have in mind when I redefine "alienation" as a precious individuality that doesn't require justification.

I am always moved to see the predicament of those who internalize "sins" of which they are innocent. But I am even more interested in the motive of those who produce an atmosphere that intentionally induces the self-contempt that afflicts so many people. I want to know the methods and motives of those who devise and enforce concepts of transgression that determine goodness and badness. And I want to try to understand why people who believe in a specific set of moral, religious, and scientific values feel such unbridled and profound dread for those who transgress.

Finally, I want to know why so many of the lauded Western beliefs about good and evil are so profoundly evil.

BEYOND THE
3 WALLED CITY

The final belief is to believe in a fiction, which you know to be a fiction, there being nothing else. The exquisite truth is to know that it is a fiction and that you believe in it willingly.
Wallace Stevens, Opus Posthumous

Had I been born into the dominant society, had I been coached in its norms and mores—in short, had I been conditioned to see myself in the Western mirror of reality, I probably would have experienced lifelong despair and confusion about the homosexual molestation I encountered in the orphanage. But because I was a child who had been relatively remote from orthodox Jewish, Christian, and Islamic perceptions of morality and normalcy, my childhood abuse had little impact on me, even when I reached sexual maturity.

I recall thinking about those "wrestling matches," if at all, as simply another type of human experience, neither good nor bad, normal nor abnormal. Of my many emotional and physical experiences in the orphanage, the fact that I was fondled by a young man seemed rather insignificant, especially by comparison to an event that took place one Sunday in spring—an event I have remembered with distress and pain all the years of my life.

On Easter, during my first year in the orphanage, I became very excited by the announcement that we were going to have an Easter egg hunt. I knew nothing about Easter. I had never been inside a church. I had only the faintest idea of who Jesus was, and I had never heard of his resurrection. But the children had told me all about the egg hunt, and my anticipation of searching the deep grass for candy and prizes hidden by a wise and magical animal filled me with a rare happiness. I couldn't sleep the night before Easter Sunday. There are few Western holidays centered on the magic of animals. In my naiveté, I imagined that the hunt for eggs hidden by an enchanted rabbit would be the equivalent of a vision quest.

The boundary of a vast field at the edge of the orphanage property had been cordoned off while the eggs and prizes were hidden in the grass and bushes. Usually, the orphans were strictly forbidden to venture beyond the low fence that marked the boundaries of the orphanage. I may have been ignorant of the divine laws of Western religion, but I was fully aware of the rules of the orphanage. The perimeters of the orphanage marked a boundary *never* to be crossed.

So as I faced that forbidden field at dawn, long before anyone else had awakened on Easter morning, I realized with some astonishment that the hunt for the rabbit's prizes would not only take us on a marvelous quest, but it would also allow us to cross a prohibited boundary where we were never allowed to wander by ourselves.

Apparently, in my excitement, I trespassed the barrier and went into the field before the appropriate signal was given, and so I was not allowed to take part in the egg hunt.

It was a trifling and just punishment, but the memory of that April morning still haunts me. It is not an overstatement to say that of all my difficult experiences at the orphanage, nothing so deeply wounded me as being *excluded* from the quest for the magic rabbit's eggs. I cannot say with certainty exactly what I felt, because I recall so little about my childhood, but feeling this rejection was exceptionally damaging. I suspect that I suddenly became aware that my exclusion from the egg hunt had somehow turned me into an outsider among outsiders, that I was alien even amid the quintessential "alienation" of orphans.

I am still troubled with a sense of guilt and shame by my recollection of that event. Frankly, I do not recall the actual trespass, though

I have no doubt I was guilty of it. The orphanage staff probably intended nothing more than a harmless penalty that would teach a disobedient child a lesson. But their aim was not achieved, because I was completely untouched by the lesson they intended. What I do vividly recall of that distant day is the feeling of *exclusion and disenfranchisement*.

What exactly did the punishment on that Easter Sunday teach me? It taught me almost nothing about the rules, nor did it awaken in me that "sense of morality" that some insist is an inborn aspect of "human nature." What the punishment did teach me was a great deal about the retaliations that must be endured by those who break the rules. It did not teach me to respect or to understand the rules. It did not arouse in me some mystic or innate moral sensibility. But it did arouse my inherent capacity to feel condemned and rejected. Whatever inborn human nature I possessed, it responded and understood remorse. But it knew nothing about "respect" for the rules.

Is that the purpose of punishment: to enforce the rules by disempowering those who break them?

Being fondled and sexually exploited by a young man at the orphanage left no apparent scars, but being humiliated for trespassing became one of the most persistent and disturbing metaphors of my life. On that Sunday morning I found out that every step of an adventurous life risks a trespass with dire consequences. Even if the rules are unfair; even if the rules are not of your own making; even if the rules muzzle or exclude you; and even if the rules prevent you from being who you are. If you defy or break those rules, you become a transgressor.

There is always something standing in the way of idiosyncracy. There is always someone bristling with moral indignation whenever we question the rules or attempt to change them. Yet, the only way the rules have ever been successfully modified has been when someone dared to defy and disobey them.

Our most profound legends and our holiest epics are filled with wonderful accounts of transgressors and their fabled acts of disobedience. They are stories about a whole trove of mythical characters, who discover a secret and are admonished never to exploit the power of that secret. They are, in essence, urged by their maker to express their free will, only to be severely punished each time they dare to assert themselves. In virtually every myth, legend, fairy tale, and epic there is one thing the heroes are told not to do. And, inevitably, that is the one thing they always do, because without that infraction of the rules there can be no heroic adventure and there can be no story to tell.

Elsa, the princess of Germanic legend, must not ask her mysterious protector his name, but she cannot resist the urge to discover his identity; so she asks the forbidden question, and Lohengrin sails away forever on his swan boat.

Fatima, the wife of a chevalier named Bluebeard, is forbidden by her husband to open the door to a certain room in his castle, but she does so anyway, and discovers the remains of her husband's six former wives, and for her disobedience she almost loses her life.

Remus and Romulus, the mythic founders of Rome, were suckled by a she-wolf and reared by a shepherd. The twin brothers were staunch allies until the day Romulus was marking the boundaries of the new city of Rome. Remus mocked his brother's meticulous labors. Though warned not to step over the line that Romulus was marking on the ground with a plow, Remus did what was forbidden; he jokingly jumped across the shallow trench. Enraged, Romulus killed Remus.

Prometheus defied the Greek gods by giving fire to human beings. In retaliation, the gods sent a spiteful gift to earth: a handsome woman named Pandora. She brought to her human husband a jar or box that the gods had forbade her to open. But one day her curiosity got the better of her, and she opened the container, releasing all the diseases and evils that had never before been known by human beings.

Another Greek hero, named Orpheus, succeeded in liberating his wife Eurydice from the underworld on the condition that he not look back at her as he led her back to the surface of the earth. Again, he could not resist the one thing that was forbidden, so he glanced back at his wife, and she vanished forever.

Lot's wife was turned to salt for looking back. Uzza died for touching the ark of the covenant. And, of course, there is the most famous tale in Western religion: the picking of the forbidden fruit from the tree in Eden.

Everywhere in mythology there are forbidden acts, forbidden words, and forbidden objects: doors that must not be opened, places in the forest that must not be entered, words that must not be spoken, a flower or a potato that must not be picked, a hoop that should not be thrown into the air, a drum that must not be touched, the sunrise that must not be seen, the twelfth stroke of midnight that must not be exceeded, a boast that must not be spoken, a creature that must not be looked on, a bride and groom who must not see one another before their wedding, a path that must not be taken.

Such taboo motifs are found in thousands of stories, in every society and in every period of history. Equally pervasive is a special kind of person who willfully breaks the taboos. At heart, these ubiquitous stories of defiance of a rule are really stories about *transgression*.

As we shall see, the mordant symbolism surrounding the idea of transgression has been a central taboo motif of both religion and science, particularly in eras when the ideologies of religion and science have collided. The religious transgression might be called the "Eve motif;" while the scientific transgression could be called the "Frankenstein motif." In both cases, a person or a group has "gone beyond the bounds of nature"—which is the very essence of a transgression.

Despite the Frankenstein cliché, this scientific transgression, this defiant exploration *beyond the bounds of nature,* is serious business. So it isn't by accident that Western myths, legends, and fairy tales have consistently recapitulated the warning: "There is just one thing you must not do"—whereupon, the protagonist immediately does that one forbidden thing.

The heroes of mythology transgress for very much the same reason that we unlock a door—in order to leave one place and enter another. It is this venture into the unknown that defines the hero's quest. It is not surprising, therefore, that the forbidden act is one of the abiding metaphors of myth. Without undertaking the forbidden, there can be no adventure, and without the adventure there can be no story, no revelation, and no moral lesson. One of the unique aspects of modern Western culture is the presence of the antihero—the hero who will not or cannot be a hero. The hero who does not act. The hero who is hesitant or timorous. Such a persona was a rarity until the middle of the nineteenth century, when the astounding and insightful psycho-theater of *Hamlet* emerged as one of the moody and pervasive perspectives of modern art forms. Just such a motif of stultification is seen vividly in modern theater, film, and literature, but perhaps nowhere as obsessively as in the works of Franz Kafka, whose cabalistic allegories are filled with references to characters incapable of "answering the call" to their mythic adventure; characters frozen by trepidation into a spiritual inertia; characters who cannot transgress, but must await permission to step over the line.

The inability to transgress prevents the people in Kafka's world from knowing experience firsthand. They have no access to the secret that is only discovered beyond the bounds of convention. Kafka calls that secret the Law.

In one of the concluding sections (called "In the Cathedral") of his novel *The Trial*, Kafka created an extended speech for a priest, in which he repeats the allegorical message found in several of Kafka's works, but, particularly, in the parable entitled "Before the Law."

Before the Law stands a doorkeeper on guard. To this doorkeeper there comes a man from the country who begs for admittance to the Law. But the doorkeeper says that he cannot admit the man at the moment. . . . The doorkeeper gives him a stool and lets him sit down at the side of the door. There he sits waiting for days and years. He makes many attempts to be allowed in and wearies the doorkeeper with his importunity.

Eventually, the man grows older and older, and, finally, he dies. But he is never allowed to pass through the door to the Law.

Many readers see Kafka's parable as an evocation of the tragic state of the modern world of the West, having lost the basis of its faith and having failed to embrace a new mythology to replace it. According to literary analyst Philip Rahv, "Kafka's obsession was an inordinate sense of inadequacy, failure, and sinfulness—a sinfulness corresponding to nothing he had actually done or left undone, but lodged in the innermost recesses of his being."

What Rahv said about Kafka could as readily be said about the general state of Western sensibility during the first decades of the twentieth century, before the birth of generations for whom the law (divine or otherwise) has become a tacit fiction.

For Kafka, original sin becomes the basis of a cosmic retaliation. As Kafka himself said in his notebook: "The summary court is in perpetual session." And, apparently, Kafka believed that he was in the worst of all possible human states: suffering a self-incrimination that left him guilty but uncondemned.

In *The Trial*, *In the Penal Colony*, and *Before the Law*, Kafka is obsessed with a mysterious and inscrutable law that methodically judges and punishes people for unknown crimes. In his novel *The Cas-*

tle, however, the law is presented as being absurd and indifferent, as if humankind is too trivial even to be judged or to be punished.

What marks Kafka as the quintessential literary neurotic of his era is his inability to transgress—to defy the gatekeeper and pass through the door on his own volition. Instead, Kafka, like his repressed heroes, K. and Joseph K., remains the captive of an unappeasable power to which he impulsively returns again and again, to face a judgment that never comes, a victim of his own willingness to succumb to self-doubt, self-contempt, and self-incrimination for a sin he did not commit.

Kafka's emotional claustrophobia was perfectly epitomized by a childhood experience that had a persistent impact on his personality, very much as the Easter egg hunt at the orphanage affected my life. When sent to bed one night, he repeatedly asked his parents for water. His father, Herman Kafka, became exasperated and pulled young Franz from bed and locked him in a glass-covered porch.

This experience of exclusion so horrified Kafka that he saw it as a metaphor of his lifelong submissiveness. It engendered a dread of his father so great that it influenced his works and his relationships. But he was never able to rebel against Herman Kafka; instead, he turned his fear of his father inward as self-contempt, and he began to see himself as the sniveling weakling his father said he was.

It is, of course, an oversimplification to say that Kafka was an outsider eternally waiting to be let inside, but, in the context of this discussion, such a reduction has a certain amount of resonance, especially if we identify Kafka with people for whom marginality is comprehended as a life sentence.

Literary critic Erich Heller has said that Kafka was "the most alienated alien among the swarms of alienation. He hardly ever blamed his suffering upon the world. No, *he* is, he thinks, the culprit and accepts the judgment that concludes his 'trial.' "

As a Jew born in the Jewish ghetto of Prague in 1883, Kafka was preoccupied by a boundless sense of estrangement. The anti-Semitism of Prague added to his "alienation." But he was a secular Jew whose piety was paradoxical: "a servant of a God not believed in" (Blei). Even among alienated central European Jews, Kafka had a quixotic sense of identity: "What do I have in common with the Jews?" he asked himself. "I don't even have anything in common with myself," was his sardonic answer.

From his self-appointed position as both victim and sinner, Kafka became a metaphor of victimization, but it was a predicament resulting from an alien's refusal to rebel against those who excluded him. Part of Kafka's emotional paralysis must have resulted from the fact that he condemned himself for breaking imaginary "rules" that were incomprehensible to him because they didn't exist.

If we compare the walled mentality of Kafka with the libertine attitudes of a poet like Arthur Rimbaud (Highwater, 1994), it becomes clear that, whereas Rimbaud mythologized and aggrandized his "alienation," Kafka saw his "alienation" as an appropriate punishment for his delusive sins. Rimbaud reveled in being an imaginary outlaw. Kafka was a moral hypochondriac who could not be cured of the disease from which he suffered because he didn't have the disease in the first place.

Rimbaud's story was about a life lived. Kafka was about a life constantly seeking to apologize for itself. Yet, paradoxically, Rimbaud and Kafka shared a similar vision and creative process, a verbal alchemy born of equal measures of despair, intuition, and irrationality. Kafka saw his creative sensibility as nightmare and divine retribution; Rimbaud saw his gift as revelation and boon.

Kafka could not transgress. Rimbaud epitomized transgression. He was a maverick who made metaphors of his "alienation": *"Je est un autre* . . . I is another . . . I had to give up my life in order to be!"

Kafka was a hunger artist. "My life has shrunk and goes on shrinking." But Rimbaud vividly depicts the dizzy plunge from grace. This is a quite different kind of alienation from that of Kafka, who endlessly treads water, fearful of the depths to which Rimbaud lunges with a deranged delight.

Kafka was ostensibly a secular Jew and a latent heterosexual. Rimbaud was a renegade Catholic and an unabashed homosexual. Clearly, in terms of a capacity for transgression, these two exceptionally important artists of the early twentieth century were antithetical in almost every way, except for the correspondence between the irrational and visionary rituals they created in their writings.

Kafka epitomized stultification. A Jewish Hamlet, imprisoned behind a wall of glass. A freak who loathed his freakishness.

Rimbaud was the fool on the precipice, moving ever closer to the edge. Delighting in the danger of existence. Delighting in demonizing himself. A French Prospero, using his magic to send a tidal wave crashing down on Western certitude. A deranged Dante with a one-way ticket to hell.

In highly contrasting ways, the West's predicament is depicted by both Kafka and Rimbaud as a conundrum built on irony, paranoia, depersonalization, and self-incrimination. It is a dark, defenseless world, whose walls have come down, and where hopelessness and disintegration are the only realistic visions of the future.

Such depressing news about the future is not limited to the works of Rimbaud and Kafka. In one form or another, philosophy and the arts have been making pronouncements on the theme of Western disintegration for over one hundred years. But the collapsed mythologies of the West are not the only mythologies in the world. Perhaps, if we venture into a completely different culture, we might discover a parable about "alienation" that expresses a different future from the one created by artists such as Franz Kafka.

Among the Navajo Indians there is a fascinating cycle of legends built around a hero called Changing Woman. She is an important Navajo mythic figure miraculously born of a cloud. Her two sons were conceived while she bathed in a stream. One was conceived when she was touched by the radiance of the sun, and the other when she was touched by the radiance of the moon. One child was called the Killer of Enemies, a warrior; while the other was called Child of the Water, a shaman.

When the twins grew to manhood, they realized that the world was greatly troubled by monsters. So they decided to leave their familiar homeland and go in search of the sun, in order to gain his blessings for their battle against these monstrosities.

Before their departure, Changing Woman told her sons, "The world is dangerous. So take my advice. You may go to the south, and you may go to the east, or you may even go to the west, but there is one thing you must not do . . . you must not go north."

After listening to their mother's instructions, the twins immediately headed for the forbidden north.

For our purposes, now comes the most important part of the story.

When the twins arrived at the end of the known world, they were confronted by a terrible demon who guarded the boundary of the Navajo cosmos—a sentry not unlike the doorkeeper faced by Kafka's hero. The guardian of the gate in the Navajo legend is called White Sands Boy, a creature with long arms that enable him to seize trespassers and bury their heads in the sand until they suffocate. It is White Sands Boy who sees to it that Navajos do not go beyond the bounds of their mythology.

But the twins are crafty. Instead of retreating or patiently awaiting permission to pass the guardian, they flatter him. So great is their flattery that White Sands Boy allows the twins to go beyond the bounds of the known world.

During their adventure in the world beyond the world, the twins encounter three other guardians, and on each encounter they manage to appease them with flattery. And so they are allowed to continue their journey into the unknown.

Eventually, after finding their way through many obstacles, the twins arrive at the house of the sun. The sun puts them through several tests of virtue and courage, and then guides them through an initiation ceremony that prepares the twins for their battle with the monsters.

Now, with the blessing of the sun, they begin their journey home, through the vast sea of mythology, where they encounter Talking God, who gives them the weapons they will need to destroy the monsters.

Talking God is the ancestor of the *female* line of the gods. But it should be kept in mind that in the Navajo language, there are no gender pronouns. Thus this god is a combination of male and female qualities, made up of "male rain" and "female mist." The pervasiveness of androgyny in world mythologies suggests that gender ambiguity has an important spiritual implication in cultures in which there is not the rigid dimorphic notion of masculinity and femininity, which is an idiosyncratic concept in the West.

When the Navajo twins encounter Talking God, they are given talking prayer sticks made of "male" and "female" corn. These prayer sticks become their spiritual guides, leading them on their precarious journey back to the realm of humankind. The twins are also given double weapons—one "male" and one "female."

The adventure beyond the boundaries of the world has taught the twins many things, but chief among them is the integration of qualities that the Navajos understand metaphorically as "maleness" and "femaleness," terms that have far more to do with variant spiritual powers than with the West's strictly anatomical connotation of gender differences. From a traditional Navajo point of view, the whole realm of sexuality is understood in metaphysical rather than purely physical terms, which helps to explain the pre-Christian ambivalence about gender among the Navajo and many other primal peoples.

In their mythic encounter with Talking God, the twins are spiritually armed for their battle with the monsters. And, of course, that battle is won.

Mythologist Joseph Campbell has pointed out that the Navajo legend of the twins is a typical mythological adventure: "Leaving the bounded world in which they have been brought up, going beyond all that anybody knows into domains of transcendence, and then acquiring what is missing and coming back home."

The result of the hero's journey is revelation. And yet the hero is not "heroic" in the modern sense of the term. The hero is daring, but the hero is not necessarily courageous or noble or strong. The men and women who are heroes are those who are wiling to act out their sense of self. They do not act out their sense of duty. Dutiful persons are heroes of an entirely different kind from those I celebrate in this book. As Henry Miller said, "The ordinary man is involved in action, the hero acts. An immense difference." That metaphoric difference is the mythological difference between compliance and transgression.

The entire mythic adventure of the hero has tremendous cultural and psychological significance, but the crucial turning point of any adventure is that moment when a man or a woman breaks away from the commonplace world in order to act out a sense of self. It is this decisive act of disjunction from the commonplace, of departure from the known world, that represents the essential act of crossing the line, of breaking the rules and trespassing beyond the familiar world. That trespass expresses the hero's willingness to pierce the protective walls of the community. It represents the daring to make a precarious passage beyond the walls by doing that "one thing" that is forbidden.

In short, the adventure of the hero depends on *transgression.*

The adventure results from a behavior very different from the behavior of Kafka's man from the country, who stands inertly and helplessly, pleading with the doorkeeper to allow him to pass. The transgression of the Navajo twins is reminiscent of the subversive assertiveness of Rimbaud, who met and challenged obstacles and eventually came face to face with a revelation.

When I speak of transgression, I do not simply mean an act that is in violation of religious mores. There are vastly different kinds of transgression.

The commonplace definition of the word "transgression" is a violation of morality. We use the word "transgression" almost entirely as a description of a breach of religious doctrine. Most of us understand a transgression as a sin. We customarily say that people transgress when they are guilty of an infraction of religious teachings—like disobeying the ten commandments or some other religious doctrine governing morality. For these reasons the word "transgression" is generally understood to mean an action that is morally subversive. A transgression is closely associated with the religious idea of damnation. Therefore, we do not admire those who transgress. We reproach them as sinners. And the more "terrible" the transgression, the more we reproach them. We may ridicule them, disdain them, beat them, imprison them, banish them, or we may even kill them. But the worst of all possible punishments is doubtlessly our attempts to *redeem* them: to change them from their sinful ways to our blessed ways.

Sartre said that "hell is other people." In matters of dogma he may have been right.

In the literature of Judaism, Christianity, and Islam, there are long, itemized catalogs of sin. And in the works of sexologists like Richard von Krafft-Ebing there are equally long lists of sexual anomalies. In either case, be it religious or scientific, to step across a categorical line from goodness to sinfulness or from normality to abnormality is a transgression of the most negative kind. The religious and scientific canons of abominations and desecrations resonate throughout every aspect of our world, masked in countless axioms, moral stories, sermons, profanities, and laws.

Though religious fundamentalists are the most outspoken advocates of a literal interpretation of religious texts, anyone who has grown up in any culture influenced by Judaism, Christianity, or Islam is also biased by religious precepts and is inclined to interpret and mandate the nature of sin and punishment in religious terms. Whether we are actively religious or not, Western culture is built on religious doctrine, and we are deeply influenced by it in almost everything we say, think, and do (Pagels, 1988). The degree of subversive influence from religious dogma is astounding.

So how is it possible to think of transgression without placing it in the context of sin? It helps to distinguish between the mythic and the religious concept of transgression.

Moralists tend to mark their territories with great care and repetition. The religious concept of transgression is a theological form of territorial marking. Though it seems to me that the boundaries of religious territory are arbitrary, religious dogma insists that when we sin we cross a precise line established by God.

Transgression can also refer to social and interpersonal boundaries. In a negative context, such a transgression is what we imply when we speak of someone who "crosses the line" or a person who is "off limits." Both these figures of speech express some kind of hostile interpersonal transgression.

On the other hand, mythological transgression is a metaphor. It suggests a process similar to metamorphosis: an act that brings about transformation. The line crossed by a mythic transgression is a boundary of consciousness at the same time that it is a boundary of collective mores. The hero of mythology crosses from a familiar to an unfamiliar world, and in so doing the hero challenges profound social ideals and transcends the unassailable boundaries that the community assumes are a reflection of cosmic order. Groups as well as individuals have a consensus about boundaries: the points at which a group's or a person's walls of defense are located, beyond which an outsider's approach is perceived as a threat.

Anthropologist Mary Douglas has made it clear that a society is a self-defined enclosure with boundaries that are carefully protected against both entry and exit. Such boundaries constitute the limits of a specific view of the world that, at least in the West, people are inclined to call "reality." Cultures are, by definition, ethnocentric compounds ruled by an ideology that, with rare exception, places the home-group at the center of the cosmos. Every national and ethnic group has mythologies suggesting that the cosmos exists in order to accommodate their existence, usually at the expense of all other groups. Our cosmologies protect us from outsiders, but they also imprison us. So, once again, we return to the motif of the Great Wall that keeps out the barbarians.

"The human body is common to us all. Only our social condition varies. The symbols based on the human body are used to express different social experiences" (Douglas, 1985). Those experiences frame our world and define each of us as a member of that world. Invariably, the same cosmology that defines our social experiences also confines the range of our choices.

In the context of a closed social group, nonconformity is disorder. Disease is also envisioned as a form of disorder, the result of a breach of conformity to the rules of the group: "Thus we find that certain moral values are upheld and certain social rules defined by beliefs in dangerous contagion. . . . Just as it is true that everything symbolized the body, so it is equally true that the body symbolizes everything else" (Douglas, 1985).

It is not surprising, under these circumstances, that physical deformity or deviation in behavior is a central issue in the lives of most groups. But physical and behavioral deviation does not necessarily result in censure and rejection. In many cultures, deviation has quite the opposite effect, producing respect and awe rather than disapproval.

The notion of deviation can be radically different from one culture to another. Often the person or act or physical appearance that is deviant in one culture may be regarded as normal in another culture. Deviance may be ascribed to individuals or to entire groups. For instance, women are almost universally regarded as dangerously vulnerable gaps in the cultural walls that form masculinized societies: "In a patrilineal system of descent, wives are the door of entry to the closed group. Through the adultery of a wife, impure blood is introduced to the lineage" (Douglas, 1985). Women and female biological functions are often regarded as "unclean." In this way, a female is a taboo comparable to the left hand among peoples who traditionally use that hand for "unclean" actions, and are deeply offended if touched by or offered food by the left hand. In Indonesian Hindu societies, the feet represent a similar "unclean" taboo.

Such cultural boundaries are everywhere, because they define a culture's extremities. It seems to me that in the Western world, homosexuals, like women, are perceived as gaps in the defensive walls that bound a society's cosmological ideals about decency and normalcy. Gay men and lesbians are perceived as the doors through which impurity—in the form of moral imperfection and physical deformity—enter an otherwise pure and closed world. Just as women challenge the patrilineal imperative of male dominance, homosexuals challenge the cosmic concept of dimorphic balance, with dominant males on one side and subordinate females on the other.

As Mary Douglas (1985) observes, "Any culture is a series of related structures which comprise social forms, values, cosmology, the whole of knowledge and through which all experience is mediated."

An assault on these metaphysical structures can be either feared or venerated. In either case, the assault is a form of transgression. In this way, transgression can have an ambivalent nature, like the Hindu god Shiva, who is both destroyer and creator. So, depending on the culture, one type of transgression may be esteemed while another type of transgression may be rejected.

The creation mythologies of countless groups contain tales of heroes who assault the boundaries of their defined cosmology, in very much the manner of the Navajo story about the twin sons of Changing Woman. Inevitably, the birth of the tribal or ethnic group is understood as the result of a transgression, even though such transgressions endanger the entire series of related structures that comprise social forms, values, cosmology, and the whole knowledge of a group by which all experience is mediated. A transgression, in its most epic form, attacks, destroys, and then replaces an established paradigm. So it is not difficult to grasp the perceived danger inherent in the process of transgression.

At the same time, as we have seen in the story of the Navajo twins, a transgression has the potential of facilitating the most daring and inventive adventures of the human spirit. Yet this creative aspect of transgression has been almost entirely neglected by Western societies. Even the word "transgression" has been vilified, and its original intent lost. The term comes from the Latin word *transgredi*, which means an action that carries a person across a boundary, into other worlds, including the mythic realms of demons, gods, and spirits. For me, this ancient definition is far more compelling and complex than its moralistic, modern connotation.

In the most positive sense, transgression, like "alienation," can be redefined as the act of crossing a metaphysical boundary—a conceptual barrier—and venturing into new worlds, like the world Alice found on the other side of the looking glass and the cosmos that a Copernican astronomer, like Galileo, discovered on the other side of his telescope.

In the context of this book, a transgression is not a "sin" but a rebellious act that breaks conceptual barriers. And "alienation" is not necessarily a negative experience. It can also represent an individualist experience, a form of creative rebellion, driven by imagination and knowledge. The Copernican revolution was such a transgression, bringing revelations that reconfigured the heavens of the Western world and awakened us from an exhausted cosmic model dictated by biblical dogma. Copernicus gave us the bad news that we are not the center of the universe. That transgression turned Copernicus into an alien among his peers, because it was "alienation" that drove his imagination. It did not defeat or silence him.

Today no scientifically educated person would seriously claim that the sun and the other stars revolve around our planet. Unfortunately, we have made far more conceptual progress in astrophysics than we have in regard to many social attitudes, which are still bounded by the exhausted norms and models of Cartesian cosmology.

For this reason, I believe we must redefine our ideas about transgression. Murder and rape are not transgressions; they are calamitous social regressions. Where we find genuine transgression today is in our startling revelations about cosmology, on the one hand, and about sexuality, race, and gender, on the other hand. Almost everything we have known and believed in the West is being redefined by biology and astrophysics. The little cosmos of our daily commonsensical lives is desperately trying to catch up with Copernicus and Darwin, but there are still a great many people who are having difficulty recognizing that they can no longer define everything and everyone with antiquated and obsolescent norms and rules.

We can dispute a wide range of definitions for words like "abnormality" and "evil" and "perversion." We can search the wisdom of all the world's religions and all the schools of science in an effort to understand the bounds of our freedom to live and die our lives and deal with our deaths. But we don't seem to get anywhere with such investigations until we are willing to explore the countless mythologies of transgression that lurk somewhere *behind* our beliefs. I have said it before, but I must say it again: *We cannot change our minds until we change our mythology.* We cannot truly know what we think until we truly think about what we are thinking, with the courage to search behind the facades of intellectual boundaries that we take to be divine law, natural law, or any of the other "laws" whose origins are lost somewhere in the deep shadows of both time and mind.

At the end of the twentieth century, it seems to me that the most volatile transgressions of all are those acts that resist the community's authority to determine the fate of our bodies: what we put into them, what we take out of them, how we use them, with whom we use them. Clearly, not everything that is possible is desirable. But regulations that are supposed to protect us from ourselves too often result in impositions on our right and our capacity for self-realization. One of the most unfulfilled maxims of American mentality is the slogan: It's my body and it's nobody's business what I do with it. Unfortunately, there has never been a time when there have not been people who go out of their way to claim that what we do with our bodies is very much their business.

Religion and behavioral science have somehow become competing mediators in determining the power we have over our lives. Religion and science are equally caught up in battles about the control of life and death, about abortion and capital punishment, and about gender differences that are supposed to be the basis of "normal" social roles and "normal" personal behavior. It is perhaps symptomatic of the obsolescence of Western civilization that we are engaged in an endless debate about the truth or falsity of an everlasting law of God or an equally unreproachable law of nature that is supposed to be the final arbitrator of all human conduct.

This religious and medical battle over the ownership and control of our bodies has become something of a holy war, involving brutal public beatings and assassinations as well as rabid rhetoric about norms and standards that are purportedly found in science or religion or in those frail and fabulous concepts we call "natural law" and "human nature," though they do not seem to exist either in nature or in any demonstrable statutes of the cosmos.

Under these circumstances, it is not surprising that some of the most inflammatory debates of our time are concerned with abortion, euthanasia, homosexuality, and capital punishment, issues that radically impact our control of our lives and bodies.

I believe that of all these controversies, the most complex and the most apt to arouse psychopathic wrath is the debate over homosexuality, because it seems to challenge *every* familiar value and *every* convention of Western religious and scientific paradigms.

Homosexuality does not serve the perpetuation of marriage, reproduction, and the nuclear family, which are favorite fixtures of the three dominant Western religions. It doesn't perpetuate the genetic imperative of evolution, a focus on procreation that is an obsession of many Darwinists. Like left-handedness, it doesn't seem to serve any evolutionary purpose, even though it occurs in, debatably, the same percentage of human population—about 10 percent.

As we will see, left-handedness has been considered an abnormality by some societies. Even in the West, until fairly recent times, there were practitioners who tried to help people overcome their left-handedness. But few civilized people today would be willing to call left-handedness an anomaly or an abomination.

On the other hand, homosexuality is widely viewed as an anomaly or even as an abomination. Some pragmatic people go so far as to claim that same-sex partners don't even have anatomical parts that "fit" one another. Others, reading the Bible as history, point out that "God didn't create Adam and Steve," and feel nothing but disgust when they try to imagine the intimate things that gay men and lesbians do with one another.

Yet, through all of this antagonistic reaction, there are a great many enlightened people who are frankly amazed that "homosexuals" have somehow managed, in great disproportion to their numbers, to be among the most creative and influential members of a great variety of societies that apparently date back to the beginning of recorded history.

We learn a great deal about the contemporary world when we try to understand the complex mythology of transgression that informs and impels our attitudes about homosexuality. We have to step through the glass in which we see familiar images if we are to understand something that lies beyond our acculturated reflections. We have to cross a gigantic social boundary—for the greatest distance between people is not space but culture. We also have to expect the unexpected if we hope to encounter it on a cultural exploration as mysterious and beguiling as the most audacious research in astrophysics and biotechnology.

There are countless battles about homosexuality currently underway in many different fields. There is a great deal of admirable and heroic political activism. There is also a great deal of demented political backlash. There are cants and recantations among those who specialize in classifying "normal" human behavior. There is debate among ethicists, geneticists, among sociobiologists and naturalists, and there are more and more factions within and outside the world of gay men and lesbians competing for attention and validation.

The stories of many of these forays will pass briefly through the pages of this book. But they are not my central concern. I don't want to know if homosexuality is genetic. I am far more interested in knowing why some people believe they need to find a gene to validate homosexuality. I don't want to know if homosexuality is normal any more than I want to know if heterosexuality is normal. I don't want to know if homosexuality is a sin, insofar as I am convinced that "sin" is a social construction.

What I really want to know is why homosexuality seems to require any type of explanation or justification. I want to know what buttons homosexuals push, causing such explosive reactions from people in a vast variety of fields.

Precisely what sacred boundaries are transgressed by homosexuality? And why are these transgression so inflammatory? To put it another way, I don't want to know *if* homosexuality is hateful. I want to know *why* so many people spend so much time and energy hating it.

I want to explore the dark motives hidden *behind* various attitudes about homosexuality. I want to investigate our particular mythologies of transgression. And I want to try to understand the cultural relationship between transgression and homosexuality.

TRANSGRESSION

4

Behold, the man has become like one of us, knowing good and evil.
               Genesis

The arrogance of sex is the punishment and consequence of the arrogance of man. The sexual parts of his body were the first to rise up in disobedience to God.
    Michel Foucault, The History of Sexuality

What is this knowledge of good and evil that got Adam and Eve into so much trouble?

At the center of the Western vision of the cosmos is a silent teleology. The conviction that design lies hidden behind the dense veil of creation is usually called *divine law*, because it assumes that the basis of the cosmos is one of intelligently directed purpose. It is on the basis of this cosmological law that Western culture devised its rules of conduct that are, presumably, reflections of divine authority. Thus the ten commandments are no less than the authentic word of God; while many other moral precepts are said to be based on revelations gleaned from religious scripture.

But why does homosexuality represent what Foucault calls the "arrogance of sex"—one of the most detested transgressions of divine law?

For many centuries such a question was not asked and could not be answered, because divine law was supposed to be inscrutable. Faith was blind because people didn't want to recognize that faith is different from fact. But once people of exceptional curiosity and insight began to ask questions, the veneer of the Judeo-Christian-Islamic cosmic models began to erode. Once rebels dared to make visible the normally invisible basis of our beliefs, many people began to have doubts about the rules of conduct expected of them. Other people became zealots, disdaining any critique of their dogma.

A great many strongly held beliefs are grounded in religious mythology, even though they are rarely attributed directly to dogma. It is a commonplace to hear people justify capital punishment with the ancient biblical code of vengeance "an eye for an eye." The notion that God and only God can give or take life is the often unconscious basis of most of the arguments against suicide, abortion, and euthanasia. Even birth control is widely regarded as an intrusion on God's supreme right to control the process of procreation, even though God apparently delegates to juries and courts the right to take the lives of those who have transgressed the biblical concept of "innocence" by taking another's life. Behind most of our profound decisions and attitudes is a subversive mythology—and I say subversive because most of us are entirely unaware of the mythological basis of the decisions and attitudes we uphold as a matter of blind faith.

Today, 47 percent of Americans declare that they are religious fundamentalists; not to mention the startling fact that 73 percent of people ages twenty-seven to forty-five and 80 percent of people ages forty-six to sixty-four "agree the Bible is the 'totally accurate' word of God."[1]

Yet, according to another poll, "half the people who tell pollsters that they spend Sundays in church aren't telling the truth."[2] So it would seem that a great many people, who are not actively religious, feel a great deal of pressure to pretend that they are religious, which only underscores the power of a persistent sense of religious guilt even during an era when religious faith is theoretically declining.

Consider for a moment the possibility that human moral beliefs have a basis in cultural and religious mythologies not unlike the way certain aspects of human personality are based on personal genetic history. From a purely social point of view, it's my belief that mythology has a far greater impact on our points of view than genetic heritage. Metaphorically speaking, a myth is the intrinsic basis of our spirituality in much the way that DNA is the intrinsic basis of our physicality.

Because we live in a period of immense cultural fragmentation, we are inclined to envy those who lived at an earlier time, and who possessed religious and moral certitude. Today, that certitude is the political force behind a retrograde mentality of several religious sects politely called "fundamentalism"—a term that implies that religious faith is no longer metaphysical but physical, that mythology has been transformed from metaphor into historical fact. The fundamentalist state of mind is one of "blissful ignorance" that many of us view with more than a degree of both contempt and longing.

Despite the fundamentalists' battle against a doctrinal revolution, the historical record implies that such cultural revolutions are inevitable. There is a great deal of reason to believe that all human communities have finite existences, built on the limitations of their capacity for paradigmic change and adaptation.

Every culture is built around a tenuous social model. In his landmark study *The Structure of Scientific Revolutions*, Thomas S. Kuhn approached such models in science as paradigms, a term that has subsequently come into very wide use in the social sciences. A paradigm is a consensus about reality that is almost completely unconscious until it begins to erode and collapse. There has probably never been a time when *everyone* in a specific culture believed in *exactly* the same things. But there have been a great many times when the great majority of people in a society shared a common ideology.

The major force behind such an ideology is a creation story that provides the basis of the whole society's cosmology, and, as I have already noted, also answers its most urgent questions: Where did we come from, what is the purpose of our lives, why is there pain and suffering and death, and what happens to us after we die? Collectively, these cosmic stories are the mythology that provides the underpinnings of a society, while various ritual activities offer a society the capacity to make its mythology both visible and experiential.

One of the unique tendencies during the paradigmatic decline of a society is a sweeping deterioration of certitude and a renunciation of old answers by at least some people, while a great majority of other people engage in an equally inordinate reassertion of old answers. This kind of factionalism and this kind of ideological debate between progressive and reactionary groups are found in every collapsing society, from the time of Periclean Greece and Imperial Rome, the Hindu collapse under Islamic invasions of Southeast Asia, the Americanization of Japan, and the British retreat from its worldwide colonies. In his lauded television series, *The Western Tradition*, UCLA historian Eugen Weber spoke of the ancient Greeks in this way: "Their insatiable curiosity paid off in instability, in insecurity, and also in greatness." It is precisely this penetration of cultural boundaries that is a compelling force both for the mythic hero and for societies themselves. Perhaps the most curious result of the inevitable process of social decline is the fact that the rituals that enliven a mythology often outlive the mythology that give them substance. For instance, hopscotch was once a religious ritual; but while the ritual survives as a children's game, its original meaning is entirely lost. Only biological experience like birth, death, and various forms of intimate relations endure, but their meanings and the rules controlling them are constantly changing.

What I am suggesting is that, in a similar way and to a very great extent, Judeo-Christian-Islamic moral rituals have survived beyond the lifetime of the mythology (the cosmic model) that provided them with religious significance.

There are always polemical debates in productive societies, but there have rarely been debates as violent as those that are taking place during the decline of the mythic superstructures on which Western societies are built. During the last three centuries, from the time of the seventeenth-century Enlightenment, there has been in the West an aggressive questioning of the very nature of "reality" itself—that is, at heart, a questioning of the connotations of *divine law*—concepts gleaned from various interpretations of the first three books of Genesis, from Hebraic religious law, and from the ideas attributed to Jesus and Muhammad.

To question divine law is the ultimate transgression, because it attempts to cross the boundaries laid down by a religious cosmology. It is, so to speak, an argument with God. And of all forbidden acts, there is none as strongly prohibited as transcending a society's religious mythology and thereby calling into question its most tenaciously held attitudes about divinity, morality, normality, and the ultimate nature of reality.

Even as the metaphysical authority of religion steadily declines and the naturalistic authority of science expands into a new worldview, the turmoil of the old and the new attitudes have accelerated into a pitched battle between those who cling to a safe but obsolete vision of the cosmos and those who insist on alternative points of view.

Virtually everything in our lives resonates with the impact of this debate. But nothing is more influenced by twentieth-century skepticism about divine law than our attitudes about our dominion over our planet, its creatures, and our own lives and bodies. By this I specifically mean to bring to mind the heated debates about ecology, conservation, capital punishment, abortion, euthanasia, sexual orientation, and the right of one society to mandate social and moral ideals for other societies with different mythologies and different points of view.

Today's most dramatic revolutions are taking place in fields of science and philosophy that are intent on the deconstruction of the entire Western concept of reality. Yet, these arcane debates greatly impact everyday life, even if they do so subversively. Growing skepticism about the divine law of the Judeo-Christian-Islamic tradition has advanced in many direct and indirect *social* manifestations: women's rights, civil rights, racial equality, gay and lesbian rights, and a good many other issues that were not allowed a voice by the old ideology. Despite these important social rebuttals of divine law, faith in old ideas has also intensified, becoming more insistent as it becomes aware of its vocal critics: Jewish and Muslim women who don't like their assigned roles in the Hebraic and Islamic cosmos; Catholics who are uncomfortable with the infallibility of the pope; nonwhites who reject white supremacy, Manifest Destiny, and colonialism; as well as homosexuals who repudiate homophobia.

British physicist L. L. Whyte has said that *thought is born of failure.* The failure of a cosmography forces its adherents to re-ask all of their urgent metaphysical questions about origins, destiny, and purpose all over again. It was the failure of the congruity of Western paradigms that ushered in radical forms of thought. And it was the questioning of the validity of a once absolute value system that brought about both the collapse of traditional cultural values and launched an unrelenting series of bitter debates about the nature of reality.

Among fundamentalists, the most scandalous transgressions are linked, directly or indirectly, to gender and sexuality. Social conduct, by which I mean responsible community relations, has become far less important than a moral conduct based on religion. Fundamentalists believe that only with the authority of divine law can there be community values. They reject the humanist conviction that people possess the will, intellect, and dignity to control their own actions. And they insist that legislative law (law without God) does not have the power to deter anarchy. And when fundamentalists claim that social justice refutes God, they believe they are excused from obeying the rule of such justice. In short, they are exceptionally possessive about their God: They speak in his behalf, they interpret his messages, they classify his categories of sin, they use his name to deny the Gods of others, they claim a God-given right to break the laws they believe are ungodly, and they elect themselves as the indisputable arbitrators of God.

Unfortunately, virtually everyone is touched to some degree by the inclination of Western fundamentalism to read metaphor and mythology as historical fact and to interpret morality as divine law. Such prosaic evangelism has strong appeal because most of us cannot imagine the existence of a cosmos without an intrinsic, intelligent design, which we presume provides our very humble lives with both importance and meaning.

Jesus and his disciples understood that their religious ideas were revelations from somewhere beyond the religious model of the then two-thousand-year-old Jewish world. They also understood that the new lessons they wished to teach were complex abstractions that defied many of the fundamental concepts of Judaism. The early Christian leaders knew that lofty abstractions wouldn't be of much help in converting a huge, barbarous Roman population into devout Christians. So they commissioned religious "picture books"—frescoes and stained-glass windows—that illustrated mythic tales from the Bible for the largely illiterate flock. They told simple parables and allegorical stories that taught their congregations complex beliefs about the nature of good and evil. In images and parables they managed to express the inexpressible and speak the unspeakable: about mystic prophecies, revelations, and visions totally beyond the grasp of everyday people. They used realism to deal with things that were *not* real; they used the physical to define the metaphysical. And because of their insistence on the transformation of their mythic ideals into understandable physical facts, they transformed Christianity from a visionary sect into a worldly institution with prosaic rules and prosaic ideas about the nature of reality. In the end, they changed the world.

Today, many Christian believers rely on the premise that mythology is factual history. It is the kind of transition from revelation to mediocrity that is found in many religions: in Buddhism, in Islam, and in the ultra-orthodox wing of Judaism. In each of these cases, there is an inflexible standard used to make moral judgments about those who break rules that are perceived as the eternal, unchallengeable laws of a specific deity.

It seems essential to me that we see important social issues, like the conflicts surrounding abortion, homosexuality, and euthanasia, against this background of the *literal* interpretation of divine law, rather than beginning with political agendas that merely respond and react to biblical interpretations and dogmas, but fail to challenge the Kafkaesque "law" that presumably lurks somewhere beyond and behind prosaic moral interpretations.

We haven't arrived at our current conflicts simply because there are people in the world who are bigoted. To the contrary, it took a very long time to teach people to be bigots. But that education in prejudice has had a very inconsistent basis, shifting constantly as it became socially and politically expedient to alter the rules governing divine law. The reason, for instance, that scholars like the late John Boswell found little evidence of homophobia in the early years of the Christian Church is probably because the Christian attitude about "homosexuality" didn't exist as a distinctive designation of "deviant" sexual behavior. Christian attitudes about gender and sexuality changed from era to era, just as the Christian attitudes about martyrdom and social freedom changed. In fact, it is becoming increasingly doubtful that our connotations of sexuality and gender have any relevance to the attitudes and even the terminologies of other eras and other cultures.

During the early Christian period, when Christianity was a small persecuted sect, the dominant concept of divine law was built on the ideal of self-sacrifice and the virtues of martyrdom. For many tribes and nations that were subjugated by Rome, the notion that suffering was an expression of piety and spiritual freedom had been a great boon. From the time of Nero, the embrace of such a validation of misery under Roman rule had been a great comfort to the politically brutalized Christians of the Roman Empire. Then, about three hundred years later, this frame of mind completely changed, when the emperor Constantine sanctioned Christianity and the Roman realm was Christianized. Thus when Christianity became the official religion of the Roman world, the powerful Christian philosopher Augustine nimbly changed the concept of divine law to accommodate Christianity's new political privilege.[3] In short, the status of divine law is highly flexible and politically accommodating. In one intellectual transformation, Augustine revised a mentality that for centuries had given persecuted Christians the right of spiritual and moral freedom into a story of human bondage. Augustine deconstructed the highly influential story of Adam's sin. In his revisionist version, Augustine contended that Adam's sin had forfeited the right of his human descendants to be free. This highly amended version of divine law became a sanction for the limitations placed on the political freedom of newly Christianized "barbarians," a forfeiture that the followers of Jesus paid to Rome for its sanction of their outcast religion (Pagels).

Augustine not only cost humankind its free will, rendering the Christians of Rome incapable of genuine political freedom, but also contended that Adam's sin had made sex irreversibly corrupt. It is this sex-negative model that greatly impacts on the twentieth-century attitudes about homosexuality. According to Elaine Pagels, "Augustine's theory of original sin offered an analysis of human nature that became, for better and worse, the heritage of all subsequent generations of Western Christians and the major influence on their psychological and political thinking."

The twentieth-century effort to reshape the Christian view of homosexuality has been a process of religious and political persuasion. It has rarely attempted to reverse the fundamentally homophobic reading of divine law inherited from Augustine, who viewed all forms of sex as an evil. Gay and lesbian activists have addressed important matters of civil liberties. Some have sought validation from revisionist views in the fields of psychiatry, neurology, and biotechnology. Others have sought biblical accommodation, publishing essays built on the scriptural validation of homosexuality in booklets like *What the Bible Really Says About Homosexuality*—a curious reversal of the methods of those who use scriptural passages to attack homosexuals as blasphemers.

For reasons that have far more to do with social expediency than with changes in the fundamental attitudes about divine law, there have been some liberalizing shifts in Christian and Judaic dogma. But there have also been a number of shifts that have been ruthlessly reactionary. Many of the most violent acts of our era, from bashings to bombings and assassinations, are repercussions of a religious resistance to change in the moral model of Christianity, whether the rhetoric of that resistance is dressed in pious or political jargon or in hate speech.

Gay and lesbian activists have too often accepted Judeo-Christian dogma as a given, fighting their battles on an unlevel field. They have acquiesced to somebody else's arbitrary rules, instead of rejecting the entire basis of the deeply ingrained sexual morbidity of Christianity. As a result, gay liberationists have not fully addressed the mythology *behind* the bigotry that castigates sexuality, in general, and homosexuals, in particular. Gays either ignore divine law, as if it were not a tremendous obstacle, or they try to find an all-embracing, affirming God lost somewhere in Jewish, Christian, and Islamic cosmologies.

Meanwhile, most homophobic people have no idea why they find homosexuality abhorrent. If pressed to be rational, some homophobes will speak vaguely of divine law (of nature and of natural law), but when asked for details about their beliefs, they really don't know exactly why they fear or disdain homosexuality. Ironically, they believe that their abhorrence is so profound it must, therefore, be "biological" or, as they like to say, "natural."

Apparently, hatred, like faith, is blind. The faithful are not aware of their beliefs because they regard their beliefs as unquestionable truths that require no explanations or rationale. Every question about conduct is answered by some insinuating quotation from scripture, as if the supreme authority of all biblical concepts were somehow beyond social, historical, or rational challenge. Clerics may argue among themselves about their widely dissimilar interpretations of biblical texts, but the ultimate authority of the Bible as the word of God is rarely contested.

It is only when people are required to defend their "truth" that they become aware that faith has never been blind, except among the ignorant. Faith has always had a rationale, and every religion is built on a philosophical and mythological premise. More than a century ago, Nietzsche made it clear that the quagmire surrounding most moral debates is caused by the fact that the rules are discussed but the premise *behind* those rules (*beyond good and evil*) is rarely confronted.

According to Alexander Hehams, "Nietzsche's ambitious aim was to undermine the moral tradition. . . . His main objection to morality is its absolutism, the fact that it exhibits what he calls 'the worst of tastes, the taste for the unconditional.' "

As I have already pointed out, until we change our mythologies, it is impossible to change our rules, especially if we are unaware that some of our most doggedly held opinions are the result of a mythology we have long forgotten or that we never knew or embraced or fully understood. A long succession of early civilizations demonstrates that a mythology is subtlety or radically changed when the people who live under its spell become aware that their mythology is only one of many possible mythologies. In other words, we change a mythology simply by becoming aware of its existence. That is precisely what has happened since the times of Copernicus, Darwin, Freud, and Einstein. Whatever the intentions of these remarkable innovators, the fact remains that their revolutionary points of view revealed the existence of a distinctive Western mythology and, consequently, their viewpoints revolutionized the cosmic model of civilization in the West.

If religious dogma is a rationale hidden within a specific mythology, then I must ask: From the point of view of the Judeo-Christian-Islamic model, where exactly is the mythological beginning of homophobia?

I think that myth must have originated with some of our most fundamental attitudes about our bodies, those unruly organisms that bring us such sublime pleasure as well as such terrible suffering. We know the world through our bodies. We enter the world through our mothers' bodies. And when our bodies are gone, we are gone. For virtually every society, the life and death of the body have been a primary mystery.

One of the first principles of Buddhism is "pain exists." From that premise a complex ritual mentality of asceticism evolved, embracing the ancient Hindu concept of a succession of incarnations that deliver the spirit, presumably entombed within the body, to a sublime state of Nirvana, the Hindu/Buddhist realm of pure spirit. Though vastly different in theological detail, the body-negative model of Buddhism is similar to the negative Christian precepts of the body.

Anthropologist Mary Douglas (1985) confronts the religious renunciation of the body by emphasizing the primacy of our bodies in determining social values: "Rituals work upon the body politic through the symbolic medium of the physical body. . . . The human body is common to us all. Only our social condition varies. The symbols based on the human body are used to express different social experiences."

In most of the world's major religions, the body has a very bad reputation. Sex is easily the body's most maligned function. Virtuous men are supposed to be moderate or ascetic, using self-control, reason, or meditation to triumph over the pleasures and afflictions of their bodies and the demonic compulsions of sex, which are usually blamed on the sexual insinuations or aggressions of women. As Semonides of Samos reported in the seventh century B.C., women are "the worst single thing Zeus made for us."

By and large, the negativity about our bodies and our sexuality is a resonance of a prevailing contempt for women, who are always associated with wild nature, animality, and sensuality; men are associated with restraint and reason, which presumably achieve the orderly structure of the city—the *polis*—that stands as the triumph of males over uncontrollable nature. Unquestionably, in the West and many other cultures, the so-called passivity of women is looked on with contempt and is seen as the basis of the male homosexual's "effeminate" behavior. So, by default, gay men are held in greater contempt than women, because, supposedly, they are people with the high rank of males who have chosen to behave in the "lowly and passive" manner of women.

In the almost worldwide cultural crisis leading to the need to explain the existence of suffering and death, sex somehow became an enigmatic symbol of all adversities among a great majority of organized religions. About 600 B.C., there occurred what Joseph Campbell (1962) has called "the Great Reversal," when the prevailing worldview shifted from an affirmation of life to a negation of life, from the expectation of reward, comfort, and innocence to the acceptance of punishment, discomfort, and guilt. The Great Reversal was an epic, worldwide moment in history, when an unprecedented, negative conception of destiny arose, eventually being embodied in that Judeo-Christian Original Sin that makes pain and punishment an implacable aspect of Western life.

The most direct line of descent of the sex-negative philosophy in the West begins in the ideas of the Christian apostle Paul, who only reluctantly consented to congenital union in marriage, commanding his flock to "propagate without pleasure." In fact, he was reluctant to sanction *any* form of sexuality. "The flesh lusts against the spirit, and the spirit against the flesh; and these are contrary the one to the other. . . . To be carnally-minded is death; but to be spiritually-minded is life and peace." (Galatians 5:17; Romans 8:5–6).

Augustine eventually took an even more radical stance against sexuality, instructing early Christians that "the world must be used, not enjoyed." Most remarkably, Augustine claimed that semen itself is "shackled by the bond of death" transmitting from generation to generation the damnation incurred by the Original Sin of Adam. Augustine concluded that every human being ever conceived through semen is born contaminated by sin. The single exception to this tragic predicament, of course, is Jesus, who was "immaculately" conceived without semen.

The term "immaculate" is derived from Latin by way of Middle English—*immaculata*—and means "unblemished"; this, of course, suggests that less miraculous forms of sexual conception are blemished or unclean.

It is against this startlingly pessimistic background that we must explore the mythic and philosophical context of both homophobia and the contention that AIDS is an expression of devine retribution.

Such a negative view of sex was abhorrent to most historic Jews, who believed that their God commanded them "to multiply and be fruitful." Celibacy was unthinkable to all but a very few Jewish sects, like the Essenes in Palestine and the Therapeutae monastic groups in Egypt. So primary was God's commandment to multiply that most historic Jews disapproved of any form of nonreproductive sex, such as masturbation, prostitution, and homosexuality. The Hebraic commandment to be fruitful was a focus on the special privileges of men in a patriarchal culture, making polygamy and divorce acceptable for men because such privileges increased a man's chances of producing sons.

The censure of nonreproductive sex in modern religious thinking began with the Hebrews, but the censure of all forms of sexuality began with Paul and Augustine.

Eventually, Jewish attitudes changed greatly through the influence of various reform movements. Christianity also faced a Reformation, but the sex-negative precepts of Paul and Augustine persisted as fundamental aspects of Judeo-Christian mythology through all the upheaval of Western religions, and such precepts still have an immense, if covert, influence on us today.

The dismal Christian model of sexual contamination and paranoia begins in the Gentile interpretation of the mythological story of Adam and Eve in its rhetoric of a primal transgression. There is a great deal of religious debate about the exact nature of that transgression. In general, Jews and early Christians believed that Adam's mythic sin was one of disobedience, and his subsequent suffering was a testament of a *freedom* gained at the expense of paradise. But, after Augustine, it became the orthodox view of Christianity that Adam's sin not only caused human mortality but also corrupted human sexuality.

In Augustine's view, human disobedience gave rise to death and sexual desire, and, in the process, it also deprived the progeny of Adam the freedom to choose not to sin. In other words, sin became compulsory in a religion that saw sin as damnation.

Of course, the unique power claimed by the church is the ability to carry out rituals that absolved the faithful from damnation. Such deliverance gave the early Church great attractiveness. In retrospect, the sex-negativity of Christianity seems highly convoluted, but Augustine was very persuasive in his theological arguments. He had come out of North Africa, from the town of Hippo, where he was a bishop. During his youth he had been an adherent of a Middle Eastern religion led by the prophet Mani. The cult of Mani, called Manichaeism, was one of the first world faiths to evolve a highly dualistic concept of the eternal battle of good and evil, body and soul. It was this negative dualism of Manichaeism that Augustine brought to Christianity.

Augustine's views were so perverse by even the standards of most orthodox Jews and Christians of his time that we can only wonder how he managed to persuade the majority of Christians that sexual desire of all kinds is essentially "unnatural"—an act resulting from the transgression of Adam and Eve.

> From the fifth century on, Augustine's pessimistic views of sexuality and human nature would become the dominant influence on Western Christianity, both Catholic and Protestant, and it would color all Western culture, Christian or not, ever since. This cataclysmic transformation in Christian thought from an ideology of moral freedom to one of universal corruption coincided with the evolution of the Christian movement from a persecuted sect to the religion of the Roman emperor himself. (Pagels)

This historical context sheds a great deal of light on the ways in which Christian dogma approaches events in the modern world. Given the insidious doctrine of Augustine that sin is endlessly transmitted by semen from generation to generation, it is little wonder that religious fundamentalists have seen something ominous in the fact that a virus that is devastating homosexual men is often transmitted in semen. It is a dismal coincidence that facilitates the mythological theme of divine retribution. And it has a long history in the Judeo-Christian tradition, which associates sin and disease as expressions of divine punishment.

When we become aware of the mythological basis for at least part of the aggressive attitudes of fundamentalists regarding gay men with AIDS, we begin to grasp the power of myth in blindly shaping social attitudes. From Augustine (who lived almost sixteen hundred years ago), we have acquired a view of semen and sexuality that transforms the AIDS pandemic into divine retribution against the transgression of homosexuality.

The view of the body as corrupt and sinful is by no means limited to Christianity. In a remarkable number of religions, the body and sexuality are disparaged. But Christianity has given a unique emphasis to the retaliatory nature of God when it comes to acts of disobedience to the divine laws that catalog bodily sin and then resolutely punish transgressors. Ultimately, we can discover behind virtually every Christian category of sin the pessimistic influence of Augustine's view of the corruption of the body and sexuality. So ingrained is this contempt for the body that it has repeatedly surfaced in a whole succession of Western concepts, even those of biological science, that supposedly reject and preclude all inferences of religion.

Though religious documents appear to contain direct and indirect references to the prohibition of homosexuality, I think we make a considerable error if we assume that homophobia is an ancient bias that was singled out by the church for special contempt and punishment. It's important to understand that the sexual pessimism of the West disdains *all* forms of sex. It has only been in relatively recent history that a category of sexuality such as "homosexuality" has even existed. Originally, it is likely that even the term "heterosexuality" was a reference to sexual debauchery (Katz, 1995).

As Mary Douglas (1982) affirms, the major concern of Christianity, as with all bounded traditions, was the protection of its community from *impurities*. And the orifices associated with excrement and sexuality were viewed as dangerous breaches in social and tribal boundaries. Even the most cursory look at the cynical paintings of the fifteenth and sixteenth centuries (particularly Bosch and Brueghel) reveals an inordinate preoccupation with body orifices as well as excrement, including many visual references to an evil omen popularly called "the Devil's Fart." According to art historian Helen Gardner, "Bosch seems to show erotic temptation and sensual gratification as a universal disaster."

The problem of sex for Christianity was not same-sex violations of moral boundaries. Instead, the problem was founded on all forms of sex not directly associated with a Pauline consecration of marital procreation. As for homosexuality, it is debatable that it even existed as anything other than one of many possible kinds of debauchery, but certainly not as a "lifestyle."

It is doubtful that there was such a thing as specific and fixed categories of sexual identity in the early history of Christianity. It is far more likely that long before there were any specific issues concerning homosexuality, there was a deeply entrenched negativity among Christians about sex of *all* forms. At issue was adultery. It was of secondary importance what person or beast the adulterer pursued. Though we tend to think of adultery as sex with any person other than one's spouse, the Latin and Old English meaning of the terms derives from *adilterare*—to pollute, to contaminate by adding extraneous, improper, or inferior ingredients—*to compromise the purity of the tribe*. So, once again, we are reminded of Mary Douglas's (1985) concept of transgression as the breach of tribal boundaries that control cultural purity and lead symbolically, if the boundaries are breached, to personal and cultural pollution as well as something akin to "racial" impurity. In the Douglas cosmos, what is pierced by transgression is the mythology of the tribe that defines reality.

In this way, homosexuality was probably a "sin" submerged and greatly overshadowed by the immense and all-consuming Christian disgust for the body and *all* forms of sexuality.

Because of the intense negativity toward nonreproductive sex among the Hebrews and the repulsion of any form of eroticism and sex among early, doctrinaire Christians, it seems likely that classifications of blasphemous acts, like homosexuality, were invented, *if at all*, less to disdain those who transgressed sexual boundaries, and more to lift some of the moral burden of sexual sin from the conscience of those who eventually created a "sanctified" gender identity for themselves— a context for sex that was viewed as procreative conduct sanctioned by God. I am speaking, of course, of monogamous heterosexuality, though, admittedly, the specific modern context of the term "heterosexuality" was probably not used until 1892 (Katz, 1995).

Because the Western world is not monolithic and has always been composed of many layers of socially and ethnically diverse populations, the Church Fathers, despite all their moral enthusiasm, had an exceptionally difficult time mandating the social and sexual conduct of the ribald "barbarians" who composed their flocks. There is far more evidence in the early Christian era of undifferentiated sexual attitudes than there is of the sanctioned kind of marital "heterosexual" sex that we have lived with since categorical sexual practices were invented in the nineteenth century. In fact, there was such moral upheaval in the Middle Ages that there was little time for moralists to designate any one sexual act as more sinful than another. In the fourteenth century, at the same time that religious miracle plays and parables dramatically deplored the body and sexuality, it is estimated that about 40 percent of the children born in Europe were illegitimate (Muller). Obviously, Augustine's asceticism could not easily capture the minds of the huge converted barbarian population of Europe that knew nothing about the "perils" of pleasure. "At no time in the world's history," concludes medievalist James Bryce, "has theory, professing all the while to control practice, been so utterly divorced from it."

The vain efforts of high-minded churchmen to curb excesses provide an inkling of the paradox of medieval life. That same paradox has continued into our time, becoming, as we shall see, one of the most fascinating sources of the heterogeneity of modern sensibility. A great deal of the robust culture of the pre-Christian world managed to survive two thousand years of religious vivisection, thanks to the continuity of a healthy "barbarism"—a vast variety of primal and indigenous traditions that have endured among all of the world's peoples, but especially among the financially deprived and the ethnically disenfranchised. The transgressions of such alien and pre-Christian influences have been persistent transgressions of divine law. It is significant that many of the cultural "innovations" of the West have actually represented a resurfacing into the mainstream of Asian, African, and ancient Near Eastern traditions, like the African basis of American and Caribbean popular music, or the mannerisms of early-twentieth-century modernist painting, or various emulations of the classical world, like the Italian Renaissance and the revolutionary "Greek" dance style of Isadora Duncan. These infusions of alien influences were also transgressions of divine law that challenged and changed Christian doctrine by pointing out the persistent paradoxes of Christian theory.

Divine law may have claimed dominion over the Western world, but the culture of outsiders was never truly vanquished. It simple went underground. The barbarian subversion of Christianity began almost as soon as Paul embarked on his evangelic mission among the tribes of Europe. Local "pagan" gods resisted destruction and were accommodated as "Christian" saints. The Near Eastern rituals celebrating the birth and death of Jesus were infused with Gallic, Norse, and Druid symbolism. Evergreen trees and sprigs of mistletoe found their way into the rites of Christmas. Rabbits, eggs, and other symbols of rebirth and fertility emerged as emblems of Easter. The wide cultural diversity among primal peoples who lived at the time of the Middle Ages may have been masked by religious propriety and the social invisibility of the underclasses, but that culture's subversive resonance triumphed again and again in Western history, shaping many aspects of modern sensibility. There is something very familiar to the people of the late twentieth century in the description by historian Herbert Muller, when he depicts the contradictory world of the European Middle Ages:

> In theory, life was regulated by elaborate forms and codes, hedged in by religious rules that had the most awful sanctions. In fact, life ran wild in uncouth freedom, with a reckless defiance of all the rules upon which salvation depended. Social records indicate that vice and crime were far more prevalent than they are in the skeptical, cynical modern age. Furthermore, much of this lawlessness was condoned.

We may look on the religious solemnity of Dante (1265–1321) as representative of the mentality of the Middle Ages, but, in fact, it is the luminous, bawdy, and homoerotic works of both Chaucer (1340–1400) and Boccaccio (1313–1375) that provide a truer and more vivid illustration of the ribald mentality of the era—a time when sexual experimentation seems to have been a way of life practiced with equal abandon by both laity and clergy, aristocrat and peasant.

During this tumultuous period of Christian indoctrination, church scholars disregarded the life-affirming activity all around them and concentrated on reforming the lively parlance of the common people, *the vulgate,* by Latinizing vernacular terms that the church regarded as crude and profane. The censure of words and ideas readily became a censure of acts. The blushing Latinists provided the West with a trove of peculiarly bloodless words like "penis," "vagina," "fornication," "coitus," "fellatio," "semen," and "cunnilingus." In this way, language was thoroughly Christianized, and, by extension, sexual anatomy and physiology were sanitized. The so-called Anglo-Saxon terms that were replaced by Latin became "dirty words" that described "dirty acts." The Christian history of language betrays a revolutionary revulsion for the body. There is, for instance, speculation that the word "fuck" may have originally been borrowed from the perfectly respectable Norse terms *fukkar* or *fockar*—which referred to the sex act. The Christian attempt to vanquish sexuality by encoding such "pagan" vernacular has had a highly negative impact on our ability to think and talk about sexuality. For this reason, it is impossible to describe twentieth-century homophobia without speaking of the linguistic censure that underlies all European languages when it comes to *all* subjects of sex and gender. Homosexuality was by no means the only "love that could not speak its name." It is far more to the point to say that *all acts and all organs associated with sex* could not speak their names—except in quaint, antiquated Latin. There is something unbearably coy about the fact that people use expressions such as "the F-word" or "F——ing," when everyone fully understands that what they are really saying is "fuck" or "fucking." Words are simply sounds and written signs that bring acts and ideas to mind. So "F-word" and "F——ing" serve exactly the same purpose as the forbidden terms "fuck" and "fucking."

Even when people disavow the canons of divine law that control language, still many Europeans and Americans persist in using Latinate terms for sex as a matter of salacious courtesy rather than for reasons of true piety. It is this pervasive duplicity and timidity about sex that has made it difficult to speak plainly and openly about sexuality in general but particularly about homosexuality.

For all the verbal restraints of Catholicism, it is Protestantism that seems to be largely responsible for the sad present state of profanity. "Where the most taboo words in Roman Catholic countries tend to be the blasphemous ones—oaths in the name of the Father, Son, or Virgin Mary—the truly offensive terms for Protestants are those that refer to intimate parts of the body and its functions" (Rawson). Through the manipulation of words, sexuality became something that was not merely worldly and hedonistic; it also became unclean, impure, and obscene.

Presumably the vernacular names for parts and functions of the body are embarrassing to righteous people because, from the Western perspective, our bodies are embarrassing. Yet even this Protestant anatomical censorship is strongly biased. We cannot politely say that someone is a "dickhead" or a "fuckface," but we are allowed to refer to someone as a "birdbrain" or a "sweetheart." That is because the brain and the heart are not among condemned organs. But all the red flags go up when we approach the geography of sex and excrement.

Words and images are often accused of transgression, despite the fact that of themselves they are not harmful or unwholesome. They simply allude to things that are arbitrarily designed as unwholesome and deleterious. The association of nakedness and shame, of sexuality and guilt, is so intricate to Western culture that we are inclined to accept it as a transcultural norm and look down on peoples of the world who wear few garments, because we supposed that nakedness is an inditement of crudity and "primitivism."

Some theologians tell us that if we are righteous, we inherently possess a mysterious set of rules collectively called *conscience*—a genetic edition of the ten commandments that is supposed to be an inborn aspect of our divinely granted status as the only creatures in the cosmos in possession of what the pre-Christian Stoic philosopher Epictetus called "a distinctive portion of the essence of God" and that Christians later came to refer to as "soul." Interestingly, there are also some biologists who believe that our recognition of good and evil is a genetic legacy. I am, however, every bit as uncomfortable with the idea of allowing science to arbitrate conduct as I am with the notion that religion be allowed to grant sanctions or penalties for behavior.

Medievalist Johan Huizinga is the source of a rather gloomy evaluation of the late twentieth century. Huizinga was capable in 1930 of foreseeing the consequences of our loss of imagination. He detested the secularization of society: the tendency to turn our mythologies into factual histories, the reckless rejection of ambiguity, and our prosaic discomfort with the poetic and the ineffable. For him the world went sour in the nineteenth century, when a naive realism fortified by an equally naive technology destroyed our myths simply because no one wanted to believe in a fiction that they knew to be a fiction. "They killed all the mysteries and [still tried to] acquit man of his guilt and sin," Huizinga lamented.

But, Huizinga insists, such acquittal is an illusion, for the gullible realism that destroyed the orthodox and redemptive religious faith of the past possesses so little mythology of its own that those who once believed in original sin can never completely believe in the possibility of their acquittal. As a consequence, many people are stripped of the redemptive promise our old mythologies once provided, at the same time that they continue to be burdened by a fanatical sense of religious guilt that is constructed on a mythology in which they no longer consciously or actively believe.

> And what rough beast, its hour come round at last,
> Slouches towards Bethlehem to be born?[4]

It seems to me that the beast of which Yeats spoke is far more ancient than the demons born of Judaism and Christianity. Even among peoples whose names and histories have long vanished from Western memory, there is the remnant of a freakish shadow of something both sacred and profane, a recollection of hallowed abominations, of the monsters in the labyrinth, of half-human creatures, whose strangeness has aroused countless generations to respond with both awe and terror, astonishment and disgust, wonder and repulsion at the wonder of "nature's mistakes." Everywhere in human recollection is an unbridled wonder and fear of the cataclysmic and unruly process that underlies nature itself—the same process that, in its horrific randomness, makes evolution possible—*makes even a creature as unthinkable as you and me a biological possiblity.*

As much as the circumstances of homosexuality were unquestionably shaped by the Christian concept of divine law, there are far older and more furtive reasons for humankind's fear and wonder of "nature's oddities." It is when we *believe* that nature itself has defied its own "natural law" that the most fearsome and awesome of creatures is born. There have been many names for such creatures—some divine and some names too sacrilegious to be spoken aloud. But in our conventional world such social and biological mutants are usually called *freaks.*

It is possible that if we explore the long social history of such anomalies, we might begin to find that the connotation of homosexuals as "freaks of nature" was built by Christianity on a reverence and a loathing far older and far more complex than Judeo-Christian divine law.

TRANSGRESSION

5

AS DEFORMITY

In *Member of the Wedding,* Carson McCullers created a highly autobiographical tomboy in the character named Frankie. In McCullers's novella, there is a touching and telling scene in which Frankie finds herself confronted at a carnival sideshow by the person called "Half Man/Half Woman," or, as Frankie says, "a morphodite and a miracle of science."

Frankie's fascination for this and other sideshow freaks is gradually overwhelmed by an intense fear of what she sees.

"She was afraid of all the freaks," McCullers says of Frankie, "for it seemed to her that they had looked at her in a secret way and tried to connect their eyes with hers, as though to say: *We know you. We are you!*"

Literary critic Leslie Fiedler realizes that "Carson McCullers finds [in the freaks] a revelation of the secret self." What Frankie fears is the recognition of her own "oddity"—her homosexuality—in the sideshow creatures whom her community regards as monstrosities. They are *freaks*, whose only employment is the job of being ridiculed and stared at by people who are convinced that they possess a God-given ordinariness that reflects the perfection of the divine design of the cosmos. In the rural world of Frankie's childhood, to be other than ordinary is to be deformed, to be "freakish"—to represent a strange and frightening transgression of God's cosmic plan.

In the 1940s southern settings of Carson McCullers's fiction, it is not surprising that the recognition of herself as a freak awakens fear and embarrassment in Frankie. Though she is clearly unaware of the "name" for her predicament, Frankie feels certain that, except for the freaks in the sideshow, there is not another person in the world like her. The freaks are her only role models. And she is deeply aware that her neighbors considered them abominations.

The freaks look and act like freaks. But what most terrifies Frankie is the fact that she is certain that somewhere hidden inside of her is a freak disguised as an everyday human being. This freakishness is not an identity she has invented and cultivated, but one that has been thrust on her. For Frankie, her differentness is a tragic burden.

The dramatic impulse that drives Frankie's adolescent experience of "deformity" not only is her typical struggle with the confusion of suddenly becoming very tall and unexpectedly developing breasts, but also is caused by her growing realization that she is not "typical," that she somehow doesn't conform to the idealized ordinariness of the community in which she has grown up and whose values she shares, even if those values produce a blinding sense of self-contempt.

Frankie has never had a frame of reference other than the behavior she has encountered in her little town, and though that commonplace conduct seems to be taken for granted as acceptable behavior, at the sideshow Frankie is abruptly struck by the fact that she is not like the other townspeople. She is a freak among the freaks. This realization makes her painfully aware that her neighbor's expectations of "normality" exclude and isolate her. In several bittersweet scenes, Frankie slowly comes to the conclusion that she is an outsider, hopelessly infatuated with a young woman who is about to get married and go off forever with her new husband.

The isolation of gay youths, growing up with little or no awareness that they are not freaks, is still a problem in many countries, and adolescent suicide among gay boys and girls is pandemic. It will remain a major social problem as long as the stigma of freakishness continues to be profoundly rooted in exclusive notions of normalcy.

Many less traumatized homosexual students have a sense of solidarity; they are often outspoken about their orientation, and some of them insist on bringing their same-sex partners to high school football games and proms. And, yet, the imprint of social disapproval doesn't simply vanish in a few decades, because censure of this kind is built on a highly structured and deeply encoded bias. There seems little question that there is a persistent sense of freakishness that haunts a great many otherwise contented gay people. And it is a haunting marked by an insinuation of shame and a fear of ridicule. The current public image of gay men and lesbians has great latitude, resulting in an identity somewhere between the closet and the sandwich board.

Like all the mythic attitudes of the West, our attitudes about normality don't change quickly. The entrenched Western paradigm of "divine law" leaves little room for the impulsiveness of nature. In our illusions of a "steady-state" biology, the seasons may change and creatures may be born and grow old and die, but human nature, having been perfected by God, remains immutable and eternal. It is tacitly assumed that God doesn't make mistakes, doesn't create freaks, unless his intentions are ominous, meaning that his errors are forms of punishment. Behind every disease, anomaly, and deviation is the persistent question: "What did I do to deserve this?" Even for those who revel in their spiritual liberation, there inevitably remains the suspicion that illness and adversity are some inscrutable form of divine justice.

Even the word "freak" is a shortened form of the original Latin *lusus naturae* (freak of nature), suggesting that nature can somehow be unnatural. We rarely grasp the scope of nature's variety because we are obsessed with a model of nature that cannot easily understand anything that doesn't have a clear-cut polarization: It is normal or it is abnormal. Our comprehension of time and identity does not permit us to recognize that everything is constantly changing—passing silently through the immense space that exists between what is expected and what is possible, between what exists and what is coming into existence, between what is "normal" and what is "abnormal." By the standard of *lusus naturae*, every mutation essential to evolution and every hybrid plant or beast is a freak, because it cannot and will not *fit* into the narrow context that we take to be God's ultimate "reality."

Despite the importance of nature's whims in the earth's creative process, most of us are so intimidated by the prospect of radical change and so uncertain of exactly what constitutes a "freak" that we plead for reassurances from our peers that we ourselves are exempt from that terrifying category of freakishness. The reassurance we seek, however, is not an affirmation of our *own* normalcy, but a satisfaction that comes from designating the abnormality of *others*.

"We are the freaks!" is what we believe all the oddities of the world constantly assure us, as they look across at us from their dreadful isolation. "Look at us. Can't you see? *We* are the freaks! But not you! Not *you!*' The age-old fascination with humpbacks, dwarfs, transvestites, hermaphrodites, bearded ladies, and giants seems to be rooted in the realization of the curious possibilities of nature, which happily do not overtake the lives of ordinary people. "We are the freaks! Not you!" But this fascination is not built simply on disgust and aversion. In many societies, deformity is regarded as the mysterious connection between the physical and the spiritual. In modern Western society, freaks may be regarded as aberrations, but in many other times and places freaks were and still are regarded with fear and reverence.

So exactly what is a freak? It is the exceptional rather than the ordinary. It is something that is unusual or irregular. In this sense, left-handedness is freakish. A freak can also be an unusually formed organism, a dwarf, a giant, or Siamese twins. An albino African is a freak. Yet in each of these instances, freakishness has no implicit negative cultural significance until a negative value is attributed to specific kinds of irregularity. Freaks occur in nature, but society determines their value, that can as readily be revulsion as wonderment. In our particular society we are instructed to respond to most irregularity with revulsion. Children must be taught not to stare at disabled people. In contrast, the albinos of Central Africa are held in great regard, as exceptional rather than deformed persons.

The basis of freakishness that interests me is the one that arises from a peculiar cultural question that repeats itself again and again as we look across the chasm separating people who are different: "Who are we? Are we *us* or are we *them*?" The current wisdom insists that this apprehension about conformity is built on our inherent need to be accepted into our kinship group, but there is also a good deal of evidence suggesting that acceptance is only part of our cultural motive. There are countless societies in which acceptance is not based on our notions of behavioral and physical conformity. To the contrary, in a great many communities oddities were and still are revered.

People with crossed eyes were greatly admired by the ancient Maya. The poetry and songs of the Ethiopian peoples are filled with praise for men with gigantic dicks. One of the most revered and pervasive figures of Mesoamerican culture is the so-called Hunched Back Flute Player, who is associated with rain-making and whose image is widely found in Mexico and throughout the southwest United States. In the seventeenth century, the leaders of the tribes of the Congo were admired for their overwhelming obesity. Among the Moche of pre-Columbian Peru a favored subject of thousands of effigy potteries is a huge range of physical deformities as well as every conceivable sex act involving every possible combination of male and female participants. It is inconceivable that such pots were simply marriage manuals or "textbooks" of pathology, since they were valued funerary offerings, suggesting a more metaphysical purpose (Doig, 1980).

But, in the West, diversity is often equated with deformity. We earnestly want assurance from our peers that we are *not different*, that we *don't stand out* except in certain very acceptable ways, such as having wealth or fame, possessing social stature and community prestige, and being conventionally attractive. We don't want to be too tall or too short, too buxom or too flat-chested, too endowed or excessively underendowed, too unnoticeable or too conspicuous. That's why we follow the lead of trendy magazines, dressing and grooming ourselves in terms of the prevailing notion of attractiveness. *Above all, we don't want to be freaks.* We don't want to have extraordinary or exotic looks. We are reluctant to create an entirely new and individual kind of beauty because such beauty might be seen as an aspect of freakishness, until, that is, a person of prominence introduces it into the pop repertory. Even our ideas about what is sexy are based on consensus. And what we want more than anything else is to be a lauded imitation of that consensus. At the very most, we want the safety of being sublimely average. But under no circumstances do we want to be freaks.

The ideals of our own social identity entirely prescribe our expectations of and our responses to other people. When we sense an imperfect imitation of the consensus in a stranger, we feel uneasy, and then, as the degree of difference widens, we feel repulsed, which is a response expressed as readily with brutality as with derision. This discriminatory process is how we have been meticulously trained to respond to oddities and freaks as well as strangers from other lands. Since our social attitudes are based on the manipulation of an innate proclivity to be sociable and live in communities, we mistake our imprinted behavior for an inborn reflex; and we take it for granted that our hostile reaction to someone or something "unnatural" is simply a "natural" expression of our God-given knowledge of what is and what is not natural.

The problem with the word "natural" is very much like the problem with the word "unnatural." Such terms presume an infallibility that closes all disagreement and debate. The words alone, without qualification or explanation, represent an unimpeachable judgment. Even to question the merit of such words, we must take on the entire mythological cosmos. In order to contest the worth of such words, we must give up all hope of discussing the issue at hand, whether it be race, homosexuality, abortion, or euthanasia. Instead, we must go back to the beginning and to the difficult effort of contesting an unassailable concept of "nature" that was presumably defined by God.

This dilemma is not just an issue when we try to deal with fundamentalists, because the preconception of "naturalness" permeates every aspect of Western culture. Judeo-Christian morality is everywhere; and in its every manifestation it is, to a greater or lesser extent, a very tricky form of religious ventriloquism. It is "God" who is *really* having his say when people move their mouths and claim they are expressing their own attitudes about life and death, disease and health, reward and punishment, as well as naturalness and unnaturalness. God is everywhere in Western civilization because we could not have created our civilization until we had first created our very particular notion of God. That notion of God is what our civilization is all about, even when we revise, refute, or deny God. We hear more about God on television than we do in churches and temples. God is in our anthems and on our money and in the mouths of our politicians and presidents and on the minds of people who are in trouble, and on every side of every battle that has ever been fought. God is in our beds and in our underwear and in the trillions of reproachful eyes that watch billions of little boys and girls masturbate. So how can we argue with God when it was "God" who presumably set up all the rules governing the debate?

Until the rules change, people will not be able to escape the mythology that turns children like Frankie into freaks because, at heart, Frankie has been methodically trained to believe she really is a freak. Willingly or unwillingly, the members of a society embrace the consensus that targets some people as freaks, with the result that children like Frankie wish they were somebody else. Some people will do almost anything to *naturalize* the unnatural impression they make on those who find them odd or repulsive.

That process of *naturalization*, which I will discuss in detail when dealing with social metaphors, can involve all kinds of self-abuse and self-deception: anything from steroid therapy and obsessive bodybuilding, to implants and cosmetic surgery, or hair straightening and skin bleaching. It can also involve the change of an ethnic family name or an altered personal history, a marriage of convenience or an appropriate "sweetheart" of the opposite sex for display at office parties. And it may also be the motive, in some cases, for radical gender surgery and sex hormone therapies.

To the extent that we can neutralize a stigma, we may feel that we can evade persecution and provide ourselves with a semblance of social conformity. But, at heart, the normalizing process is a form of self-censorship and denial that simply disguises the stigma at the cost of our own identities. For instance, Leslie Fiedler has asked if transsexuals undertake radical surgery for the purpose of self-realization or if they do so simply to accommodate a bourgeois institution, if not of marriage, then, at least, of the polarity of maleness and femaleness, that was an inevitable part of the tidy invention of heterosexuality. Are transsexuals always people who feel like they live in the wrong bodies, or are they often people who are *made* to feel profoundly uncomfortable with their orientation, and who undertake virtually any action to resolve (naturalize) traits that arouse the ridicule and contempt of their society?

Leslie Fiedler has a keen insight into this normalizing process:

What monsters men have needed to believe in, they have created for themselves in words and pictures when they could not discover them in nature. And it is with this psychic need that we should begin: seeking prototypes neither in history or anthropology, nor in embryology or teratology, but in the depths of ourselves, and in our most basic uncertainties about the limits of our bodies and our egos.

From my point of view, "the depths of ourselves" is explored only when we confront the mythologies that are the basis of our fundamental beliefs and values. Such an exploration is difficult, because the Judeo-Christian attitudes about divine law are resistent to change to such an extent that reformations and reforms have caused serious riffs in Western religious communities. And yet dogma cannot shield us from an inkling that unexpected things, freakish events, are always happening. Meteors plummet to earth. Two-headed calves are born. The caterpillar mysteriously changes into a butterfly. In fact, wherever we look we see evidence of change and mutation despite the fact that we are taught that we are sheltered under a fixed and finite sky.

Our observations of change, in conflict with our faith that the cosmos is in stasis, create a peculiar kind of metaphysical schizophrenia in the West. Because we ignore the process of natural modification, *we often mistake variation for deviation*. In fact, the perfectly acceptable word "deviation" has assumed a sinister connotation when applied to sexuality. And because we identify deviation with distortion, we suspect that despite the perfection of the world, somehow there are still some things that are imperfect. This knowledge of deviation and transgression impels us to define and defend our standards of normalcy. Those standards are unmistakably aimed at condoning those who are part of the mainstream while condemning those who are marginal, racially, ethnically, and in terms of gender and sexual orientation.

Despite all the evidence to the contrary, in our minds the world remains a motionless island at the center of the cosmos, and our particular ethnic and religious and gender group remains at the center of all the populations of the world, because we persist in using ourselves to connote as well as to denote human normalcy. It is in this sense—in a prolonged and mindless bias regarding normalcy—that deformity has been institutionalized as a moral and spiritual transgression in the West.

Still, even such arrogant ethnocentrism is inevitably haunted and humbled by a glimmer of doubt that is always flickering somewhere deep within the human psyche. Even at the height of Christendom, when Europeans declared that the cosmos is immutable—the perfect celestial machine created and set in motion by God—there was, nonetheless, a trace of a long and lingering memory of other gods and other worlds that seemed to question all that was supposed to be unquestionable. In the age of exploration, Europe began a continuous series of encounters with peoples and cultures with entirely different models of reality. "Freaks" were beginning to be discovered everywhere. They were no longer just rare anomalies, hidden in closets, in museums, monasteries, and orphanages. They seemed to have found a life of their own.

Missionaries, such as Padre Bernardino de Sahagun, whose intent was to save freakish pagans from eternal damnation, became so intrigued by the unexpected and alien worlds they discovered that they became the major repositories of the very cultures they were sent to destroy. This intrigue for the forbidden lore of paganism was as compelling at home in Europe as it was in strange "new" lands. For even in the safety of their own Christian nations, there remained a trove of barbarous legends that streamed, like underground rivers, from generation to generation. Pre-Christian rituals, vaguely disguised as holy sacraments in honor of Jesus, survived the sternest prohibitions of the church. Good Christians continued to toss spilt salt over their shoulders. They continued to carry rabbits' feet. They kissed under mistletoe and decorated evergreen trees in honor of a son of God born in a territory where there were few conifers. Clearly, Europe had its own legacy of freaks and heathens that ruminated on the hearth and in the nursery of every home.

The freak and the heathen retained the power to subdue religious caution and call people back to the beginning, like a forbidden word never spoken but everlastingly remembered. Because the West, despite herculean effort, has never overcome the primordial belief that the power and mystery of nature are boundless, the people of Western societies have continued to respond with both wonder and terror when confronted by the many "anomalies" of the natural world. Nature keeps slipping free of the shackles with which we wish to restrain it. And, because we are an intrinsic aspect of nature, we too continue to slip free of the restraints of the arbitrary norms with which we attempt to define ourselves and the world.

It is only when we approach an entirely different culture from our own that we sometimes discover a disparate model of reality and a different definition of gender identities that strike us as shameful at the same time that we are undeniably fascinated by oddity. It is not surprising that in such alien societies the most fundamental rules of conduct are often at odds with the Judeo-Christian rules we take for granted as a matter of divine revelation.

In the heart of the deep south of the United States, long before the battles for civil liberty made any progress, there was a pre-Columbian tribe called the Natchez. They were untouched by Western religious dogma until as late as the 1750s, when a Frenchman named Dumont de Montigny encountered them in the territory then called *La Louisiane.*

> Among the Natchez and perhaps also among the many other Indian nations, is called "the chief of the women." It is certain that although he is really a man he has the same dress and the same occupations as a woman. Like them he wears his hair long and braided. He has, like them, a petticoat or *alconand* instead of a breechcloth. Like them he labors in the cultivation of the fields and in all the other labors which are proper to [women]. . . . When a party of warriors or of Honored Men leaves the village to go either to war or to the chase, if they do not make their wives follow them, they always carry with them this man dressed as a woman, who serves to keep their camp, to cook their hominy, and to provide, in short, for all the needs of the household as any woman might do.

Depending on the tribe and its localized culture, gender variance was widely accepted among Native Americans. Instead of viewing deviation as deformity and transgression, an openness to gender identities persisted wherever traditionalists resisted Christian assimilation, sometimes well into the first decades of the twentieth century.

During the last years of the nineteenth century, anthropologist Matilda Coxe Stevenson conducted a great deal of fieldwork among the Zuni Indians of the American Southwest. Her chief source of information, and her close friend, was an Indian named We'wha, a Zuni *Ihamana*—or male transvestite, whose biological gender was unknown to Stevenson until We'wha's death. That We'wha was a biological male was also unknown by President Cleveland and other politicians whom the Indian visited during a six-month stay in Washington, D.C.

We'wha was greatly admired by the members of her tribe. At an early age she lost her parents and was adopted by a sister of her father. She belonged to the Badger clan. Owing to her intelligence, We'wha was often asked by her clan to memorize and recite the long prayers used at Zuni rituals. She was both a religious and a tribal leader. Only when she died did Stevenson know with certainty that We'wha was a male. For her funeral, We'wha was dressed in women's clothing, with the addition of men's trousers. The ambiguity of gender in the Zuni worldview is emphasized by the fact that We'wha was buried on the men's side of the cemetery. This was the only biological demarcation of social gender that countered the gender she had chosen during her lifetime. Her behavior had determined her gender in life; her anatomy only was the determinate of her gender in death. From the Zuni point of view, We'wha's spirit was that of a woman; only her body was that of a man.

Stevenson eventually asked one of We'wha's close friends: "Why didn't someone ever tell me about We'wha?"

It was a question that would have made a good deal of sense to any Anglo whose notion about gender is anatomical and whose notion of reality is a matter of physical facts. The serene answer given to Stevenson came from a very different point of view. "Tell you about what?" responded the Indian with an expression of perplexity .

For the Zuni, We'wha was not stigmatized because he/she was a *Ihamana.* To the contrary, her tribe always referred to her as a female, and the people viewed her as a divine freak. To be different in the way that We'wha was different was understood as a blessing, as the designation by the Great Mystery of a being of extraordinary spirituality and power, to be revered, admired, but also to be feared.

It is fascinating that the Zuni both accepted and honored a person of nonspecific gender. But what seems far more interesting is the mythic basis of the divine law that probably prompted such acceptance among the Zuni.

Awonawilona is the primeval Zuni deity, whom the Zuni referred to as *He-She,* a gender neutrality of the Zuni language that permeates the entire Zuni cosmos and provides, both in words and thoughts, an attitude about gender entirely different from the Western connotation. In English, we may refer to objects, like ships and automobiles, in terms of gender, but, ultimately, our language calls on us to describe only a living creature by either male or female gender, and then only if and when we are aware of the creature's genitals. There are secondary characteristics of gender, like tone of voice, absence or presence of facial hair, dress, and grooming, but the essential qualification of a male or a female in the West is purely anatomical. For the Zuni, the connotations of maleness and femaleness are closely linked to spiritual powers and are not references to genitalia.

The rich mosaic of male/female power possessed by the supreme Zuni deity Awonawilona is at once omnipotent and omniscient. It is, in Western terms, an androgynous energy that transcends identity and endows Awonawilona as a naked singularity—exiting alone, without beginning or end, in a vast nothingness.

Awonawilona is called "the supreme giver of life"—he/she who made everything in creation. This mysterious Zuni spirit first created itself out of nothingness, and then began to think outward into eternal space. Those primordial thoughts became the blue vault of heaven. Awonawilona also scattered parts of his/her body into the nothingness, and a sea was formed. From the foam of the sea, Awonawilona created the sky father Apoyan Tachu and the earth mother Awitelin Tsita, whom he separated into male and female from the androgynous mi-asma of the cosmos.

Such androgyny is not a deformity but an integral part of many of the world's creation mythologies. Primal people saw the cosmos as a divine unity of male and female, and this unity was perceived as the basis of the generative powers in nature. Many androgynous deities were worshiped as emblems of the life force. There was the bearded Aphrodite, a classic hermaphrodite representing the union of the Evening Star and the Morning Star, the spiritual connection between light and darkness.

There was also a Middle Eastern deity of the Moabite called Baal-Peor—a double-sexed deity addressed both as Baal, meaning "Lord," and as Asherim, meaning "Mother." During the worship of Baal-Peor, priests dressed as women and priestesses dressed as men. Such priestly cross-dressing is found in countless religious rituals throughout history and around the world.

In Assyria Baal-Peor was known as Belphegor. Medieval storytell-ers borrowed the name Belphegor, and demonized the god by creating a tale about a time when he was called out of the infernal regions in order to mediate the quarrels of married couples on earth. After study-ing all the intimacies of humans, Belphegor fled in horror and returned to the depths quite pleased that female companionship did not exist there. But, for the Assyrians, the original Belphegor contained the har-monious elements of both the male and the female.

An exploration of world religions makes it clear that undifferen-tiated gender was often regarded as a sacred and mysterious manifes-tation as well as a supernatural source of life. In a great many cultures, the differentiation of gender seemed to be an unlikely attribute for a primordial deity who was somehow capable of creating the world out of nothing but divinity itself. In the minds of the ancients, creation required a wholeness of generative powers contained in both male and female form. So it is not unreasonable that a great many creator deities were equally male and female.

This is not to say that there was not categorization of gender and dimorphism of sexuality among many societies. Nor is there any lack of contradiction between the mythological attitude and the social attitude of a multitude of peoples. For instance, the Japanese are one of the few cultures to designate and honor the sun as a female deity, yet the social status of women in Japanese history has been far less than magnanimous. It is difficult to explain how the same mentality that imagined a supreme female deity could also imagine the subjugation of women, nor is it possible to pinpoint if and when the matrocentric mythic point of view of Japan was countermanded by a patriarchal mentality. The same difficulty arises in attempts to explain the specific social causes of the decline in the West of agrarian cultures and the rise of the patriarchal regimes launched, mythologically speaking, by Zeus (ca. 2500 B.C.) and Abraham (ca. 1800 B.C.). The apparent global transition from a female-centered to a male-centered model is a paramount consideration in any exploration of gender polarization. By extension, we can assume that the invention of the "idea" of aberrant or deviant transgression probably arose as a social infraction—a "breach" of the hierarchical mentality that was created by the patriarchal cultural revolution.

The extensive demystification of women and the erosion of a primordial, agrarian culture may have introduced the polarization of gender and greatly elevated the male as the sole and rightful parent of his offspring, but the invention of homosexuality (though unquestionably built on such a patriarchal revolution) would not take place for another four thousand years. The efforts to use anthropological and historical records to speculate about alternative lifestyles and sexual orientations are inevitably flawed by Panofsky's theory of "disjunction"—the meaning and social context of language change even though the words may not change and the similar terminologies used by different societies may describe very different acts and attitudes. We are apt to read too much or too little into historical documents, especially when we have no context for their contemporary meanings. Archaeologist Sir Arthur

Evans certainly did just that at his excavations in Knossos. And there is suspicion that Margaret Mead and Ruth Benedict invested their field-work with a good deal of personal idealization. Until quite recently, it was a standard approach in the field of social research to make the unsupported assumption that contemporary tribal peoples, like the Australian Aborigines and African Bushmen, are "living fossils," whose twentieth-century customs and communities supposedly provide insights into how the people of late paleolithic Europe lived forty thousand years ago. Such an unfounded assumption completely ignores the fact that tribal peoples evolved no less than other human groups, though their particular kind of social evolution did not necessarily result in what Western observers assume to be the ideal social "goals" of all humankind. To imagine that there is only one possible form of "civilization" is very much the same as assuming that there is an ultimate, transcendent, and easily recognizable single basis of human gender and sexuality.

Endearing salutations in correspondence between men were formalities of the sixteenth and seventeenth centuries, and have no proven homoerotic significance even though, in our particular context, they may seem a bit bent. By our standards, there is something effete about the cosmetics, lace, wigs, and courtly behavior of the rakes of the period of Louis XIV. Yet, if those seventeenth-century Frenchmen could observe American males, they would probably find them irredeemably course and vulgar.

It has become evident since the time of anthropologist Franz Boaz that the records of Western scholars are heavily influenced by their own cultural biases. The result of this misinterpretation is, in its way, a reduction of "otherness" to either an Edenesque fantasy or a voyeuristic freak show—idealizing the "noble savages" or denigrating them as freaks of nature. What is worse for historians of sexuality is the discovery that the presumably authentic transcripts of rituals and ceremonies of aboriginal peoples still relatively untouched by Western biases were extensively expurgated and far less than candid about issues of sex and gender. Even when the earliest field reports of the major Americanist Fletcher, Coxe, Stevenson, Cushing, and Matthews were explicit and candid, their work was routinely purged by their publishers (Duberman, 1991). It is not difficult to be skeptical of such records when we consider the biases and omissions of the once extolled translations into English by Benjamin Jowett of the Greek classics, that were not fully discredited for their sexual deceitfulness until the 1970s (Tripp).

Clearly, the model of sexuality and social conduct among the people of any group is as variously structured as any other community standard. And yet, among most non-Western cultures, even in the most solemn religious rituals, there has long been an almost universal inclination for open and unrestrained humor closely associated with all matters of sex—a frame of mind reminiscent of the keen sensuality and casual vulgarity of Chaucer, Boccaccio, and their contemporaries.[1]

Despite the appalling social situation of women in many Asian societies, there is abundant evidence of a time when the Asian "idea" of woman possessed the same loftiness found in the unique poetic revelations of the troubadours of the European age of chivalry.[2] The entire thrust of Asian religion revolves around the prehistoric concept of yin/yang, the cosmic harmony of female and male principles, symbolized by a circle divided into a white comma (yin) and a black comma (yang)—entwined inextricably into a whole. Kuan Yin, one of the most celebrated Chinese goddesses, was a transformation of the far earlier deity Avalokitesvara, a disciple born from a tear shed by Buddha when he witnessed the sorrows of the world. Until the twelfth century, Kuan Yin was a male figure, and even modern images of the goddess often show a trace of a mustache, another example of a "freak" who is revered.

Kwannon is the Japanese name for Kuan Yin; she was, like her Chinese counterpart, originally a male deity who became a female, the Goddess of Mercy, who is now one of the most popular deities of Japan.

It has often been pointed out by mythologists, like Frazer, Eliade, and Campbell, that Jesus was also an androgynous deity, an aspect of a number of vegetative, generative deities of ambiguous gender, such as the Greek god Adonis. Jesus, like all vegetative spirits, possessed the dual qualities of strength and compassion—"male" and "female" powers symbolized in the Middle Ages by a mermaid, denoting the dual nature of Christ as god and mortal, male and female.

Clearly, Yahweh, who is the tribal god of Judaism and became the Father (Jehovah) of Christianity and the Allah of Islam, is not an androgynous deity. Yahweh is the *baal* of the Hebrews, baal being the generic name of numerous ancient Semitic gods, especially of Syria and Palestine, each usually the local agricultural deity bestowing fertility on his tribe's lands and flocks. The word "baal" is derived from Semitic terms meaning "master" or "owner" as in the "owner of land." Even in modern Yiddish, this ancient meaning of baal survives, as in the expression "baalboos"—meaning "a big boss" or "a master of the house." Underscoring all this religious and semantic history is the basis of the potent *masculine* bias found at the heart of all Western civilizations since the days of Rome. Interestingly and ironically, the first of the powerful Western religions to rescind the negative connotation of homosexuality was Reform Judaism.

If we look deeply into Semitic mythology we discover that at one time, before the unification of the ancient Hebrew tribes, Yahweh was not alone. He had the company of angels, one of whom was vain or competitive or both, and apparently fell from grace, becoming Lucifer. And despite a great many rumors to the contrary, God also had a wife, whose name was a feminized form of the same name for Yahweh. She was probably the most important deity of the ancient Jews before the rise of the patriarchs Abraham and Moses (Graves and Patai).

The compilation of the Hebrew Testament was the result of generations of appropriation and revision. Part of that process was the extermination of both the female and the androgynous aspects of the earliest tribal mythologies of the Semitic peoples. The wife of God vanished. The hero Judith was delegated to the Apocrypha—the collection of uncanonical biblical tales. And Lilith, the rebellious first consort of Adam described in the Babylonian Talmud, a woman created simultaneously with Adam from the same dust who rejected his supremacy, also vanished into demonhood. And all vestiges of the bisexuality of Yahweh, whose combined male and female attributes had created the world, were eradicated.

The transformation of androgynous spirituality into a patriarchal cosmology did not disrupt the kinship system of the Semitic peoples, whose leadership was built on the power of men, but whose lineage depended on tribal descent from women, resulting in a curiously matrilinear patriarchy. In short, the son or daughter of a Jewish male cannot be an Orthodox Jew unless the mother is a Jew; while a Jewish woman's children are Jewish no matter the background of their father.

If we compare the mythic basis of the cosmology of Awonawilona of the Zuni Indians and the Yahweh of the Judeo-Christian-Islamic cosmologies, there is little wonder, on the one hand, that the divine law of the Zuni honors We'wah as person of divine spirit; while the masculinization of divine law in Western cultures eventually deemed sexual ambiguity an abomination, even in the figure of Jesus—who is usually regarded as asexual rather than androgynous. Among the Zuni, sexual ambiguity confirms the creative power of divine law, whereas, among many Christians sexual deviation breaches the male-centered hierarchy of a different kind of divine law.

That consequence is not written in the stars; it is written in the invented cosmologies on which disparate cultures build their rules of conduct and their notions of norms. The cosmologies of societies that revere sexual ambiguity are usually life-affirming cultures because they give great significance to the procreative abilities of their feminized conception of nature. Even if we explore the period in which Christianity was born, we find remnants of an earlier, androgynous attitude toward sexuality. The New Testaments of Christians contain no explicit passages of sexual negativity. And, as Lawrence Osborne has observed,

> Nor, contrary to popular belief, does the peculiar ferocity of later Christian thought find its roots in the Old Testament. . . . What is different about later Catholic theology is that sexual love is fully equated with death. . . . Sexual pessimism, then, is the equation of sexual love outside the prerequisites of reproduction with death.

In the opinion of many outstanding scholars (including Denis de Rougemont), the same Christian mentality that built the boundaries beyond which only freaks exist is itself rather freakish—a psychology that equates sexual passion with death.

The sexualization evil and the demonization of sex by Christianity have persisted through the years. Witches and Jews were denounced as demons. The notorious reign of the Inquisition, between 1230 and 1430, was principally aimed at the destruction of religious nonconformity. Women who for centuries had been midwives and herbalists were accused of witchcraft. It was widely believed that it was through acts of sex that demonic forces entered the human world. Virtually every fiend was given a sexual connotation, most famously the *incubi* (the sexually aggressive demons) and the *succubi* (the sexually passive demons). But these demons were not designated as male or female. They were envisioned as deviants who could take on the appearance of either gender, depending on their lust and their victim. But the most sexualized of all the Christian demons was Satan: "There is a grudging awe at the Devil's enormous organ . . . while the witch was a kind of supernatural whore" (L. Osborne).

Nature can be regarded as limitless, so every process of nature is accepted as a blessing. The West, however, devised a very limited religious perspective of nature, so any deviation from the narrow precept of normalcy has been denounced as a blasphemy and a crime *against* nature. This Western process is a powerful vehicle of slander and demonization. For example, if we follow the process of the demonization of Jews, we find a striking historical correlation between anti-Semitism and homophobia.

The early record of anti-Semitism is filled with both medical documents and folklore that insinuates that Jews are not fully human, that they are forever blemished by original sin, and that they lack the potential of absolution because of their refusal to recognize Jesus as the Messiah. Later, in the late nineteenth and early twentieth centuries, as we shall see in the next chapter, the ever-changing Western concept of normality and abnormality was drastically shifted, becoming a matter of judgments based on medical law instead of the license of divine law. Under the assault of this new "science," anti-Semitism and homophobia were seen as aspects of the same kind of pollution. Therefore, Jews and homosexuals were accused of being the kind of unnatural creatures who are contemptuously called freaks. While the new "science" of German physician Richard von Krafft-Ebing (1840–1902) was pathologizing homosexuality, in his treatise *Textbook of Insanity*, he also claimed that "the percentage of insanity among the Jews is decidedly higher." He then linked Jews, insanity, sexual excess, and homosexuality: "Concealed under a veil of religious enthusiasm there is abnormally intensified sensuality and sexual excitement that lead to sexual errors that are of an aetiological significance." This "medical" defamation of Jews was the extension of a long-standing bigotry, easily joining a multitude of other anti-Semitic fabrications, like the pervasive European folklore that imagined that Jews were freaks of nature, with horns hidden in their curly hair.

This history of the demonization of Jews and homosexuals as freaks has persisted into the twentieth century. In 1919, the Jewish anti-Semite Arthur Trebisch declared that Jews had invented homosexuality. Two decades later, Hitler invented the notion that Jews were carriers of syphilis, claiming in *Mein Kampf* that "with satanic joy in his face, the black-haired Jewish youth lies in wait for the unwitting girl whom he defiles with his blood."

By the twentieth century, sex had earned such a terrible reputation in the West that it was possible to slander an entire group of people simply by identifying it with sexual taboos.

We have realistic reason to celebrate the changes that have come about in the West with regard to racism, even though we must admit that attitudes about race remain dire social problems. We can also begin to envision a time when women might be treated as the equals of men. And yet, these crucial changes have been largely cosmetic or ideological. Regrettably, they have not been the result of any fundamental changes in our approach to religious law. It is difficult to imagine any time in the near future when we can hope for changes in the role of divine law in setting our social agendas. And, without changing that story, homosexuals will continue to be regarded as outsiders and freaks, and their human reality will continue to be subverted by a mentality that mistakes conformity for equality.

Howard Becker has observed, "Before an act can be viewed as deviant, and before any class of people can be labeled and treated as outsiders for committing the act, someone must have made the rule that defines the act as deviant." It is the amplification of Becker's statement that has been the focus of this chapter, so it warrants repeating that it is only such arbitrary rules that define deviation as deformity and deformity as transgression. The rules, and not nature, create freaks.

Any definition is built on a prototype—a model of reality. And, as the historian of religion Elaine Pagels has affirmed, there is no Western prototype as confounding or as influential as the events that took place in Eden. One typical result of the Eden prototype was the long-standing debate about the origin of Native Americans. Since Christianity has attempted to answer all questions about the origin and conduct of life with literal biblical interpretations, Christians were confused by the fact that there seemed to be no mention of Native Americans in the Bible. They asked, "If God didn't create Indians, then where did they come from?"

Christians and Jews were entirely unaware of the existence of the peoples of the Western Hemisphere until 1492. Therefore, their existence had to be validated in terms of Christian divine law. The labored declaration, after years of deliberation, that Indians are the remnants of the "lost tribes" of Israel was not an effort to discover the truth; it was, instead, an effort to create a new fiction in order to accommodate the existence of Indians in a mythical history described in the first three chapters of Genesis.

With Eden as a prototype, there is very little chance a biblical scholar will ever announce that there was a homosexual in Paradise. And, if not in Eden, then homosexuality must have arisen from some abominable and freakish mistake of nature—*lusus naturae*. Indians were theologically legitimatized as "the lost tribes of Israel," while homosexuals have been stigmatized as freaks who are not intended to be part of God's creation.

It is important to repeat that, with rare exception, what we mean by the word "homosexuality" was a meaning left uninvented by most societies, including many cultures of the Western world. In fact, the Classic anatomist Galen claimed that the sexual anatomy of men and women were identical except for one point: reproductive organs in men were external, whereas they were internal in females. Even the dimorphic model of what we perceive as strictly male or strictly female "gender" was a relatively late invention. Biologically speaking, "Renaissance doctors understood there to be only one sex" (Laqueur). Yet the social categories of sex—the superiority of males and the inferiority of females—were construed as "natural," even though they were at odds with the biological concept of sex. Such a biological connotation of one *physical* sex divided into two *social* sexes was a reflection of the attitudes of the Greeks, the Romans, as well as the Christian scholars of the Middle Ages. Until the last few centuries, biology and not divine law has been the arbitrator of what physiques and behaviors are abnormal, deformed, and freakish.

In the political life of the West, the concept of *gender as culture* has had a far longer history than the concept of *gender as sexuality*: "A penis was thus a status symbol rather than a sign of some other deeply rooted ontological essence. . . . It would be construed as a certificate of sorts, like the diploma of a doctor or lawyer today, that entitled the bearer to certain rights and privileges" (Laqueur). But, contrary to all we think and feel about gender, the concept of biological gender polarity, the dimorphism of males and females simply was not an issue until relatively recently. And if we see sexual deviation in light of this one sex model, it becomes clear that much of the consternation toward homosexuality that we think we find in historical records is largely a matter of misinterpretation and errors in translation.

When, in 1980, John Boswell expressed his view that homosexuality has not had a long history of social condemnation and abuse, his premise became a political hot button. But subsequent research in a number of fields seems to corroborate rather than refute Boswell's position. There were always freaks, but homosexuals were not specifically numbered among them until the nineteenth century.

It was *not* homosexuality, but *any* unconventional nonreproductive sexual behavior and any departure from the so-called missionary position that were looked on as "corruptions of the soul" (Aquinas). Pre-nineteenth-century Western literature provides evidence that those who practiced any kind of "deviant" sexual activity were denounced as "sodomites," which was a generic term often having no specific reference to anal sex. In short, they were freaks. The sexual freaks of Western history, however, were rarely condemned because of the objects of their desire. There was, in the opinion of Galen and Avicenna, the major medieval medical specialists of both the Christian and Arabic worlds, "no inherent gendering of desire and hence of couple. . . . The male body, indeed, seemed equally capable of responding erotically to the sight of women as to attractive young men" (Laqueur).

Presumably, to the Greeks and Romans, a freak was a male who continued into adulthood to desire the *passive* role in sex. The Classical notion of disgrace, by and large, was not unlike the attitude among many macho gay males today who believe that there is no greater stigma of emasculation than "getting fucked." Much of the hostility of various curses involving the word "fuck" or different gestures signaling the word "fuck" is the implication of emasculation through passivity.

Gender, then, was a matter of *social* boundaries, the demarcation of rank, authority, and assertive masculinity, rather than a matter of genitalia. By virtue of these boundaries, it was possible to rationalize the subjugation of women as a mandate of "nature." Women, after all, are not men. And, at least for a time, the visible phallus was the crown and scepter of gender domination.

Not until late in the eighteenth century was sex as we know it today finally invented: "The reproductive organs went from being paradigmatic sites for displaying hierarchy, resonant throughout the cosmos, to being the foundation of incommensurable difference" (Laqueur).

The medical wisdom of the day deemed that women owed their personalities to their "internalized" sexual organs. It was decided that the classical doctors, such as Galen, were mistaken in believing that female organs were an inferior form of the male genitalia and, by implication, that women were socially and biologically inferior to men. The hallmark of this anatomical revolution was the decision that "a woman is a woman"—a fully human and distinctive person. Thus two sexes were invented as the new foundation for gender. The issue of equality, however, would continue to be resisted on the basis of the "natural" superiority of men.

By the time of the nineteenth-century French forensic physician Ambroise Tardieu, the question of gender had become strictly biological. Any notion of sexual ambiguity or neutrality was regarded as nonsense, because all questions of gender were supposed to be answered by the direct and unquestionable evidence of anatomy. This distinction of male and female sexual identities seems so commonsensically "natural" and obvious to us today that we find it difficult to believe that it was a recent cultural invention and not the result of an inherent knowledge of divine law.

Only with the polarizing of the sexes came the gradual realization that a specific "type" of gender deviant existed, "lost" somewhere in limbo between the strict polarities of biological naturalness. The neutrality of the word "deviation" (to mean "variation" or "difference") was abolished, and "deviation" became synonymous with terms like "deformity," "degeneracy," "perversion," and "freakishness." Only at this moment of history, supported by declarations of the nineteenth-century forensic physician Ambroise Tardieu, were almost all undifferentiated sexual and gender behaviors, no matter how irreconcilable, clustered into a single category of presumed deformity and freakishness called *homosexuality*. As Foucault said, "The politics of truth had changed." Ever since that cataloging of sexuality, Western society has continued to redefine what is meant by the term "freak of nature." This change has been monumental in its scope and impact. "In the late sixteenth century, the situation was very different—a woman taking the man's role in lovemaking with another woman was assumed to be a tribade (*fricatice*). . . . She stood accused as a woman who had violated a law of social gender by playing the man's part during intercourse" (Laqueur). But the breach was not one of "perverse" sexuality. It was a breach of social boundaries: a woman daring to act like a man. Before the eighteenth century, the lesbian was not a lesbian. She was, instead, a female who dared to cross a forbidden social line by usurping the "superior" sexual role of a male. The crime was not called homosexuality. It was called "immoral lust" or "sodomy." In fact, a woman named Marie de Marcis came close to being burned at the stake for this social transgression.

As for women in general, until the mid-twentieth century, they were, as Freud said, "the dark continent"—a mere footnote in the history of human sexuality that was written entirely by men. Women were regarded either as "whores" and sexual predators or as "mothers" who were supposedly sexually anesthetized. This stereotyping of females is at least part of the reason that female homosexuality was rarely a moral issue, as were other forms of deviation. The men in charge of public morality knew very little about both the female body and the possibilities of female sexuality. If women were so trivialized that their intimate behavior went largely unnoticed, male sexuality, by comparison, came under constant scrutiny. Before the age of naturalistic science, almost any male act of nonreproductive sex was condemned as "sodomy." Only with the nineteenth-century dimorphic model of gender was the notion of "homosexuality" invented.

That invention announced a seemingly drastic redefinition of deformity. It was a change marking the end of one era and the beginning of another, in which Christian attitudes about nature and naturalness were recast into what passed as a different and secular point of view. But the so-called revolution of science was not a real rebellion. It was a very gradual process of accommodation between religious and secular scholarship. The divine law of the church was transformed into the natural law of science, with far more changes in terminologies than in ideologies, at least until the time of Darwin. The transgressive attitudes about deformity shifted from religious revulsion to scientific curiosity. The religious freaks, the heretics of Christianity, did not simply vanish. Instead of being freaks of divine law, they became freaks of natural law. As we will see, that difference was superficial—merely a rethinking of religious "condemnation and atonement" as medical "diagnosis and cure." But the story of deformity as transgression was not yet concluded. What ends here is the unlimited authority of the church and the ascendancy of medicine as the arbitrator of medical, and, by extension, moral laws still presumed to emanate from God.

The advent of naturalism was spawned by several revolutions in science, but the most crucial were the revisions made by Newton and the mechanistic metaphor devised by René Descartes. Such points of view drastically changed the model of Galen, who had understood the body as a correlation of cosmic order. Now the body had its own mechanical nature—a nature born of nature. But for all its secular terminology, the science of Descartes was Christian science. Only the language of procreation changed: the term "generation" (implying a human replication of God's act of creation) was replaced by the mechanistic word "reproduction." But God was not banished from scientific research. His existence was simply veiled by a spurious claim of objectivity.

The mechanistic view of Descartes, supported by elaborate mathematics, deduced that the cosmos and all the things in it ware automata. Gary Zukav puts it this way: "From Descartes' time to the beginning of this century, and perhaps because of him, our ancestors began to see the universe as a Great Machine. Over the next three hundred years they developed science specifically to discover how the Great Machine works."

Descartes laid the philosophical foundation for physiology by advancing the notion that the bodies of humans and animals can be regarded as machines. But since moral principles obviously do not apply to machines but do apply to Christian human beings, Descartes thoroughly Christianized the machine by assuming that humans must therefore be more than automata in human shape. The element that makes people more than automata is the soul, "a spiritual agency that is not itself part of the body."

This cleaving of body from soul, like the earlier dimorphizing of male and female gender, has remained an indelible revision of Western consciousness, and the cause of most of our philosophical dilemmas. Descartes informed us that without belief in the soul's ability to make moral choices, there would be no basis for Christian ethics. "For the purpose of dealing with the intersection of morals and human biology, nothing has thus far replaced the Cartesian body–soul dualism" (Stent).

Descartes became the scientific ventriloquist of religious dogma. As Aldous Huxley said, such religious facts disguised as science are like the pronouncements of a ventriloquist's dummy. "Sitting on a wise man's knee, they may be made to utter words of wisdom, elsewhere say nothing, or talk nonsense, or indulge in sheer diabolism."

Descartes was not looking for a new truth. He was actually trying to revamp a very old one. For him, a deviance from divine law was still a transgression. Oddity was deformity. His cause was the same cause as Paul and Augustine's. Descartes was the benefactor of a concept that did not really change the world as much as it provided a new political basis for the old religious biases: new "scientific" rationales for a great many aspects of Christian dogma. The Cartesian model affirmed that the mind (soul) is distinct from the body. It is the mind and not the body that thinks and makes moral decisions. From that premise, it was deduced that the mind (soul) has no sex. Gender, the social division between men and women, between heterosexual and homosexual, must therefore have its basis in the body and not in the mind. Eventually, psychology would attempt entirely to reverse this idea.

What Descartes did in separating the soul from the body, Freud would later do in separating the psyche from the body. The contradictory impact of both of these dimorphic notions of the body placed homosexuality in the position of being a "sickness" not of the body but of "the psyche," creating the modern impression of homosexuality as a psyche living in a body that it is sexually incompatible with: "a woman living in a male body," or vice versa.

The Christian doctrine of the corruption of the body was validated by Cartesian science. As in all things technological, calibration became the basis of social doctrine. So in the wake of Cartesian science came every conceivable form of calculation, all in the service of ancient dogmas that refused to disappear. At the same time that science was inventing race, it also invented superior and inferior races based on calibrations of the brain and the skull. At the same time that science was inventing the polarity of male and female, it announced new empirical evidence of the superiority of men. And at the same time that science was placing white males at the crown of creation, it also cataloged all the myriad perversities of gender and sexual orientation that fell outside the gender dimorphism that is the essential anatomical mark of Descartes's mechanistic model. On the basis of that Cartesian mechanism evolved the stupendously naive notion that men and women were meant for each other because their parts fit together.

Such Cartesian ideas have had an enormous and continuing impact on our most complex and most simplistic thinking, to such an extent that many of us are convinced that the Cartesian point of view is "natural." But, despite its scientific tone, Descartes's dualism and his depreciation of the physical world as "dead matter" were not ideas in conflict with Christian dogma. Cartesian science was, to the contrary, simply a novel remapping of the same old Judeo-Christian worldview. It still resonated with Augustinian pessimism and Pauline asceticism. But it claimed a scientific rather than a religious basis. In essence, what Cartesian philosophy really achieved was to make Christian dogma the premise on which a supposedly nonreligious and objective science was built. Though seemingly incongruous, this marriage of scientific technology and Western Christian dogma was inevitable:

> Unlike the deities of paganism, the Christian god was a creator God, architect of the cosmos, the divine potter who shaped men from clay in his own image. In the Christian conception, all history moves toward a spiritual goal and there is no time to lose; thus work of all sorts is essential, and becomes, in a way, a form of worship. Such ideas created a mental climate highly favorable for the growth of technology. (Casson)

L. L. Whyte has observed that whatever lip service we pay to other philosophies, and however certain we are of the falsity of Descartes's ideas, after three centuries we still behave "as if we live in a Cartesian world." That anachronistic attitude has had a profound impact on our conceptions of both the body and sexuality. As science writer Gunther S. Stent has said, "Cartesian dualism is very much alive today and remains the unstated metaphysical premise of medical ethics."

The freak is still an outcast. Deformity still constitutes a transgression. Descartes merely changed the medical model from a religious to a secular dogma. With the advent of "science," the freaks have lost only their magical place in the West's mythic life. Freakishness is no longer mysterious and sacred, and it is no longer an abominable distortion of God's law. Today the freak is a mere irregularity of scientific expectation. The Western intelligentsia entered the nineteenth century with the illusion that their bonds with Christian metaphysics had been broken and that the "superstition" of the past had been replaced by a naturalistic science whose mission was to define a new reality. Just at the moment when religion began to lose its role as the absolute arbitrator of what is normal and virtuous, along came science, delighted to usurp the function of the church and replace its divine law with the naturalistic model by which we are now judged. The rule of science is far more fearsome than anything devised by Paul or Augustine. The new authority of mechanistic science in defining human normalcy and abnormalcy occupies the same territory once defined by God. It holds the same metaphysical power. It retains the same intensity of dogma. And it is as unapproachable, ineffable, and irrefutable as God. Now, however, divine law is called "natural law." In the eighteenth and nineteenth centuries there emerged a new kind of expert who professed to have the ability to decode the hitherto hidden "laws of nature." Mechanistic science innocently laid claim to empirical knowledge of all the mysteries theology had not been able to explain. It was at this crucial junction in Western history that the religious reading of mythology turned into a materialistic decoding of "nature" that claimed to be entirely unencumbered by mythology.

TRANSGRESSION

6

O miserable Mankind, to what fall
Degraded, to what wretched state reserv'd!
Better end here unborn! Why is life giv'n
To be thus wrested from us? Rather why
Obtruded on us thus? Who if we knew
What we receive, would either not accept
Life offer'd, or soon beg to lay it down,
Glad to be so dismisst in peace.

John Milton, Paradise Lost

I abhor myself. But when I discovered that he, the author at once
of my existence and of its unspeakable torments, dared to hope
for happiness; that while he accumulated wretchedness and de-
spair upon me he sought his own enjoyment in feelings and pas-
sions from the indulgence of which I was forever barred, then
impotent envy and bitter indignation filled me with an insatiable
thirst for vengeance.

Mary Shelley, Frankenstein

Two sorrowful protests, one spoken by the wretched Adam to the God who created him, the other voiced by the equally wretched monster created by the science of Dr. Frankenstein. In these outcries there is a haunting expression of the West's preoccupation with the powerlessness and victimization of human beings, beings created by forces beyond their control and then sent blindly into a life of confusion, pain, and illness. The stories of Frankenstein's monster and Adam are tales of those who are eternally forsaken, stories in which the mythology of science and the mythology of religion merge. The mythic imagination may be transcendent, but, despite the undeniable distinctions between God's Adam and Frankenstein's monster, both characters are the subjects of pervasive Western myths that describe much the same cynicism. The characters of history are always changing—even the identities of their creators change—yet the essential myth of human victimization persists as one of the underlying relationships between people and their creators.

The mythology of Western religion and the mythology of Western science share a distinctive claim to realism. In many other societies, mythology is a conscious expression of the imagination. In the West, mythology has learned to play a different game with the imagination. It is the kind of mythology that does not believe in mythology. So it persistently passes itself off as empirical truth or as a curiously ineffable hermeneutical reality—a circular kind of truth that cannot be directly experienced. Like all final ideas of *truth*, the Western attitude must constantly reinvent itself in order to keep pace with changing facts that relentlessly and irresistibly refute whatever is meant by the word "truth."

The mythology of the West professes to change its facts and their meaning; while all that really changes is the tellers and the telling of the same tale. Our mythology seems to be in a rut because we refuse to acknowledge its countless deaths and transformations. As psychologist John Rajchman points out in his correlation between the Christian theology of the flesh and the revisionist science of sexuality, instead of abandoning old truths and moving on to new models, we simply reconstruct old models and insist that they are reflections of one ultimate reality. We deny that mythology changes and, therefore, we deny that it has a history. We insist that it exists in an immutable *now*. As such, our mythology is the kind of geological model that changes too slowly to betray the enormity of its motion. What this neglect of change tends to promote is an inclination to mummify and pass along the corpse of our *single* materialistic myth, like morticians who use a perverse, cosmetic craft that allows them to create the semblance of life in something that is unquestionably dead. We have trained ourselves to obliterate from memory our primordial past; thus we can convince ourselves that we have never been anything other than what we are today. What we have carefully forgotten is our animal genealogy. What we have lost is the awareness of the possibilities of life. No longer the sacred freak of the ancients, an honored outsider who is transformed into the quintessential insider by a sublime unnaturalness. That myth of the extraordinary has escaped our memories and slipped into a *subversive forgetfulness*, the province now of dreamers, poets, and perverts.

What remains of myth for most of us are the moral monstrosities created by Christianity and the psychopathic degenerates created by science. As much as we would like to claim that all the demons have vanished, they can never vanish as long as we continue to demonize people with narrow categorizations and a regulatory taxonomy. It is possible that the immoralist and the monster are simply two versions of the same fiend, a two-headed creature created by religion or science. The truth of God has been replaced by the truth of Nature. Instead of having just one sinner, we now have two—one is a god-fearing beast infused with soul by divine law; the other is a fragile brute evolved out of mud and blood, an invention of natural law.

But what kind of distinction is this? How, really, does natural law differ from divine law? Are they conflicting attitudes or simply two different names for very much the same assumptions?

As I have already noted, phenomonologist Maurice Merleau-Ponty has said that "man is a historical idea and not a natural species." But a good many philosophers and biologists insist that human beings are a replications of forces hidden within a transcendent, cosmic mechanism called "Nature." As such, natural law is supposed to be a set of principles, based on what are assumed to be the permanent characteristics of the life process—principles that can serve as our standard for evaluating conduct and designating social decrees and appropriate punishment for the transgression of those decrees. To breach divine law is to act immorally. To breach natural law is to act unnaturally. Both transgressions are built on the same mythology, except one calls itself religion while the other calls itself science.

The pre-Socratic philosopher Heraclitus spoke of natural law in sixth century B.C. as "a common wisdom pervading the cosmos . . . for all human laws are nourished by one—the divine." According to the later Stoics, the universe is governed by a rational principle variously called Logos, God, or Mind. The Stoic Epictetus, who lived about A.D. 55 to 135, attempted to find a relationship between divinity and morality. "You, O Man," he wrote, "are God's principle work. You are a distinct portion of the essence of God, and a certain part of him exists in you. . . . You do not observe that you profane God with impure thoughts and unclean actions." And so it goes, even as the faces and names of the gods continually changed and even as the notions of what is and is not pure and clean were endlessly revised, natural law itself remained a consistent, religious doctrine built on an unfathomable divine will. The pragmatic Roman orator Cicero pointed out that natural law "is of universal application, unchanging and everlasting. . . . There will not be different laws at Rome and at Athens, or different laws now and in the future, but one eternal and unchangeable law will be valid for all nations and for all times."

Later, the philosophers Aquinas, Spinoza, and Leibniz interpreted natural law as the basis of Judeo-Christian ethics and morality. But the "nature" in their natural law was monomaniacal, expressing an exclusive and distinctive metaphysical bias. Aquinas, of course, was a devout Christian theologian who developed the idea of the "Eternal Law"; Spinoza was a Jewish pantheist with an "intellectual love of God," while Leibniz invented "the best of all possible worlds"—a concept built on his belief that the world was perfected by God and could, therefore, not be improved. In the romantic era, Rousseau believed that people are born wise and good "by nature." By the nineteenth century, this persistent impact of natural law was briefly silenced by various naturalistic attitudes that claimed an alliance with various ideologies of science: positivism, empiricism, and materialism. Gradually, natural law became an extension of another Western platitude, the one called "human nature," that presumes that people everywhere and at all times are the same—not just in their blood types and anatomies, but in their countless behavioral distinctions. In this way, it was assumed that Plato, Louis IV, and Einstein were interchangeable examples of human nature, different only because they happened to have lived at different times. This imperfect conspiracy of "human nature" and "natural law" began very early in Western history, with the words of Paul, when he speaks in Romans 2:14 of the Gentiles, who did not possess Mosaic law but did "by nature what the law requires," suggesting that goodness is an innate knowledge ("instinct") possessed by all human beings as part of their "human nature." In order to advocate an inherent morality, it has been necessary also to advocate a continuity and singularity in human nature. The seventh-century encyclopedist Isidore of Seville elaborated on that concept when he affirmed that natural law is observed everywhere by *natural instinct*. He cited as proof of the universality in human nature the "eternal laws" ordaining marriage and the procreation of children. The sixth-century Catholic clergy consecrated marital abstinence in the laity and celibacy in the Catholic clergy. It condemned masturbation, prostitution, and adultery. From the beginning, natural law was built on the arbitrary norms that the West claimed as the "will of nature."

It was not until the seventeenth century that the Dutch jurist Hugo Grotius attempted to break the bond between divine law and natural law. To achieve this, he suggested that the law would have validity even if there were no God. In place of divine law, what Grotius suggested was an objective or abstract type of universal law, knowable through pure reason in a way, Grotius explained, that abstractions of mathematics are known to us. Grotius wanted abstract truth without an ineffable God. As such, he opened the way to the rationalistic theories that dominated the seventeenth and eighteenths centuries, allowing both Hobbes and Locke to propose something they called "an original state of nature" from which they supposed a binding social contract naturally arose.

Without saying it in so many words, the consensus of the seventeenth century was that procreative, marital sex between a male and a female was an expression of "an original state of nature." Locke also understood this *natural law born of the original state of nature* to provide human beings with certain *inalienable* rights that could not be violated by any governing authority. But the democratic implications of natural law didn't last long. Like the divine law provided by God, the "new" truth *without* God began to erode. By the nineteenth century, jurists and philosophers came to regard the existence of a natural law unprovable. They decided that there could be no ultimate truth without God.

In the absence of a God-given law or a law that was an intrinsic aspect of nature, a new skepticism about morality and the law arose. Women and peasants gained unprecedented liberties as a result of the urbanization of the Industrial Revolution. The family unit, which had represented the core of rural society, began to erode as young people were allowed to consort without chaperones, inventing the unprecedented, modern idea of "dating." The invention of the automobile and the dark motion-picture theater moved romance from the supervised privacy of the living room into public places. The creation of public bathrooms in Paris in the nineteenth century had an unmistakable influence on male homosexuality. Single people of every orientation congregated in amusement parks and dance halls and taverns. Sexuality became an aspect of both fashion and culture, even if it remained largely subversive. And as sexuality became a more visible aspect of the social world, professionals began to specialize in sexual research, with the inevitable results that they produced a typically Western categorical approach to sex. The twentieth century opened with a utilitarian approach to the whole question of morality and law, a concept that became the oligarchic position called legal positivism, that is, *it is the law simply because the person in charge says it's the law.*

At least in theory, positive law largely replaced both natural law and divine law. It was a throwback to the classical Greek ideal that, as historian Eugen Weber has noted, "believed that law and institutions were the result of reason and not some sort of divine revelation." Both morality and civil obedience were understood in a relativistic framework—we legislate laws that serve the public interest and protect the individual, and we obey these laws voluntarily both because they are a consensus and because their infraction carries civil and criminal penalties. At such a juncture, God and nature have supposedly nothing to do with law.

But the West is profoundly uncomfortable with ambiguities; so positive law was bound to be contested by those always seeking something or someone larger than life. Even within the fields of science, a great many Judeo-Christian biases persist today—particularly about *purpose* and *progress* in the cosmos. These biases were doubtlessly the basis of the distinction that arose between the deterministic attitude found in biology and the ambiguities inherent in the theory of relativity in physics. Many of the continued debates about gender and sexual orientation are propelled by these two highly contrasting worldviews in science.

As often pointed out by social scientists, the Theory of Relativity, like many innovations of quantum physics, was not intended to create a shift in social, cultural, or religious attitudes. But, intentionally or not, the socialization of theoretical physics has been unlimited as well as being highly influential in countless fields.

The British physicist Paul Davies provides a brilliant framework for the debate that arose between physicists and biologists. He begins with the revolution in astrophysics that suddenly brought into question the fate of the cosmos:

Eventually the sun will run out of fuel and cease to shine. The same slow degeneration afflicts all the stars in the universe. In the mid-nineteenth century, this dismal fate came to be known as the "cosmic heat death." The thermodynamic "running down" of the cosmos represented a significant break with the concept of the Newtonian clockwork universe. Instead of regarding the universe as a perfect machine, physicists now saw it was a gigantic heat engine slowly running out of fuel. . . . This second law of thermodynamics introduces an arrow of time into the world because the rise of entropy seems to be an irreversible, "downhill" process. By an odd coincidence, just as the bad news about the dying universe was sinking in among physicists, Charles Darwin published his famous book *On the Origin of Species*. Although the theory of evolution shocked people far more than the prediction of a cosmic heat death, the central message of Darwin's book was basically optimistic. Biological evolution also introduces an arrow of time into nature, but it points in the opposite direction to that of the second law of thermodynamics—evolution seems to be an "uphill" process.

Whereas thermodynamics predicts degeneration and chaos, biological processes suggest an inherent progress in nature, producing order out of chaos. Biology represents procreation and life, while physics predicts erosion and death. The impact of this collision of ideas was so damaging to Western mythology that it resulted in profound denial, with the result that there are still a great many informed people clinging to obsolescent notions of normalcy and morality fundamentally at odds with the pervasive scientific vision of human life and cosmic process.

Despite many debates to the contrary and Darwin's own confusion on the subject, Darwin clearly believed that there is an innate drive in nature toward improvement and complexity. The entire platform of Darwinism is built on the universal natural law of an essentially heterocentric and "natural" procreative process. "As natural selection works solely by and for the good of each being, all corporeal and mental endowments will tend to progress toward perfection," Darwin wrote in *The Origin of Species*.

In *The Selfish Gene*, Richard Dawkins argues that successful genes—those that persist from generation to generation—are those that, by sheer luck, happen to improve the chances of their own organism's survival and thus of the gene's own perpetuation. In this context, survival of the fittest is not built on progressive purpose but on a fortuitous moment of sheer luck in the otherwise chaotic ruminations of the cosmos. Cosmologist Alexander Vilenkin was deeply impressed by this evolutionary notion and used it as the foundation of his approach to the anthropic principle in cosmology. Dawkins believes that a gene's existence is all the justification needed for whatever odd-seeming function the gene embodies; similarly, the anthropic principle

says that our very existence justifies the odd-seeming constants of nature that make our universe possible.[1] Perhaps biologists might adopt
this same position and declare that the mere existence of homosexuality
is all the justication needed to explain its evolutionary existence.

Clearly, the paradigm of biology was different from the paradigm
of physics. And this difference has had a powerful influence on Western
attitudes about sexuality, gender concepts, and morality. In a process
strikingly similar to the attitudes of Judeo-Christian theology, biology
has been predisposed to identify norms and hierarchies. Early on, biologists began to talk about a "ladder of progress" with microbes at
the "bottom" and human beings at the "crown of creation." Sexual
orientation as well as aspects of Judeo-Christian morality became a
fixture of this ladder of progress, a revelation possible to biologists only
because of the "superiority of human intellect." Even before sexuality
became a biological issue, sexual orientation was already part of the
hidden agenda of biology. Sexuality could not possibly avoid the implications of this ladder of progress and its valued judgments about
hierarchy. The cosmic plan was not supposed to be religious, and yet
the mythology of duality, hierarchy, and the Cartesian ghost in the
machine remained essentially unchanged in science except in name.

Although the theory of evolution rejects the idea that God designed
and made every creature in one miraculous week of creative labor, it
nonetheless leaves abundant room for some kind of cosmic designer,
functioning behind the scenes and guiding the course of evolution over
billions of years, *upward* from algae toward the triumphant arrival of
human beings. This progressive point of view is based on a concept
that is both subversive and morally loaded—in order to survive you
must adhere to the "law" of natural selection—that is merely another
recycling of the imperatives of *procreation* as an essential aspect of
natural law.

As we shall see, in the few instances when Darwinists and sociobiologists are willing to talk about nonreproductive sex, like homosexuality, they seem stunned and perplexed that an indisputably
nonreproductive behavior has persisted throughout history, even
though it has no apparent incentive to assist the "ascent of the ladder
of progress" or engage in the evolutionary "competition" that allows
survivors to pass on their genes from one generation to the next.

Darwinists are inclined to explain things in terms of survival. For
example, they point out that the bright plumage of male birds arouses

the interest of a mate, while the drab coloring of female birds provides camouflage while nesting. Or they observe that male mammals who achieve dominance in a group are inclined to kill the newborns of other males, apparently in order to assure the survival of their own genetic line. Or they point out that the suicidal behavior of the male Australian redback spider "must offer an evolutionary advantage or it never would have become entrenched."[2] The male redback spider turns a somersault and places his abdomen in front of his mate's jaws so she can devour him while the couple is still copulating. Similar efforts to explain homosexuality in evolutionary terms have been highly controversial.

If biology is apt to look for commonsensical evolutionary survival motives, physics searches for a reality that "exists" beyond common sense—a conceptual rather than a perceptual reality. Biology appears to perpetuate the West's naive realism (the observed world is the real world), while physics appears to deal with a reality that has much in common with the Asian notion of *maya* (the perceived world is illusion).

Since the turn of the century, physics has attempted in various ways to deal with a mythology of *chaos*, while many philosophers and biologists, who assume that linear progress is an implicit aspect of the life process, have attempted in various ways to deal with a mythology of *order*. All such linear and progressive philosophies see evidence in the universe of an intrinsic ability of "nature" to evolve order out of chaos. Heterosexual generation, procreation, or reproduction are viewed as unquestionable aspects of that biocentric attitude, putting homosexuality at a great disadvantage.

As Paul Davies notes, "Unfortunately, progress in nature did not mesh well with blind thermodynamic law of chaos.... Tension between the concept of a progressive biosphere on the one hand and a universe destined for heat death on the other produced some confused responses."

Some biologists, especially in France, emphasized Darwin's implication that evolution works progressively and downplayed his central thesis of chaotic and random mutation. The result was a mysterious quality called *élan vital*, or life force, responsible for driving organisms in the direction of a progressive and linear process that denied the chaotic cosmological views of astrophysicists. This impasse between biologists and physicists has been a very heavy burden on the West during the late twentieth century. Physicists stood firm with their vision of chaos, chance, and cosmic death. But, even in the face of such astrological skepticism, biologists have remained determined to prove that life on earth *makes sense*.

In this way, the twentieth century began with a wide schism between physicists, who were startled to discover chaos at the heart of the cosmos, and biologists, who seemed, at least in some instances, to espouse an almost religious attitude about an element of "design" inherent in the evolutionary process—even though such a point of view was a basic betrayal of Darwin's fundamental doctrine of randomness.

Darwin's insistence on the randomness of the evolutionary process has been the source of conflict among Darwinists because that doctrine of randomness seems in conflict with Darwin's own statements: "Natural selection works solely by and for the good of each being, all corporeal and mental endowments will tend to progress toward perfection." The terms "progress" and "perfection" have apparently impacted generations of biologists far more than Darwin's conviction that random choice—pure chance—drives evolution.

As Paul Davies indicates, this battle still rages. Though a great many biologists have abandoned the notion of a "life force" that directs evolution, other scientists, many of whom have been influenced by the work of Ilya Prigogine, still insist on the existence of *self-organizing* processes in nature, and maintain that advancement toward greater organizational complexity is a universal law-like tendency. So, at least in biology—and by extension, in the study of sexuality and gender—God and natural law appear to be desperately clinging to life.

One of the potential problems of such a teleological point of view in biology is that it is inclined to moralize "nature" in exactly the same way that psychoanalysts in the United States have tended to moralize "human nature," suggesting that some behaviors are normal (good) and others are less than normal (bad), and that "bad" behaviors need to be changed through various processes—like genetic splicing or by dredging up painful secrets from the ineffable unconscious with the help of a psychiatric shaman.

Ultimately, such moral agendas bring about a confusion between observation and evaluation. As biologist Bernd Heinrich has observed, "Reductionism is to biology as fundamentalism is to religion, or totalitarianism to government." For Heinrich, biological research has nothing to say and *should* have nothing to say about morality, because "natural is what *is*, nothing more." Lost beneath the survival history of every living species is a great legion of mutations that were an essential part of a random process, even if they were doomed to extinction. Unless human beings somehow mange to thwart that process, no life form seems to escape the finite operation of evolution. Under the circumstances, it seems more than a bit monomaniacal that a science that essentially *specializes* in *extinction* has often lent its name and its research to a moralistic categorizing of human sexual behavior and to a process of gender and racial discrimination that have been among the most retrograde interpretations of the twentieth century. When, as belatedly as 1974, the American Psychiatric Association finally removed homosexuality from its official list of mental disorders, it was an astoundingly self-congratulatory act, sadly reminiscent of the recent announcement by Pope John Paul II that he pardoned Galileo for his sin of 350 years ago, when Galileo proposed that the sun does not revolve around the earth.

Wherever we look, we find that a consuming idea of transgression is at the heart of Western mentality. The idea that there are moral laws of nature is so deeply entrenched in the West that we tend to see breaches of those laws every time someone's behavior confuses or outrages us. The language of transgression changes from time to time, but the process of vilification remains very much the same. Whatever the categories of sin, whatever the categories of normalcy, in the West we seemed to be continually on the hunt for offenders. It seems to me that we are famished for demons, as if our very sanity depends on a kind of moral cannibalism. Whether we speak of the wickedness of breaking divine law or the degeneracy of breaking natural law, essentially we are describing the same transgression—the violation of a boundary established by a mysterious power variously called God and Nature.

In the 1920s, many astrophysicists joined Niels Bohr's admonishment of Albert Einstein's cosmic teleology. When Einstein objected to the concept of a nonpurposeful cosmos, it was Bohr who famously advised Einstein to stop telling God what to do. This was one of the rare and legitimate instances of a radical and fundamental change in Western thinking. But radical change does not come easily. In astronomy the existence of meteorites was doubted for generations. It was considered ridiculous to suggest that rocks could randomly fall from the sky. If such an occurrence could really happen, it would betray a chaos inconceivable in an orderly cosmos. Then, following a spectacular meteor shower over Paris, the French Academy changed its position about the reality of meteorites, marking the beginning of what Paul Davies has called "the death of materialism." Davis also points out that scientists have often seen things that aren't there, and, in other cases, scientists have failed to see things that were right in front of their noses.

Since the time of physicist Niels Bohr, all fields of science have drastically changed. Scientific "investigation" no longer refers to research defined by objective common sense. Astrophysicists are delighted when they encounter something that is so random and purposeless that it seems to do what Einstein believed to be impossible: "to play dice with the universe." For this new breed of postquantum scientists, the chaotic—the "unnatural"—is the gateway to discovery.

On the other hand, biology has had some difficulty breaking its longtime bond with religion. Indeed, the deep faith that there are laws sanctioned by a creator of the universe provided the basis for the flowering of early biology. In the nineteenth century, biologists were thought of as "natural theologians" who sought to discover God's mysterious logic through the study of nature. In fact, nature was to biology very much what scripture was to theologians. The Bible was the word of God; religious scholars were intent on interpreting the word. Nature was also the handiwork of God, and presumably it too reflected his thoughts. It was the biologist's job to "read" nature in order to find out God's plan. As Bernd Heinrich has said:

> In this view, the bee wasn't just fooling around on the flowers. It was working to carry out God's plan to make more plants. And animals didn't engage in sex for the fun of it. Sex was strictly business. Eventually these ideas became accepted without question—as if they were laws created by us.

It is this kind of unconscious bias about a "plan" in nature that puts the whole subject of sexual orientation in an impossibly contentious cultural dilemma. If sex is "strictly business," it is not surprising that many researchers have a "reproduction bias" that makes them inclined to believe that people aren't supposed to have sex for the fun of it. Somehow the antique idea of God's hand operating in nature has become fossilized not only in the church but also remains the basis of what is inevitably meant in science and philosophy when people speak of "purpose in nature." At every turn, our religious and secular mythologies entwine and imprison us. Science has often been in the service of the ruling paradigm, authenticating it and setting up barriers of expectation sufficiently rigid to exclude the unauthorized and unthinkable. Again, we find ourselves within the walled city. The poetic conceit of René Char merits repetition: *For those who are walled up, everything is a wall—even an open door.*

Physicist Werner Heisenberg is renowned for his observation that "natural science does not simply describe and explain nature; it is a part of the interplay between nature and ourselves; it describes nature as exposed to our method of questioning. This was a possibility Descartes could not have thought, but it makes the sharp separation between the world and [the observer] impossible." It appears to be a possibility that many of us still cannot accept. Because we cannot readily make a distinction between the world of reality and the reality of ourselves. Instead, we tend to make a great many distinctions between ourselves and "others." As already noted, in the nineteenth century, the mentally ill were referred to as the "alienated" and psychologists were called "alienists." These uses of language offer a fascinating insight into covert meaning in the field of behavioral psychology. The "contrary" or the alien has always been suspect in the West. Some social scientists believe that because human beings have an innate social nature, they "naturally" resent people who do not conform to their social norms and hierarchies. The stranger, like the foreigner, is supposed to be a dangerous outsider. But the insider who *behaves* like an outsider is not simply a "stranger" or a "foreigner." Something more perplex and menacing is at work in the perception of insiders who act like outsiders. They are seen as "nonselves" living covertly in a community of selves. Such nonconformists—such nonselves—are not viewed as incomprehensible strangers, but as sociopathic insiders—as transgressors.

So insistent is the Cartesian focus on distinctions between self and nonself that for almost the entire second half of the twentieth century immunologists have thought they understood the fundamental purpose of the immune system: "It was to recognize the difference between self and nonself, and to defend the body against the alien invader."[3] Thus, even modern immunology was motivated by an attitude that discriminated between insiders and outsider, between us and them. Immunology simply assumed the validity of the ancient notion of the inherent danger of the alien—the threat of the nonself, and the perils brought into our world by outsiders. Today that reductionist and biased "self versus nonself" concept of immunology is widely contested by specialists who point out that the immune system is a rather lax border guard when it comes to keeping foreigner organisms out of our bodies. Pregnant women do not ordinarily reject fetuses. None of us attack the food we eat despite its abundant component of alien antigens; nor do we reject the millions of bacterial organisms that colonize our gut and are an indispensable part of the symbiotic functions of the life of our bodies. These "aliens" are, indeed, *nonselves*, but they are also essential to the survival of *self*.

Transgression takes many forms, growing out of differences of coloration, gender, mannerism, shape, height, facial expression, body language, and the use of jargon and vernacular language that betrays social status and education as well as locality and tribe. At heart, the problem seems to be that few of us can imagine the possibility of being anybody other than who we are. We can't imagine being somebody truly different—racially, culturally, or sexually. Everything in a bounded society conspires to affirm our biased views of identity and normalcy. If we are urged to consider being someone else, we do so with the belief that to give up our social identity would mean relinquishing something of our worth. Clearly, then, *we* are somehow superior or more complete than the "other." Doubtlessly, all "others" would like to be who we are, but we would not want to be "them." In fact, we are profoundly fearful of being suspected of being "one of them."

Because human beings are deeply influenced by visual and kinesthetic experience, physical appearance and physical behavior are widely used to identify someone who is part of the social or gender group as opposed to someone who is not. There are researchers who are convinced that there are innate, transcultural physical qualities that are universal designators of attractiveness and beauty: large eyes, high cheekbones, prominent chins, long headedness, and so on. On the other hand, it is clear that pigmentation has played a very negative role in social attitudes. So has obesity and nontraditional gender behavior, like "masculinity" in females and "effeminacy" in males. And yet, as we have seen in the discussion of freaks, difference and nonconformity do not always illicit censure. Sometimes deviance has quite the opposite impact.

People have been interested in "handedness" for as long as there have been folktales and legends. Left-handedness was often looked on as an unnatural deviation from the unique right-handedness of human beings, who, among all creatures, predominately favor the right hand.

There is a curious correlation between attitudes about sexual orientation and attitudes about left-handedness. As I've pointed out, right-handedness is unique to humans. Other animals may favor one side over another, but there are essentially equal numbers of left- and right-sided animals. The unique right-handedness among humans appears to arise from the nature of the human brain. Handedness depends on which hemisphere of the brain is dominant. If the right hemisphere tends to dominate, the person is left-handed. Left-handed people have a distinctive, thicker corpus callosum (the fiber bundle linking the left and right hemispheres). And the pattern of brain organization for activities such as speech control, face recognition, and spatial perception is unpredictable in left-handers. The same brain functions are highly predictable in 98 to 99 percent of right-handers. Handedness seems to be determined, at least in part, by genetics. But the ways in which heredity affects handedness are still unknown. Left-handedness is almost as much as a biological mystery as homosexuality. Yet these two forms of deviation from majority behaviors are treated very differently in various societies.

What is interesting is that the division of the U.S. population of left-handers and right-handers is debatably just about the same as the division of the gay and straight populations—left-handers represent about 10 percent of the population, while right-handers represent about 90 percent, with perhaps 10 to 15 percent of the right-handers displaying some degree of ambidexterity. Fossil evidence suggests that the distribution of right- and left-handedness has probably existed since the time of the first hominid who possessed hands with true opposable thumbs and nails instead of claws, such as the *Paranthropus* hominid of about 2 million years ago.

In the West, social pressures have had a negative impact on left-handedness, regarding it as an anomaly that must be changed. Until the recent past, it is believed that the great majority of left-handers were forced into becoming right-handers. But a good many people, especially exceptional people, refuse to change handedness.

Leonardo da Vinci was left-handed. In his painting, his shading is always executed from right to left, unlike that of right-handed artists.

In his countless notebooks he used what is called "mirror writing," working from right to left, and producing thousands of pages of reverse, left-handed script. Legend has it that he employed this illegible, enigmatic method of writing to avoid the Inquisition's discovery of his radical inventions and ideas, but his writing appears to have expressed a more fundamental love of secrecy and mystery. Biographers indicate that his refusal to write with his right hand was probably an expression of his love of idiosyncracy (Bramly). In other words, for Leonardo left-handedness was a cultivated transgression.

I am using handedness strictly as a metaphor, but it is an interesting context for exploring sexuality, insofar as, coincidentally, Leonardo's sexual orientation also defied the heterosexual conventions we regard as norms today.

Just a few decades ago in the United States, the use of the left hand was strongly discouraged, resulting in only 2 percent (of a statistically likely 10 percent) of the population being openly left-handed. Even today, in Taiwan, left-handedness is so socially unacceptable that only 1 percent of the population writes with the left hand.

The vilification of left-handedness has a long history. The English word "dexterous" stems from the Latin word for "right," while the English word "sinister" comes from the Latin word for "left." Clearly, left-handedness was demonized like so many other idiosyncracies. Handedness was also given a hierarchial significance. The place of honor is usually on the *right* of a host. In many European legislatures, the commoners sit on the chairperson's *left*. To this day, a value judgment is encoded in the political terms "right" (conservative) and "left" (progressive). Sexuality, like handedness, has also been encoded in judgmental terms, such as heterosexuality and homosexuality.

If a trait as inconsequential as handedness has had such a strong impact on social attitudes, turning left-handers into "sinister outsiders," it is not difficult to see why deviations of sexual orientation and gender behavior became the basis of an entire school of science during the late nineteenth century, when the German physician and neurologist Richard von Krafft-Ebing almost single-handedly invented the field of sexual psychopathology and the "medical model" of homosexuality.

Even Krafft-Ebing's successors, Havelock Ellis in Britain and Magnus Hierschfeld in Germany, who presumably attempted to decriminalize and liberalize the stereotypical model of sexuality codified by Krafft-Ebing, tended to accept the notion that homosexuality, though not a vice, is nonetheless an anomaly or, at best, a deviation or variation of heterosexuality. No sexologists seemed willing to jettison the whole dimorphic obsession of the West and embrace a *gestalt* view of sexuality, seen as a whole that is greater than the sum of its parts, and as an orientation with unlimited possibilities.

Krafft-Ebing was born in Mannheim in 1840. In 1886, he published his famous *Psychopathia Sexualis*, a collection of case histories of "sexual deviation," which was translated into a great many languages and had worldwide influence. Krafft-Ebing was not the first specialist in "abnormal" sexual behavior, but he certainly was the first scholar to set the boundaries of sexuality as we know them today. In many ways, Krafft-Ebing invented the "deviant."

He considered homosexuality a "hereditary neuropathic degeneration" aggravated by "excessive masturbation." Havelock Ellis attempted to modify Krafft-Ebing's categorical attitude about sexuality in general, and he introduced a revised attitude on the subject of homosexuality. Ellis's *Sexual Inversion* raised questions about the pathologicizing of desire. He advocated birth control and championed a view of sexuality that was not entirely based on the necessity of reproduction. He introduced a new idea about sexuality as a cultural rather than merely a physiological impulse. For all of his liberal and cultural attitudes about sexuality, however, Ellis did not denounce the dimorphism of sexuality into strict male and female categories. And he did not insist on a reversal of the pathological views of his contemporaries. It was the cultural aspect of Havelock Ellis's work that had an enormous influence on Sigmund Freud. For instance, Ellis strongly shaped Freud's attitudes about homosexuality, but Ellis's pioneering work did not refute homophobia or change the polemical classification of human desire.

Krafft-Ebing, Hierschfeld, and Ellis invented the fields of sexology, building their theories on both mechanistic and social science. It was Freud, however, who revolutionized and profoundly distorted the study of human sexuality. As linguistics professor at the Université de Paris VII, Julia Kristeva observed in her landmark book *Strangers to Ourselves*, "Freud noted that the archaic, narcissistic self, not yet demarcated by the outside world, projects out of itself what it experiences as dangerous or unpleasant in itself, making of it an alien *double*, uncanny and demonical."

Freud's seminal ideas constantly changed, but at the core of his concepts was a negative attitude that turned the sexual self into an alien—"a *double*, uncanny and demonical." The Freudian revolution internalized desire, deconstructing the entire Cartesian mechanistic process. John Rajchman has asked, "How have people been brought to believe that a terrible truth about their sex resided in some inaccessible or 'blocked' portion of their psyches, and thus that, in the deepest sense, their sex took place primarily in their heads?"

This portentous question has been asked just as the Freudian revolution is ending. "For all his influence, this may someday be how we think of Freud: an old joke that everybody gets, but no one can remember how important it once was." Lest such an assertion seem unfounded, let me quote further from science historian Frank Sulloway in an article entitled "The Trouble with Sigmund."[4] According to Sulloway, "[Freuds's] model of the mind and notion of dreaming are in total conflict with modern science. His major edifice is built on quicksand."

Yet it is Freud's pernicious influences that must concern us if we are attempting to grasp the impetus behind many Western attitudes about the body, sexuality, and homosexuality. It was Freud who internalized desire, hiding it deep within a recess of a remote "Self" inaccessible to the *self*. Freudian theory dematerialized sexuality. Then, very much like priests with a privileged access to the nonmaterial world, Freud, and particularly his followers, evolved techniques for unmasking what Western culture had carefully hidden from itself. At heart, Freud suggested that locked within each of us is a perverse, uncivilized bisexual desire. In order to know that desire, we would need to make it consciousness. We had to know ourselves but, if society were to function, we also had to control ourselves by modifying desire in socially acceptable forms.

The challenge to know ourselves is a familiar axiom in the West. But when the Greeks said "Know thyself," they were not recommending psychoanalysis. Desire, like *arete*, was overtly *lived* in classical societies; it wasn't flushed out of hiding so it could be domesticated.

What Freud did, metaphorically speaking, is to sexualize the mind (the unconscious). Whereas Copernicus had decentralized the earth and Darwin had animalized the human body, reversing centuries of Western anthropocentrism, Freud seems to have done just the opposite. He mystified human sexuality and placed it at the center of human motivation, making the "mind," and not the body, the most essential human characteristic. Science had vainly attempted to secularize the world, but, by internalizing desire, Freud put the ghost back in the machine.

Each in its own way, the concepts of Copernicus, Darwin, and Freud were very humbling to the old Judeo-Christian model. The cosmic boundaries of Western worldview had been irrevocably redefined, with "mind" rather than "God" at the motivational core of human conduct. Darwin irrevocably brought body back into the human scheme of things, while Freud was inclined to desert the physiology of body in favor of a metaphysics of mind. For Freud, nothing had changed. The new psychiatric frontier was, in fact, a familiar territory, built on the same Judeo-Christian mythos that had informed several centuries of philosophy and science.

When Freud was still specializing in neurological research in the physiological laboratory of the German physician Ernst Wilhelm von Brücke, he was already inclined to view organic brain disease in a manner that had an unmistakable "shamanistic" inclination, using hypnosis instead of the customary, mechanistic diagnostic tools of nineteenth-century medicine. After the publication of his article "Infantile Cerebral Paralysis," Freud's attention progressively turned away from neuropathology—that traditionally built its diagnoses of nervous disease on empirical evidence, seeing the body as the source of neurosis much as it was the victim of infectious disease. Freud began to rechannel his interests into psychopathology—building diagnoses on subjective evidence, the largely negative impact of childhood experiences of his patients. Central to the Freudian matrix was the cultural and environmental rather than the physiological and genetic basis of human psychopathology. Psychoanalysis was possible only because Freud insisted that "*mental* disease" (already an ethereal, nonphysical terminology of "mind") was a matter of nurture not nature. Any other position on the nurture/nature issue would have rendered "mental" ailments untreatable by the shamanistic methods of psychoanalysis.

A resistance to this Freudian premise of culturally constructed neurosis ("idiosyncrasy by nurture or choice"), as we will see, has become an essential motive in efforts to *naturalize* ("normalize") deviations in order to make them socially justifiable.

I should make it clear that "naturalization" or "normalization" means something rather specific in the context of this book. I mean a process that is accommodational, that provides merely a semblance of conformity while it denies self—a pretense of conventionality and a betrayal of the final reality we summon when we speak of "ourselves." *Naturalization* implies that there is an unassailable norm that has such human centrality that we must achieve it even if, in process, we deny ourselves. In this way, "naturalization" is a term I use interchangeably with "normalization"—meaning, to become "by nature" something we are not "by nature."

There are a good many therapists who still insist, contrary to Freud's own ever-changing views on the matter, that homosexuals are really heterosexuals waiting for various treatments and cures that will painlessly return them to their "natural" state of mature, heterosexual orientation.

The Judeo-Christian myth thrives in Freud's preoccupation with *psychological* rather than *physiological* explanations for behavioral disorders. This metaphysical point of view placed Freud outside the realm of the scientific naturalism of his day. He dealt with a concept of "mind" not entirely distinct from the earlier theological concept of "soul," a model he had inherited from Descartes's Judeo-Christian paradigm. Following Freud's example, a group of disciples built an approach to behavior that, to a lesser or greater degree, placed the arcanum of sex at the core of virtually all human dilemmas. Thus, sex was not only covert, but it was also subversive. This subversiveness was mirrored in the social inclination during Freud's day (and during many succeeding decades) to regard matters of sexuality as unspeakable taboos imprisoned behind the psychic walls that are believed to make civility and civilization possible.

The church had made a correlation between sex and morality. Freudians made a correlation between sex and pathology, and, by extension, created a "moral" basis for the treatment of psychopathologies.

Freud himself deplored the invention of a psychoanalytic moralism, which became especially prevalent among therapists in the United States. He insisted that there is no connection between an analyst's diagnosis of a disorder and its moral consequences. Therapists were not supposed to be moralists or disciplinarians. Psychoanalysis was supposed to remain morally neutral. The dominant American form of psychoanalytic theory takes as its foundation an early view of Freud's that saw perversions as sexual activities that involve an extension, or *transgression*, of the limits of nature—in respect either to the parts of the body involved in sexual contact or the choice of sexual object. Many Freudians found in this view a mandate for heterosexuality as the sole basis of adult relationships. Freud may not have intended to do so, but, as it turned out, he provided a perfect ideological background against which the psychopathology of sexologists could be played out as a form of scientific moral law and, as Jonathan Katz has remarked, a form of "medical colonization."

"Homosexuality is assuredly no advantage," Freud wrote to a woman requesting treatment for her son, "but it is nothing to be ashamed of, no vice, no degradation; it cannot be classified as an illness; we consider it to be a variation of the sexual function, produced by a certain arrest of sexual development."

An urbane mentality may have allowed Freud to express an unbiased view of sexual orientation, but his words *"a certain arrest of sexual development"* betray his heterocentric bias, for, as Jeffrey Weeks points out, "a 'development' assumes an appropriate end result, and 'arrest' an artificial blockage." In short, Freud was not talking about homosexuality as an orientation but as "a condition" that represents a pathological, *unfulfilled* or *unachieved* heterosexuality. Sequential psychological development is fundamental for Freud. Maturity is achieved through a specific series of stages, the assumption being that the ultimate achievement of maturity is heterosexuality, even though much of Freud's thinking also argues against such a point of view (Dollimore).

Freud and Darwin are often misunderstood as the creators of "a code of nature." Freud is presumed to have invented a repressed libido always ready to break the surface. Darwin is presumed to have invented an equally repressed animal aggression, always ready to spring into action and aid in survival at all costs. This reductionist view of Freud and Darwin is misleading, but it does aptly describe the positions of a great many theorists who claim Darwinian or Freudian credentials. Both Freud and Darwin have been betrayed by countless demagogues and extremists—from the misuse of social Darwinism by white supremacists to the misused concept of "survival of the fittest" as a political rationale for imperialism and fascism. But even when their approaches are far less bigoted, Darwinians are often inclined to see the life process as development from simplicity to complexity, from imperfection toward an anthropocentric perfection. Freudians follow along the same ideological lines, but they tend to be heterocentric in their application of Darwinian concepts, seeing the ambiguous sexuality of human childhood deveoping naturally and inevitably into a reproductive heterosexuality.

The Freudian view of sexual maturation is built on two mutually contradictory points of view. Freud saw the primordial being as bisexual or homosexual at the same time that he devised a decidedly polarized attitude about gender—a polarity resulting from the amorphous male child's psychological disengagement from the mother (following the example of the father and, thus, becoming a male) and the amorphous female child's disengagement from the father (following the example of the mother, and, thus, becoming a female). Clearly, Freud suggests that bisexuality and homosexuality are primitive or primary issues of gender development, whereas heterosexuality is the expression of mature adulthood.

The Freudian disciple Carl Jung attempted to redress this gender polarity with his orientalist concept of the *anima* and *animus*—terms that were essentially a recapitulation in Western guise of the Asian concepts of yin and yang. Anima and animus were presumed to be ambiguous psychological forces representing contrasting male and female aspects of personality that Jung believed were combined in every human being whether male or female. The Jungian developmental goal was a fulfillment of both anima and animus in a single, unified personality. But Jungian attitudes about anima and animus have often backfired, resulting in the current trend of therapists who advise males to "realize their feminine side"—a type of advice built on a strictly dimorphic bias. It is also possible to understand the forces Jung characterized as anima and animus simply as *essential attributes of all human beings,* without any reference to dimorphic gender, except in a specific cultural context—such as cultures in which behaviors are socialized in terms of a strictly dimorphic gender model: pink/blue, dolls/guns, passive/aggressive, girl/boy, inferior/superior, verbal/mathematical, female/male, penetrator/penetrated, mother/father.

Freud and his predecessors created widely different "sciences of sex." But their research had a common core—it unquestioningly confirmed a heterosexual and dimorphic view of normality. And, though Freud himself resisted Krafft-Ebing's efforts to pathologize homosexuality, the "Freudian" idea of sexual perversion has become a permanent part of public consciousness. Long before Freud actually completed his most influential studies in the field of sexuality—*Three*

Contributions to the Theory of Sex (1910) and *The Psycho-Pathology of Every Day Life* (1914)—perversion had become an effective weapon of slander. At the age of thirty-nine, Freud must have been caught up in the sensational news about a trial taking place in England. The legal battles faced by Oscar Wilde in 1895 made fatal use of sexual slander, and, at the same time, heralded the erosion of the kind of liberalism optimized by the Napoleonic Code and began the criminalization of the homosexual, no matter the rank or celebrity of a defendant.

There is no doubt that Freud created an entirely new approach to the understanding of human personality by introducing the concept of the unconscious and by demonstrating its furtive impact on daily life. At the same time, his concept of the unconscious can be seen as a replay of several antiquated forms of Western dualism—the Platonic notion of a riff between the knowable world and the invisible realm of "ideas," as well as Descartes's notion of a riff between the sentient body and the disembodied "soul." In Plato, Descartes, and Freud we discover different concepts of various ethereal forces that use the body as a screen on which to project and test themselves. For Descartes, the body is a vehicle of the soul; for Freud, a mechanism driven by blind sexual instincts; for Jung, a carrier of subterranean archetypal memories. Somehow, such views inevitably come down to very much the same thing—a ghost in the machine.

If, for Freud, "anatomy is destiny," then his notion of destiny was entirely nonphysiological except for its genital distinctions. Freud's destiny was an ethereal kind of destiny concealed within a part of the mind that is not really mind, but something resembling a hidden hell or a lost Eden—alternately a malevolence and an innocence of "mind" lost and obscured from consciousness. For Freud the genitalia seem to have been little more than the antennae of a sequestered libido.

As John Rajchman points out, the internalization of desire, residing in some inaccessible portion of our psyches, was alien to both the Hebraic and Classical worlds. Such a notion didn't enter Western thought until the time of Christianity, as an extension of the dematerializing of sex, which is the hermeneutical basis of celibacy.

To use Rajchman's words,

It is in Christian cultures that sex would start to be linked to an arcane encoding of inner impulses it takes a "hermeneutic of the self" to unriddle. The fundamental contribution Christianity would make would not reside in its code of forbidden and permitted acts, but in the type of experience one was thought to have of oneself as an erotic being. . . . Christianity would thus be the start of the internalization of eros, or the process through which people were led to find their sexuality within themselves. . . . But that obligation is no longer commanded by the will of God but by the norms of mental health; and the authority on which it is based is no longer a theology of the flesh but a science of sexuality.

Freud, as we have seen, also modified his attitudes about homosexuality, developing a cultural basis for sexual orientation that was tied to his oedipal theories. He defined the state when the intervention of the father figure requires a child to abandon an exclusive relationship with the mother and to enter into the "structures of human sexuality," where the child is then assigned a gender and a role in the family and the community. Freud insisted that such a process of sexual maturation was the basis of mental health.

Alongside this work that medicalized sexuality, we must recall that few cultures have developed identity concepts such as "a homosexual" as a specific type of individual different from other people. In seventy-six societies studied by American anthropologist Clellan Ford and psychobiologist Frank A. Beach, fully two-thirds consider same-sex activities normal and socially acceptable, and rarely had terms like "homosexual" to designate the persons who engage in such activities. For many societies, past and present, desire is not categorized. It is only when sexual polarities and categories are invented as "normal heterosexual boundaries" that homosexuality comes into existence as an exceptional kind of act that is unquestionably off-limits.

For instance, in Mombasa the relationship between gender identity and sexuality is closer to that of the Greeks than it is to modern Anglo-Americans. Gender is assigned solely on the basis of biological sex, not sexual behavior. Therefore, in Mombasa, lesbians remain women and dress as women. In nearby Oman (despite its many historical connections with Mombasa), there is just the opposite view of sexuality. A male homosexual is regarded as a transsexual, and may change his gender and effectively become a woman. Here, the sex act and not the sexual organs determine gender. Among the people of Oman, behavior, and not anatomy, is the basis of gender identity.

Many scholars see this process of categorizing sexuality as a social activity allied to the advance of Western capitalism, giving rise to what Jeffrey Weeks has called "a perverse re-territorialization, a massive effort to regain social control in a world tending toward disorder and decoding." In the decades when social Darwinists used Darwin's concepts to justify the aggression and self-satisfaction of capitalism in their efforts to exonerate the domination of the few over the masses, it took a very small leap of faith to provide heterosexuals with the same "natural" dominion in matters sexual. What we want and what we do in any society is to a very great extent what we are made to want and what we are allowed to do. Emerson verbalized this symbiosis of the individual, the group, and sexuality when he said that the whole of nature is a metaphor of the human mind. The way the body has been envisioned and evaluated by various cultures in various eras is a history of the sexual messages transmitted by social mythologies and the rituals and customs based on such mythologies.

Clearly, the establishment of homosexuality as a specific pathological category has resulted in the basis of its repression. The inventors of homosexuality were specialists in disease. They "hunted down" homosexuality and then, assuming they had discovered it, they gave it a deleterious name. In this way, homosexuality wasn't discovered; it was invented. And with that invention, scientists helped religious and political leaders to fabricate the basis of its repression.

Because psychopathologists were looking for a disease, they insisted that they had found one when they encountered an ancient expression of desire that had rarely required a categorical name. As Guy Hocquenghem suggested in his landmark book, the creation of homosexuality was also the creation of a scapegoat that "transformed the repressed homosexual elements of desire into a desire to be repressed." The scapegoat motif of degeneracy is a pacifying tool for societies that view sexuality negatively, because the designation of "abnormality" in others lifts some of the burden of sexual guilt from everyone else.

The invention of homosexuality was readily accepted as a social reality simply because it introduced yet another repulsive demon to the long inventory of Judeo-Christian demonology. This demon aroused fantastic fear and loathing—of contagion and mutilation, of heresy and unnaturalness. Homosexuality was not just a disease waiting to inflict itself on the twentieth-century culture; it was also regarded as a infectious disorder, placing innocent children in harm's way. Logic might suggest that if heterosexuality is unquestionably the norm, how is it possible for a "normal" person to be "persuaded" to *chose* to be homosexual? Is homosexuality so beguiling that, like Satan, it tempts good heterosexuals to forfeit their normalcy? Is homosexuality so contagious that a person can be infected by a sneeze? Or is it more to the point that homosexuality is deeply feared as a hidden predisposition, and, like Charles Perrault's charming story of Sleeping Beauty, is just waiting to be awakened by a queer kiss?

Guy Hocquenghem believed that psychiatry played a vital part in the creation of homosexual guilt. So the psychiatrization of homosexuality did not simply produce homophobia among heterosexuals; it also produced self-loathing among many homosexuals. Psychiatry medicalized and legitimized both the repression and the legal punishment of homosexual acts. There are still countless therapists and researchers who make negative assessments of homosexuality, basing their negative views on the experiences of unhappy people who are convinced they are "sick" and have, therefore, sought help from specialists who enforce their self-contempt by perpetuating a two-gender hierarchy that portrays a homosexual as an unhealthy heterosexual.

If psychiatry began as a discipline focused almost exclusively on biological factors and the cataloging of abnormal behaviors, it eventually made an almost complete transition away from somatic treatment with the discovery of unconscious sources of behavior. As we have seen, Freud shifted the attention from the body to the psyche as the source of behavioral anomalies, with little regard for the biological aspects of mental disorders. Almost half a century was dedicated to a wide variety of purely psychological, rather than somatic, treatment. Then, in the 1940s and 1950s, treatment shifted once again, when controversial physical procedures such as electric shock therapy and other forms of psychosurgery came into use. In this way, the treatment of the "mind" vacillated between the dominant polarities of the Western dualism of mind and body—a troubled balance between the psyche with its inherent or socially caused problems and the soma with its biochemical disorders. By the 1960s and 1970s, new ideas about the genetic and chemical nature of mental illness became a significant force. And by the 1980s, psychiatry once again shifted in emphasis from the purely psychological to the purely biological. At this point psychotropic drugs became an essential part of the treatment and control of mental illness. Today, depending on the school of psychiatry, disorders are usually understood as a combination of social and biochemical conditions.

With the emergence of biochemistry into mainstream psychiatry, with its self-conscious endeavor to link biology, sociology, and chemistry, it was inevitable that the controversial field of sociobiology would arise from a new amalgam of scientific disciplines, heralded in 1975 with the publication of *Sociobiology* by Edward O. Wilson. The approach of sociobiology immediately met with a great deal of debate. It was a model essentially built on the contention that biology determines social behavior because behavior is genetically transmitted and subject to evolutionary processes. It was hardly a surprise that sociobiology repulsed many experts, given the racist and sexist conflicts that had been produced by social Darwinism. Barely a century before Wilson's publication of *Sociobiology*, Darwin's "survival of the fittest" had been greatly distorted into justifications of everything from political imperialism, to the cataloging of cranial measurements in order to claim the inferiority of blacks, to the allegation of innate female characteristics that proved that women were procreative organisms incapable of being educated for social activities other than motherhood and the role of homemakers.

In the 1990s, the gradual acceptance of the methods of sociobiology promoted a revival of Darwinism in American social thought and led to efforts to reclaim the biological basis of the concept of a definable "human nature." This transition in thinking about human behavior has had a decisive impact on attitudes about homosexuality.

Since sociobiology is the study of the effect of biological processes on animal behavior, including primates and human beings, sociobiologists have attempted to do with behavior what Darwinists attempted to do with evolution: to find a direct correlation between cause and effect on a purely genetic basis. Just as a Darwinist is likely to find an evolutionary survival motif in every physical attribute and every behavioral pattern, so a sociobiologist is likely to find a genetic basis for all behavior, sexual and otherwise—though, curiously, specialists like Wilson have devoted remarkably little discussion to the sociobiological or evolutionary explanation of homosexuality or other behaviors like suicide, laughter, or the whole mysterious range of subjective experience.

Art historian Roger Fry once said, "Biologically speaking art is a blasphemy. We were given our eyes to see things, not to look at them." Vision did not evolve so we could have an exceptionally *useless* subjective and aesthetic experience of the world. If we explore the sexual significance of this pragmatic value of sight and the existence of subjective visual experience, then we might ask if we were not given our sex organs in order to reproduce, and not to have an exceptionally *useless* homosexual experience. What is the sociobiological "purpose" of both subjective, aesthetic experience and nonreproductive homosexuality?

John Maynard Smith, the British biologist, has attempted to comprehend the evolutionary basis for our contemplation of things "subjectively," which is a process that seems to serve no substantial role in our survival as a species. From the point of view of both strict Darwinism and sociobiology, there is no way to explain impractical human faculties such as that complex collection of responses we call aesthetic pleasure. Despite several efforts to link this subjective experience to the attractions of sights and smells and sounds that are the basis of mating and reproduction, Maynard Smith has not been convinced that the subjective sensory experience translates easily into sociobiological determinism. Human subjective experience is far more complex than, say, the brilliant displays of plumage by peacocks or the mating rituals of cranes.

Though Maynard Smith made fundamental contributions to evolutionary theory, and is considered a rather strict Darwinist, in 1995 he conceded that he does not understand why organisms have feelings. As *Time* succinctly put it,

> After all, orthodox biologists believe that behavior, however complex, is governed entirely by biochemistry and that the attention sensations—fear, pain, wonder, love—are just shadows cast by that biochemistry, not themselves vital to the organism's behavior, they are affected by the material world but don't effect it. Well, if that is the case and feelings do not *do* anything, then why do they exist *at all*?[5]

This is hardly a trifling question, especially in the context of homosexual behavior, which, like human subjectivity, doesn't seem to *do* anything in terms of genetic survival.

If, from an evolutionary point of view, subjective experience is an optional and nonpragmatic feature of the human organism, how can it be explained with the utilitarian mentality of Darwinian theory? When pressed for an answer, John Maynard Smith says that although the existence of subjective experience may have no strictly scientific explanation, it could still have what he chose to call a "metaphysical" interpretation. And admittedly, there are other evolutionary biologists, like the renowned William D. Hamilton of Oxford, who fundamentally disagree with Maynard Smith, though they have yet to provide a widely accepted answer to questions about subjective experience, laughter, suicide, or homosexuality.

R. D. Laing, James Hillman, and several other radical psychologists might say that the sociobiologists' answers are wrong because their questions are wrong. Darwinists may be doing to a Darwinian metaphor what theologians have done to a Christian metaphor: attempting to concretize the metaphor as a commonsensical model, a process that automatically defeats the very purpose of the metaphor. Even the most pragmatic naturalists are beginning to search for terms that are less syntactical and more metaphorical. When they come face to face with the ineffable, rather than trying to force the inexpressible into concrete jargon, they are now inclined to speak in almost poetic language. What Maynard Smith calls the "metaphysical" many evolutionary biologists are now willing to call "qualia"—a Latin term meaning "an abstract and aesthetic quality."

British playwright Tom Stoppard shrewdly applies the same nonspecific terminology to the field of physics in his play *Hapgood*: "There is a straight ladder from the atom to the grain of sand, and the only real mystery is the missing rung. Below it, particle physics. Above it, classical physics. But in between, metaphysics." I'm tempted to paraphrase Stoppard by saying that there is a straight ladder from male to female, and the only real mystery is the missing rung—homosexuality—that is not a mystery if we can agree that gender dimorphism (male and female) is just one form of many possible sexual unions.

What is suggested by both Maynard Smith and Stoppard is that subjective impulses and experiences that do not have any apparent survival benefits are "metaphysical." Such an attitude seems like a very convoluted way of providing an explanation of both aesthetic pleasure as a ubiquitous human response and homosexuality as a widespread behavioral orientation among mammals. Such explanations tend to make both subjectivity and homosexuality entirely remote and abstract, very much like Freud's reductionist summation of the female psyche as "the dark continent."

Essayist Robert Wright would take exception to any biological abstraction. He believes that even the human belief in free will is an illusion made possible by a mentality provided to us by evolution. Whether it is environment or heredity that makes us do what we do, he says, the compulsion is effected biochemically. We are, by the process of elimination, the "consciousness of the cosmos"; created by evolution so we can give the cosmos substance by our unique ability of our consciousness to be conscious of its existence. According to Wright, our biochemical perceptive and associative abilities transform the random impulses of cosmic vibration and electromagnetism into sounds, sights, tastes, odors—the "qualia" we claim as a "perceived reality." But, in the end, Wright claims, "we believe the things we believe about morality, personal worth, even objective truth [because they] lead to behaviors that get our genes into the next generation."

This is the overriding paradox of sociobiology when it comes to homosexuality. Here we have yet another case of sexuality being described in terms of a model that doesn't provide a place in evolution for sexual diversity.

Helena Cronin, an evolutionary researcher at the London School of Economics, agrees with Wright that to a certain extent "it is true that all biological adaptations ultimately foster the replication of those genes that give rise to them." But she also warns that "it's nonsense to encompass all cultural invention within biology. Unless there's a relevant genetic distinction between people who adopt the innovation and people who don't, we're outside the realm of biological adaptation."

Sociobiology is highly controversial when applied to human behavior in such areas as aggressiveness, sex differences, mate selection, and parenting behavior. It tends to paint itself into corners by using loaded language like the description of human conversation with infants as "motherese." It claims some rather questionable conditions as inherently human, such as the fear of snakes, sexual jealousy, gender identity, moral sense, and object permanence, behavioral elements that many anthropologists insist are the result of socialization and not of heredity, or, at the very least, a complex combination of nature and nurture.

One of the chief opponents of extreme genetic determinism is the naturalist Stephen Jay Gould, who has repeatedly debated the validity of terms like "human nature," and has attempted to limit the extremes of biological determinism: "I am a strong advocate of the general argument that 'truth' as preached by scientists often turns out to be no more than prejudice inspired by prevailing social and political beliefs" (Gould, 1980). Kate Millett had much the same response as Gould to sociobiology. "Patriarchy," she said, "has a tenacious and powerful hold through its successful habit of passing itself off as nature."

One of the most interesting as well as one of the most untenable of deterministic speculations of sociobiology is found in E. O. Wilson's proposed genetic explanation of homosexuality, as described by Gould (1980):

> Since exclusive homosexuals do not bear children, how could a homosexuality gene ever be selected in a Darwinian world? Suppose that our ancestors organized socially as small, competing groups of very close kin. Some groups contain only heterosexual members. Others included homosexuals who functioned as "helpers" in hunting or child rearing: they bore no children but they helped kin to raise their close genetic relatives. If groups with homosexual helpers prevailed in competition over exclusively heterosexual groups, then homosexuality genes would have been maintained by kin selection. There is nothing illogical in this proposal, but it has no facts going for it either. We have identified no homosexuality gene, and we know nothing relevant to this hypothesis about the social organization of our ancestors, and have no indication that our notion of homosexuality even existed in prehistory. Wilson's intent is admirable; he attempts to affirm the intrinsic dignity of a common and much maligned sexual behavior by arguing that it is natural for some people—and adaptive to boot. . . . But the strategy is a dangerous one, for it backfires if the genetic speculation is wrong. If you defend a behavior by arguing that people are programmed directly for it, then how do you continue to defend it if your speculation is wrong, for the behavior then becomes unnatural and worthy of condemnation. Better to stick resolutely to a philosophical position on human liberty. . . . [Homosexuality] need not be vindicated—and must not be condemned—by genetic speculation.

Despite Gould's warning, the debate about the biological and genetic basis of homosexuality continues to accelerate, and biological findings have become something of a battleground among gay and lesbian activists as well as a good many feminists and scientists from almost every discipline.

I have little doubt that there is a biological basis of whatever condition we signify when we use the term "homosexuality," but I am exceptionally uncomfortable with the inclination of some people to do with sexual orientation what anthropologists once did with the fiction of "race"—when they invented arbitrary transgenerational cultures, mannerisms, styles, as well as physical and psychological traits that were supposed to divide all of humankind into categorical groups, despite enormous inconsistencies within each of the groups and huge overlapping similarities between members of the reportedly distinctive groups. Quite apart from every other consideration, there is no reason to defend or justify homosexuality, particularly since it is a wholly invented term encompassing a wide variety of behaviors and identities that are as inconsequential as the equally ambiguous and invented term "race."

Jeffrey Weeks contends that biology simply defines the possibilities of our sexual choices; it does not make those choices for us, nor does it require us to give our choices delimiting names. To accept the categorical inferences of a term like "homosexuality" might be prompted by the hope of "naturalizing" deviant sexual orientations—or, in the frame of reference of psychopathology, justifying a "disorder" by claiming that it is based on a genetic proclivity, like Alzheimer's syndrome.

According to a national lesbian and gay men's magazine,

> For biologists, the scientific implications of the new work [in genetic research] is profound. Richard Pillard of Boston University observes that, with the interest currently being focused on biological factors influencing the propensity to violence, antisocial behavior, intelligence, and cognitive abilities, and mental disorders such as schizophrenia and bipolarity, even behavioral geneticists who aren't studying sexual orientation are very interested in this kind of research.[6]

It appears that, despite the apparent biological basis of homosexuality, the purely deterministic position that sees homosexuality entirely in nature and rejects all influences of nurture plays into the cause of those who would turn any form of sexual transgression into a pathology. It would be more to the point to understand the nature of the stigmatization rather than trying to justify homosexuality. By focusing on the mythologies behind judgments, we begin to deal with the prejudice rather than the objects of the prejudice; with those who condemn rather than those who are condemned. But when people internalize rejection they inevitably accept condemnation as a given, and, like Franz Kafka, they become obsessed with the need to understand their imaginary "crime" in order to exonerate themselves.

The current enthusiasm for biological definitions of sexual orientation is raising complex social problems. Biological research into sexual orientation was not an invention of the 1990s. For more than two decades, researchers had been presenting evidence for biological mechanisms underlying homosexuality—or, more correctly, male homosexuality, since, as always, women are very rarely the subjects of any kind of research in the forefront of medical science. Simon LeVay of the Institute of Gay and Lesbian Education and Dean H. Hamer of the National Institutes of Health as well as J. Michael Bailey of Northwestern University collaborating with Richard C. Pillard of Boston University have independently uncovered some fascinating evidence of potential biological "causes" of homosexuality in males. LeVay has identified a cluster of neurons in the hypothalamus of the brain that is relatively smaller in the homosexuals studied, and, not incidentally, proportional to the hypothalamus of females. By extension, LeVay suggests that these differences tend to feminize the brain of the male homosexual. Hamer worked with DNA instead of brain physiology. He and his team identified a genetic locus (Xq28)—one gene on the X chromosome (and possibly more)—that may influence whether a male becomes a homosexual. This genetic "homosexual connection" was the result of Hamer's studies of forty pairs of gay siblings. It is important to recognize that this same DNA research has found no corroboration in studies of women who are homosexual: "Researchers examined the DNA of 36 pairs of lesbian sisters but found no common genetic pattern along the X chromosome."[7] This research with lesbian sisters suggests the rather confusing possibility that "homosexuality" may have a different biological trigger in women from the trigger it seems to have in men. So, apparently, the notion of "sexual orientation" is not easily attributed to a single factor, culturally or biologically. There are researchers who, therefore, question the biological or social validity of categories like heterosexuality or homosexuality. And yet, despite a growing doubt about the relevance of the language we use in the West to describe sexual orientation, there are ever-growing biological data that suggest a connection between sexual orientation and a genetic predisposition to be heterosexual or homosexual.

Bailey and Pillard undertook a study of non-twin biological brothers and adopted (unrelated) brothers as well as identical and fraternal twins. Their results were fascinating but entirely indecisive—some of their statistics support a genetic basis of homosexuality; others seem to refute it. With identical twins, raised together or apart, both are often gay—52 percent of both identical twins identified themselves as homosexual. On the other hand, 22 percent of fraternal (non-identical) twins were both homosexual. The implication is that identical twins, who share the same DNA, also share a proclivity to be homosexual. And yet, even the high incidence of homosexuality in identical twins who share identical genes is not high enough to conclude with any certainty that homosexuality in identical twins has a basis strictly in genes. The questions that many researchers continue to ask is: Why are only 52 percent of identical male twins gay despite their identical DNA?

The potential of biological research related to sexual orientation is unquestionably enticing and may have a great deal of merit. But there are also many reasons to be cautious about accepting a purely biological basis for homosexuality. Dean Hamer admits that there is a statistical problem in his study of identical male twins. As he says, it is only "in some families but not in all" that gay brothers inherit a suspect stretch of the X chromosome his team associates with homosexuality. Clearly, if a particular part of the X chromosome is a determining factor in male homosexuality, then the impact of an identical DNA blueprint on twin brothers should be far greater than 52 percent. So there must be factors other than identical DNA at work in homosexual behavior. As *Newsweek* reported,

> In many gays this feature of DNA is entirely absent. That suggests that the DNA is not necessary for producing homosexuality. In fact, identical DNA may be only one small part of a far larger biological and environmental influence. Of identical twins in which one brother is gay, the other twin is gay only about half the time— even though he has the identical DNA.[8]

On the other hand, according to the same *Newsweek* article, the non-twin brothers share the same proportion of genes as fraternal twins (twins who are not identical), and yet only 9 percent of these brothers are homosexual. Complicating the study even more is the fact that Bailey and Pillard found that the incidence of homosexuality in adopted (nonrelated) brothers of homosexuals was 11 percent, almost equal to the rate for non-twin biological brothers. These figures are rather complicated, but they seem to call into question the impact that familial environment may have had on the siblings involved in this research, especially the higher percentage of gay adopted (nonrelated) brothers in comparison to non-twin biological brothers.

LeVay's work is based on a sampling of the brains of about forty-one people, including gay men, straight men, and straight women. Virtually all the brain samples from gay men are from men who died of AIDS, which many critics believe may have influenced the anatomical findings. What LeVay reported is that the volume of INAH 3 cells found in the brains of gay men was only half that in the brains of the straight men and about the same as the volume in the women's brains: "The results could be interpreted to mean that the cell group's smaller volume was responsible for the sexual orientation of the males whose brains had been analyzed—or, more generally, that male homosexuality as such might be the product of the brain's native development" (Kevles).

LeVay admits that no one really knows what makes people straight or gay, but he is not surprised by evidence that male homosexuality may be innate; nor are a great many other homosexuals, because the experiential response of lesbians and gay men is an inclination to believe their sexual orientation is not a matter of nature but of nuture. The problem here, as I see it, is that a great many socialized skills and attributes, from language to aesthetic judgement, "feel" natural despite the fact that they have been culturally constructed and have been learned.

Despite the obvious political and legal advantages of finding a biological basis for sexual orientation, other social issues cannot be ignored. The question asked by at least some lesbians and gay men is why homosexuality requires a biological explanation. Many gays hold that theories like LeVay's "run the risk of pathologizing homosexuality, or turning it into a genetic defect" (Kevles). Some gay activists, however, favor the biological basis of research that results in reports like LeVay's work because the "naturalization" of homosexuality could have enormous legalistic repercussions. The law of the democratic nations usually states that people cannot and must not be stigmatized or politically disadvantaged by reason of distinguishing characteristics, such as race and gender—characteristics that are immutable. There is little doubt that if homosexuality were an immutable aspect of biology, the legal ramifications would be considerable. But as Stephen Jay Gould has cautioned, once that biological issue is opened up, if it fails to be correct, it could very well backfire, losing precious ground in the modern cultural context that insists that sexual activity between consenting adults is not a social issue. The backfire might allow homophobes to emphasis the pathology of homosexuality and dismiss the persistent and unimpeachable issues of human rights.

All theories of the biology of sexual orientation are unquestionably valuable and fascinating, but they are also highly tenuous. One of the most thorough summaries of the issues involved in the discovery of a "gay gene" was offered in an article by William Byne, who specializes in psychiatry and neurobiology at the Mount Sinai School of Medicine in New York. Byne points out that although about half the identical twins studied by Bailey and Pillard were both gay, almost half were not. Another important critique is Byne's observation that the twins in the study were raised in the same home environment, making it difficult to distinguish between the effects on sexual orientation of nurture and those of nature. Byne is also critical of the fact that, in their studies, Hamer and his associates did not examine the Xq28 region of any of the straight male siblings who had openly gay brothers. If there had been genetic matches between gay and straight brothers, the fact that there was a concordance between gay pairs would have been seriously undercut.

What is most significant to me is the fact that Byne confronts LeVay on what appears to be a heterocentric mentality, though LeVay is openly gay. As Byne reminds us, "Many researchers, most conspicuously Simon LeVay, treat [sexual orientation] as a sexually dimorphic [or polaric] trait—men are generally 'programmed' for attraction to women, and women are generally programmed for attraction to men. Male homosexuals, according to this framework, have female programming, and lesbians have male programming." Clearly, this dimorphism is fundamentally sexist, making assumptions about sexuality that are built on socialized and heterocentric attitudes about gender polarity—

the existence of a distinctive male as distinct from female sexuality. To my knowledge, such a universal, dimorphic view of human beings has not been irrefutably substantiated. In fact, Byne holds quite the opposite point of view. To use Byne's words,

> Sexual orientation is not dimorphic; it has many forms. Different people could be sexually attracted to men for different reasons. The conscious and unconscious motivations associated with sexual attraction are diverse even among people of the same sex and orientation. . . . Indeed, the notion that gay men are feminized and lesbians masculinized may tell us more about our culture than about the biology of erotic responsiveness.

If we extend the inferences of this dimorphic model of sexuality, we must arrive at the very dubious rationale that of the two people of the same sex who engage in sexual activities only one of them can be homosexual. This nonsensical conclusion is based on the heterosexual model of dimorphic gender that assumes that a male is assertive and a female is passive. Therefore only one partner in a same-sex act could be homosexual. Presumably the passive partner or the partner who assumes the so-called inferior position or who is penetrated would have to be either a heterosexual female or a homosexual male; while the active partner or the partner who assumes the so-called superior position or who is the penetrator would have to be either a heterosexual male or a female homosexual.

Byne concludes that if biology influences anything it is probably the creation of a temperamental inclination for a whole range of behaviors. As geneticist Walter Bodmer points out: "Sexual preferences come in a broad array, from the exclusive homosexual, to the heterosexual who has gay forays, to the heterosexual who only finds members of the opposite sex attractive. The idea that a single gene could control these widely varying reactions is ridiculous."

On the other hand, it is rather interesting that in his designation of various sexual orientations, Bodmer works from a heterocentric point of view. He refers to "exclusive homosexuals" and to "exclusive heterosexuals," but when he describes bisexuality he relies entirely on the heterosexual dimorphic model by describing bisexuals as "the heterosexual who has gay forays." It seems to me significant that he fails to mention homosexuals who have straight forays. He also seems to tell us that sexual orientation is a polarized identity: with males and females divided between exclusively heterosexual or exclusively homosexual persons, and an occasional heterosexual who engages in same-sex activities.

Byne offers one of the most interesting conclusions in the debate that is just beginning about the influences of biology on sexual orientation:

> Perhaps more important, we should also be asking ourselves why we as a society are so emotionally invested in this research. Will it—or should it—make any difference in the way we perceive ourselves and others or how we live our lives and allow others to live theirs? Perhaps the answers to the most salient questions in this debate lie not within the biology of human brains but rather in the cultures those brains have created.

On the other hand, it would be unthinkable not to continue the biological research that seeks a genetic basis of sexual orientation, since there is some evidence of such a potential connection. Despite the potential for biological clarification of sexual orientation, there are many legal and ethical concerns.

According to Chandler Burr: 'If we have the gene and the protein it makes, it would be only logical to think about a biochemical intervention that could return a person to the 'standard' [heterosexual] orientation."[9]

Many elements of history and culture conspire to create a dimorphic sexual model—a paradoxical heterosexual *singularity* that involves a *duality* of distinctly male and female genders. Every other kind of sexuality is supposed to be either a variation on the dimorphic model or a distortion of it. This heterosexual bias (heterocentrism) is not simply the protocol of straights. The social influence of heterosexuality has been so great that it has had an impact on many people who are not heterosexual. For instance, it is not by accident that some homosexuals and bisexuals are inclined to grasp heterosexuality as the basic, if not the *natural*, manifestation of sexuality. On the basis of that presumption, all other orientations, consciously or unconsciously, are necessarily transgressions of "nature," and this internalizing of homophobia is the basis of a good deal of confusion and self-contempt among lesbians and gay men.

This tragic inclination of outsiders to experience self-contempt returns us to our central theme of transgression. As we have seen, a very long succession of cultural devices provides consensus of a society's ideas of both reality and transgression. Divine law, natural law, science, and a reverence for seeing the world as the procreative operation of opposite sexes have been subverted, defined, and constantly redefined to create an inflexible heterosexual model that, until the late 1960s, was taken so much for granted that it was rarely discussed or explained. It didn't require an explanation. *It was just normal.* While, at a more profound level, it was a myth that didn't know it was a myth, and, of course, those are the best kinds of mythologies, except for those who are turned into transgressors by myth.

When people spoke of "sex" before the mid-1960s, what they really talked about was gender. Most people admitted knowing nothing about sex except *what* people *are supposed to be*—and that meant someone was male or female, married or single, with or without children. There was something embarrassing about being single, especially being a single female. There was also something slightly embarrassing, by implication, about couples who had no children or couples who had more than four or five children.

People freely told strangers whether their babies were boys or girls or whether their dogs or cats were male or female. But that was the extent of social conversations about sex. Though people knew the basic anatomy of sexuality, they had no intention of talking about what people did with their bodies, except for the curiously mechanistic glossary of sex—"making" love or "making" babies. Even when it came to the subject of reproduction, there was a great mental distance between "the sex act" and parenthood.

To avoid social transgression, the "science of sexuality" was covert. In such a sexless context, sexual innocence (or, at least, the pretense of innocence) allowed Americans to assume that the stereotypical heterosexual family was the totality of human sexuality. So, it seemed, to a great many people, that *any* other kind of emotional or sexual bond between human beings had to be bizarre and extraordinary. Heterosexual vaginal intercourse, with the male in the so-called superior position, was the kind of sexuality that parents awkwardly tried to explain to their offspring when the questions about sex could no longer be avoided. This kind of sex was the unconditional norm. Even to mention the existence of alternative sexual orientations to children was and still is considered a defilement. The advice of the day was the warning that boys could get girls "in trouble." But girls could not get boys "in trouble." Nice girls didn't do *it*. As for boys, well, "boys will be boys"—but, "please, if boys have to be boys, it would be best if they did so with somebody else's daughters!"

Sex was something that happened after you got married. It was such an awkward subject, even in the exclusive company of males, that it was traditionally the brunt of lewd jokes at bachelor parties. But in "polite society," everyone knew that marriage was about having children—and in-laws. That's what nice people did. And God only knew what *other* kinds of people were willing to try.

This was the sexual atmosphere of middle America on the day the first atomic bomb was dropped on Japan. It was also America's sexual mentality for an additional twenty-five to thirty years—during *Star Trek*'s long run on television, when school desegregation was finally achieved, and when the first computers went on sale. Sexual ignorance was in full force when the laser, fiberglass, Pamper diapers, and transistors were invented. Sex was still taboo when the surgeon general clamped down on cigarette smoking and when DNA was synthesized at Stanford University. As late as the early 1970s, a bland psychological virginity was pandemic in middle America—even on the day in 1969 when human beings walked on the moon for the first time.

The confluence of brilliant technologies and lamentable sexual ignorance is a dangerous mixture. Yet the science of sexuality was surreptitious. This subversiveness of serious sexual research exacerbated the pettiest notions of decency, embraced by the middle class but largely ignored by the poor, the rich, by intellectuals, and bohemians. As we will see, it was this liberalism and hedonism among bohemians that would have an immense impact not only on the creation of a so-called gay culture, but on the entire avant-garde movement in Europe and America.

The rigid barrier built by the ideal of "decency" willfully kept people ignorant. In all matters sexual, there was no distinction made between ignorance and innocence. *Not* to know was regarded as a virtue.

Then, finally, in several cases in the late 1960s, the U.S. Supreme Court revised censorship laws, lifting the ban on a wide variety of sexually explicit materials. These decisions ended a cycle of censorship that had begun with the issuance of the first official list of banned books by Pope Gelasius in A.D. 496. The "right *not* to know" had survived for fifteen hundred years.

But before the liberalization of censorship laws, it was difficult for most people even to imagine the enormous varieties and possibilities of sex, partially because the scientific language of sexuality was cloaked in obscure, latinate words, and partly because nice people didn't talk about sex. The relatively few "marriage manuals," as they were called, were kept in drawers or locked cabinets. There is evidence that even the imagination of masturbation fantasies was highly limited, particularly among working-class males (Kinsey). Presumably, people could not imagine what they themselves did not experience or what others regularly experienced. The 1948 thunderbolt of Alfred Kinsey and his team was unprecedented in American culture, and yet it took fully three decades before the Kinsey report had an impact on the general public. According to David Halberstam, "Kinsey was both fascinated and troubled by the vast difference between American sexual behavior the society wanted to believe existed and American sexual practices as they actually did exist. 'God,' Kinsey noted, 'what a gap between social front and reality!' "

Probably the most revolutionary aspect of Kinsey's report was its willingness to break the transgressive boundaries science had built around sexuality. The report was remarkable both for its scholarly candor as well as its complete lack of moral judgments. The only glaring bias was the exclusive focus on male sexuality, coming, of course, from a team of male researchers. Kinsey's report was so shocking in its day that the *New York Times* refused to advertise or review it until it hit the bestseller list. Many men saw Kinsey's survey as a betrayal of the old boys' club, that closed and clandestine "group" that began by inventing itself, and then went about the business of inventing everybody else as "women" or "perverts."

Science was a man's field, and most of the social implications of nineteenth- and early-twentieth-century science had a decidedly masculine bias in regard to the world and its peoples. The unconditional political and scientific domination of males had prohibited open discussions of sex. It was unseemly for women even to mention the subject. Sexuality was only one of several boundaries carefully guarded by men for the exclusive use of men; among the other exclusions were professional status, educational institutions, financial independence, and political activity. But of all cultural boundaries, none was as conspicuously defended as sexuality. Except when men engaged in recreational sex with "loose" women (presumably rendering such females "unfit for marriage"), sexuality was supposed to have only one purpose. It was the patriarchal basis of "family." It required strict moral barriers to guarantee the validity of a man's true progeny, and to protect his *property* (his wife and the virginity of his children) from the incursion of other, marauding males. The male outsider had to be kept from crossing the line that bounded the family. As part of the process, female adulterers had to be condemned. Female virginity had to be celebrated. The female was supposed to be kept completely innocent of sex. She was expected to procreate without pleasure. Women made "love"—they didn't *have sex*. Women were supposed to keep the rules of sexual conduct, made and then broken by men.

The fact that Kinsey's science was *comparative*—that it dared to compare one man's sexuality with another man's sexuality, instead of accepting the monolithic, heterocentric notion of masculinity—was an unparalleled affront to both the solidarity of men and the carefully kept secrets of male genital anatomy and sexuality. As far as men were concerned, women were supposed to have no inkling about the body of men except through the single example of their husbands' physiques; and that singular physique was supposed to be beyond reproach. No subject was as sensitive and restricted as male virility or lack of virility. Women whispered about their insights into male sexual vulnerability, but they rarely confirmed their knowledge that, for men, the failure to get it up was a catastrophe, the failure of masculine rank and domination.

Kinsey broke the silence and ruptured once and for all the models of the dimorphic nature of human sexual orientation. The walls outlining the science of sexual boundaries began to come down, and Kinsey launched an entirely subversive and equally innocent attack on all the things people thought they knew and understood about sex. Of course, Kinsey didn't invent sexual diversity. It had always existed, but with the rare exception of writers like the Marquis de Sade, D. H. Lawrence, James Joyce, Anais Nin, Djuna Barnes, Allan Ginsberg, and Henry Miller, it was kept carefully hidden for centuries by law, by convention, and by the male rules of censorship and transgression. People who crossed the line of sexuality were never allowed re-entry into the middle-class world. The term "outcaste" conveyed a very real and desperately feared fate.

Since the time of Kinsey, the rigid framework supporting the concept of *homosexuality* began to erode, and this fortuitous erosion of a long-held dogma is one of the reasons I often contest the viability of the term, because Kinsey's insights didn't bring about any substantial change in attitudes about gay men and lesbians. The "idea" of homosexuality changed simply because the narrow definition of heterosexuality was so fundamentally challenged by Kinsey's research. Heterosexuality was forever changed. Homosexuality remained the sexuality of outcastes. Homosexuality's only profit from the groundbreaking work of Kinsey was a profit by default.

Despite Kinsey's opening the way to an awareness of male sexuality, the resistance to openness about heterosexual male behavior is still exceptionally great. Heterosexuals have always been far more comfortable about categorizing deviant forms of sexuality than analyzing what they presumed to be their own "normal" sexual inclinations. In their power to shape social attitudes, heterosexuals represent the largest special-interest group in human history. As a result, they have been so completely shielded from acknowledging their socialized norms that they are uncomfortable, if not outrightly outraged, when having the spotlight turned on their own digressions from entirely imaginary and idealized sexual standards. For instance, there is not a great deal of media attention on research concerned with the cause of heterosexuality.

Freud's internalization of sexuality resulted in the neglect of the physiology of sex. Kinsey turned our attention from what we think and feel about sex to how we experience our sexuality—how we really behave rather than how we are told to behave. He shifted the emphasis from the internal to the external, balancing behavioral observation with arcane interpretations of our behaviors in terms of their psychiatric implications. What Kinsey helped to launch was a fundamental revision of taboos and the presumptions of science and religion in regard to sexual transgressions. He also revived the perilous inclination to study the behaviors of organisms as if they were the activities of mechanisms. He was essentially a statistician who dealt with action and the subjects and objects of actions—not dream symbols, obscured memories, and their inferred psychiatric meanings. Until the 1980s, the ramifications of Kinsey's statistical deconstruction of the former gender standards of science were far more visible in pornography and the entertainment industry than in candid, public discussions.

Though science customarily attributed degeneracy to homosexuals, a fascination for kinkiness has always been part of the straight male's fantasy. But, presumably, the actual experience of kinkiness was said to be largely limited to voyeurism, like videotapes and 900 numbers. Despite a number of surveys attesting to the straight male's interest in lesbian sex, bondage, anal and oral sex, and water sports, the science that created the "real man" continues to profess that heterosexuals stick to the missionary position in vaginal sex, and admit only one fetish—a fascination for large breasts. Everything else is supposed to be degenerate and, by extension, "homosexual."

When straight males were confronted in 1972 by Bernardo Bertolucci's erotic film, *Last Tango in Paris*, they could not deal with the realization that a heterosexual man could get a thrill out of anal stimulation. The film triggered an almost primordial rage. The media simply shut down and wouldn't discuss the subject, except in coy or snide insinuations. I recall one editor at the *Chicago Tribune*, where I wrote a series of columns, angrily asking how I could possibly think of writing an article about a film in which there was a character (Marlon Brando) who liked his girlfriend "to stick her finger up his ass."

The film refuted some of the most fundamental heterosexual attitudes that had possessed the unconditional sanction of science for more than a century. The carefully departmentalized categories of male heterosexual behavior were blurred. The science of "normalcy" was unrelentingly challenged, and the designations and meanings of transgression changed again and again. But in the last half of the twentieth century, the change was not merely a cosmetic transformation of a religious cosmic model into a science modeled on religion. This time the change was fundamental. Slowly but inevitably, the science of transgression turned its attention to the ambiguities of gender, exposing heterosexual men to a scrutiny unprecedented in Western society. As a result, science found that its unquestioned, prior standards of "normal" male behavior had to be reconsidered.

For generations, the anatomy of sex had determined that penetration was a passive and inferior role supposedly restricted to women and perverts. The only erogenous zone of a self-respecting heterosexual male was presumed to be his groin. The most devastating remark a straight man thinks he can make about homosexuals is that "gay men like to get fucked." Of all homosexual acts, it is taking the passive role in anal sex that is the most detested, because it implies to straight men that a homosexual is a female in a male body. Then, suddenly, in 1972, Marlon Brando asked Marie Schneider to "go get the butter." The expression about "buttering somebody up" took on a whole new meaning.

What was sensational about *Last Tango* was its blunt bombardment of a gender distinction heterosexual males took for granted and their behavioral sciences anxiously corroborated, generation after generation. The frank sex scenes in Bertolucci's film confused the strict rules of the straight game, and seemed, at least to many heterosexual men, to compromise their dominance—and, worse yet, to feminize them.

Even today journalists still don't like talking about the undeniable fact that males have nipples. In embryology, these "useless" miniature teats are often regarded as a vestige of the fundamental femaleness of all human fetuses. If that feminizing implication is not bad enough for insecure heterosexual males, they must also face the fact that for many males the nipples are every bit as erogenous as the nipples of females. Males reach a certain degree of sexual excitement and, in a great many cases, their hands move across their chests, caressing their own torsos and then their fingers close around their nipples.

The realization of such an erotic, male action disrupts longstanding transgressive boundaries once drawn by anatomical science. The evidence of thousands of straight and gay pornographic videos has irreparably blurred those boundaries. And yet to imply any similarities between the anatomy or the eroticism of men and women has remained a major Western taboo. It is also a taboo to open heterosexual men to the kind of anatomical comparisons and scrutiny that women have had to endure for centuries. The science of heterosexual men had rarely been comparative. Such patriarchal science didn't provide a mechanism for seeing men in relationship to other men, especially men who are more attractive, better built, or better endowed than other men. The current wisdom among straight males is that very good-looking, well-built guys are probably gay—a handy ploy used to defuse open competition between men.

Victorian science had invented the notion of women as modest, sexually anesthetized creatures. With Kinsey's report, however, it be-

came clear that it was not women but men who were often and obsessively timid, self-consciously constructing countless social taboos
that allowed them to remain sexually invisible—conservative uniforms,
pleated pants, drab suits, jockstraps under loose-fitting bathing suits.
Until very recently, the bodies of men were carefully kept under wraps
in every media—not only in films and theater, but also in advertising,
social conversation, public art, and the media. The realization of this
male "modesty" has suggested the possibility that heterosexuality is so
tenuous and masculinity so easily compromised that polite people don't
expose it to scrutiny. It is a longstanding attitude of straight men that
expresses a peculiar underlying phobia that Jonathan Dollimore has
aptly called "a fear of turning into women." Science long protected
heterosexual males from the hint of such a transgression of gender
boundaries. But that protection has lapsed as science has taken a statistical look at Western male society.

In his landmark study of paradigms and scientific revolutions, Thomas S. Kuhn provided an observation that is the cornerstone of my
view of science:

> There is, I think, no theory-independent way to reconstruct phrases
> like "really there." The notion of a match between the ontology
> of a theory and its 'real' counterpart in nature now seems to me
> illusive in principle. . . . The more carefully we study, say, Aristo-
> telian dynamics, phlogistic chemistry, or caloric thermodynamics,
> the more certain we feel that those once current views of nature
> were, as a whole, neither less scientific nor more the product of
> human idiosyncrasy than those current today. If these out-of-date
> beliefs are to be called myths, then myths can be produced by the
> same sorts of methods and held for the same sorts of reasons that
> now lead to our own scientific knowledge.

For the vast majority of intellectuals, what Kuhn synthesizes is the
thunderous collapse of all forms of certitude, a process, amazingly, still
denied by a great many specialists and pedagogues. Clearly, however,
Kuhn demolishes the naturalistic perception of science as an *objective*
progression toward the kind of "Truth" that used to be spelled with a
capital *T*. What Kuhn says seems to apply equally to subatomic particles and to genes. They are "really there" only because we claim they
are there. They are "real" only in a specific connotation of reality.

Here, Kuhn builds on a paradox that Nietzsche called perspectivism: his famous insistence that every view is only one among many possible interpretations of the same things. The paradox, of course, is that Nietzsche's own view that there are only interpretations is itself only an interpretation, and, therefore, it too could be wrong. The only current resolution to such radical relativism is the contention that there are some ideas that seem to be more valid than others simply because they do not contradict information that we now believe to be substantiated by mathematics, educated observation, and analysis.

And yet, as we have seen, nothing changes as much as the things we believe are substantiated by educated observation and analysis. My aim is not to debunk science or biology, but to try to see various fields of scientific research in a relative context—the same relative context that science itself insists is necessarily the basis of all contemporary concepts and theories. *New York Times* science writer George Johnson observes that "scientists are the shamans of our place and time, telling us what is 'real'." Johnson asks if, in the end, all scientific theories are just as poetic, metaphorical, symbolical as ancient myths. Or can we really and finally believe we are right to think we have access, through mathematical reason, to the underlying cause of all things? When Stephen R. L. Clark comments on Johnson's book *Fire in the Mind*, he reminds us that even the most profound scientific theories are tenuously built on long chains—or even loops—of inference, and that they are subject, like all human efforts, to revision and change. Though provisional attitudes in regard to reality are debatably the most irritating, baffling, and troublesome of twentieth-century paradigms, relativism is nonetheless a basis not only of the philosophy of Nietzsche and all the philosophers influenced by him, but it is also a prevalent view of astrophysicists. Physicist Niels Bohr has said that "the opposite of a correct statement is a false statement. But the opposite of a profound truth may well be another profound truth." Naturalists and biologists, being of a somewhat less abstract mentality than astrophilosophers, tend to view their empirical evidence very seriously, resisting the possibility that their particular take on Darwin's profound truth may well be the opposite of another equally profound truth.

Science, like the tribal spiritualism of primal peoples and the divine law of Judaism, Christianity, and Islam, is a territorial mentality, a self-made enclosure with boundaries that are carefully protected against both entry and exit. As Kuhn suggests, science is one of a great many mythologies on which we build our lives, surrounding ourselves with the protective fortification of arbitrary boundaries that we call reality. Science is as much a basis of moral boundaries as religion is. To cross those boundaries is as much a transgression in the world of natural science as it is in a world of divine law. And yet, in my view, scientific thinking is the best and most reliable kind of thinking we have at the moment. It is for this reason that I am exceptionally concerned about the attitudes of scientists about sexual orientation.

Once the earth was the realm of the wizard and the alchemist, the ritualist and the magician. Then it became the domain of the priest who knew how to speak to God, allowing the priest to read God's lips and understand God's rules. But since the eighteenth century, the earth has been the domain of science. Francis Yates has tried to understand the drastic transition in the custodianship of nature:

> The basic difference between the attitude of the magician toward the world and the attitude of the scientist toward the world is that the former wants to draw the world into himself, whilst the scientist does just the opposite; he externalizes and impersonalizes the world by a movement of will in an entirely opposite direction.

Thomas Kuhn makes a very persuasive case for a greatly revised view of science as a discipline heavily influenced by *nonrational* procedures. He succeeds, I think, in recovering the magician's efforts to draw the world into the subjective realm of intuition and imagination. He also succeeds in disgracing the empirical notion that there is a demonstrable correlation between the ontology of a theory and its "real" counterpart in nature. Like Gertrude Stein, Kuhn tell us, essentially, that *there is no there there.*

In doing this, Kuhn strikes a decisive blow against the most fundamental supports of Western scientism. He does not rebuke science so much as he makes it clear that scientific theory is the product of an informed but arbitrary worldview that has no more claim to the truth than any other eruditely reached point of view. On the other hand, lest I misrepresent his point of view, I think Kuhn would say, without hesitation, that evolution has a far more vital place in the world of modern thought than creationism simply because evolution is built on a current model open to the best available examination and analysis, while creationism is essentially a matter of antiquated, blind faith, a mythology whose time has come and gone, and a subject, therefore, that is beyond the bounds of productive discussion.

Despite what is clearly my admiration for science, it has still been my intention here to disavow the inclination of science to claim a natural law that declares fixity and universality. I agree with Thomas Kuhn that science is a mythology among countless other mythologies. In our time, therefore, science is a viable myth produced, as Kuhn has said, "by the same sorts of methods and held for the same sorts of reasons" as any other mythology.

In this context, the vilification or validation of homosexuality by science is not any more of a disadvantage or a benefit than the vilification or validation of homosexuality by religion. It is this deconstructive frame of mind that I hope thinking people will consider with both care and caution.

Again, until we become aware of the workings of our mythology and understand how it affects laws, values, relationships, and daily life, we cannot change some of our most fundamental ideas about ourselves and others. Until we acknowledge and explore the impulse behind our myths, we must continue simply to change the names and shapes of the things we claim to admire or despise or fear without truly grasping what motivates our personal and social responses.

The greatest obstruction to the exploration of mythology is the dogma that has made our myths inaccessible and indisputable, producing the understandable fear that any failure of faith in our myths leaves us desperately vulnerable and alone. Divine law and natural law made the same absolute claim of hegemony, implying that either we accept what we are told to believe or we will be left with nothing in which to believe. But, there are still alternative mythologies for now and for the future.

When twentieth-century physicists confronted the norms of the decrepit, materialistic science of the eighteenth and nineteenth centuries, they succeeded in making a wide breach in the boundaries of the West's walled mentality. Today the mythic hero on a quest scribbles eloquent equations on blackboards and searches the sky for improbabilities and anomalies. In ways very similar to the adventures of the countless heroes who went before them, the revelations of today's scientists tell us about the realm of possibility that lies somewhere beyond the mythology that was once our only reality.

In 1990, as one of his final and most insightful observations, mythologist Joseph Campbell proclaimed:

We have not even to risk the adventure alone, for the heroes of all time have gone before us. The labyrinth is thoroughly known. We have only to follow the thread of the hero path, and where we had thought to find an abomination, we shall find a god. And where we had thought to slay another, we shall slay ourselves. Where we had thought to travel outward, we come to the center of our own existence. And where we had thought to be alone, we will be with all the world.

It was Gilbert Ryle who, in the 1930s, first referred to the idea of a "mind" or "soul" hidden deep within Cartesian dualism as "the ghost in the machine." As Paul Davies and his co-author John Bribbin wisely observe, "Ryle was right to dismiss the notion of the ghost in the machine—not because there is no ghost, but because there is no machine."

TRANSGRESSION

7

AS SENSIBILITY

Narcissus is never ourselves; he is always the other one who cannot see us.

> Paul Zweig, The Heresey of Self-Love

Sterling: I couldn't shield him with raw silk, and tassels, and tiebacks. The limits of style.

> Paul Rudnick, Jeffrey

In the mid-1960s, when Howard Becker wrote *Outsiders: Studies in the Sociology of Deviance*, the metaphor of the "other" was just beginning to emerge as an ideological theme in the liberal American conscience. Enlightened people had always known about the estrangement, inequality, and victimization of a number of marginal persons and groups, but until the civil rights and youth movements of the 1960s, the full extent of disempowerment was not recognized, and the connections between such disempowerment and social conflicts and tragedies in the United States were almost entirely written off by the majority as the reckless and unlawful behavior of various outcast groups and individuals. The awakening of Americans, particularly young Americans, to the inequities of "outsiders" was deeply disillusioning at the same time that it pointed out the fallacy of social congruity in the United States. Since the days of Ozzie and Harriet, skepticism and cynicism have steadily overwhelmed the fabled "equality under the law" that served for almost two hundred years as an idealistic shelter from the bigoted undercurrents of American culture. Gradually, it became evident that the punishment of America's underclass was in the same heinous category as war crimes. It became evident that demonstrations and riots were not the disorderly behaviors of mavericks and outcastes, but the acts of persons who had no voice in their own destinies. Idealistic hippies and college students of the 1960s and 1970s noted that there were no lyrics in the National Anthem sanctioning racism, sexism, anti-Semitism, and homophobia. And yet, the American social mentality brimmed with bigoted attitudes, expressed blatantly or subversively in cruel jokes, belittling theatrical and advertising images, and the unthinking psychological biases hidden within the law of the land.

The admission that *outsiders* even exist in the United States has been reluctant. The undeniable fact that certain people and certain groups have been brutalized, unlawfully punished by the law, slandered, and lynched has often been challenged, in very much the same way, and probably for the same reasons, that certain people deny the historicity of the Holocaust. It was not until college students and activists opened clamorous public debates about bigotry in the 1960s that it finally became evident that the monolithic unity of our nation was something of a farce. People discovered that many of their presumptions about social justice and national congruity were built on fallacies. Many people were startled to realize that the enemies of the tribe were not strangers and foreigners. On the contrary, it was discovered that there was an intense and widespread animosity *within* the nation. There were strangers and outsiders struggling to survive in the outmost margins of the home society, some in ghettos, some in subcultures, some in closets, and others in middle-class kitchens and nurseries—outsiders who lived inside American society: Jews, Hispanics, Native Americans, African Americans, Asians, homosexuals, and women. Starting noticeably in the decades after World War II, these thousands of invisible people became a threat to the dominant society because they began to come out of their ghettos and closets in order to shed their invisibility. Voices, long silent, were heard. The outsiders issued astoundingly iconoclastic pronouncements, taking part in massive demonstrations, rioting in the cities, and intimating the possibility of the impossible—a battle *within* our nation, a confrontation between those who were stigmatized and those who stigmatized them. As it has turned out, with rare exception the battles have been fought with words rather than arson and assassinations.

It is the outsiders living within our world who have always interested me. My interest is provoked by a disillusionment I have known from childhood and that, to my surprise, I began to share with countless others in the social activism of the 1960s and 1970s. As a young man, I had looked on with cynicism as my peers were force-fed on a fantastic Boy Scout mentality, convincing them that difference—that "diversity"—was at the very heart of what they meant by words such as "individuality," "freedom," and "democracy." I knew better, and I was never a Boy Scout.

The context of any society depends on obedience to a tradition that quells and often destroys individuality, and, subsequently, builds an unspoken consensus about what is and what is not a transgression. If that congruity is shattered, then and only then does the self-conscious kind of identity called "individualism" come into existence. Among tribal peoples true individuality is rare. But in the West, where we like to attribute the concept of individuality to a Greek heritage, the truth is a good deal less idealistic. That elitist Hellenic heritage of individuality was smothered by Christianity and buried in forgetfulness until the rebellious Renaissance. As we have seen, the fragmentation of Western philosophical unity has had a long and contentious history. It is only since the time of the Reformation that the West began in earnest to speak of individuality, originality, private sensibility, and individual style, rather than presuming that everyone had the experience of a cohesive oneness with culture. Again, as we have seen, at some point in time, people realized that the law was no longer divine and unassailable. Without divinity, there seemed to be no basis for obedience, no source of the reward and punishment fundamental to the enforcement of obedience. People began to live lives of multiple choice rather than lives of right or wrong choices. The boundaries of Western mythology eroded, allowing the entry of ideas that underscored and exacerbated the failing unanimity of the West.

In tribal societies—in societies still bonded by a mythological premise, by a prevailing belief system—there is little distinction between person and culture. And, if idiosyncratic persons emerge in such metaphysically closed societies, then, as we have seen, the societies usually enlarge their mythologies to embrace, disdain, or even revere exceptional and nonconformist persons. Such cultural cohesion in regard to both the rule of law and community attitudes about persons is the most intrinsic basis of congruent societies. But when a mood of uncertainty forces people to reassess the nature of the "outsider," to take a second look at the outsiders who are within, inevitably social congruency is shattered and holes are punched in the closed boundaries that made a society a society. Outsiders who are outsiders are enemies, and there is nothing metaphysically complex or socially perplexing about such tribal enmity. But the *outsider who is an insider*, who lives among us but is not accepted as one of us, that person arouses a particularly vicious resentment because he or she breaches the boundaries that are supposed to keep insiders inside and outsiders out. The blurring of the metaphysical distinction of who is one of us and who is not one of us is among the most devastating situations in a closed, tribal society.

Apparently we deeply disdain and dread outsiders who live among us because they repudiate the nationalistic and ethnocentric notion that we are all of one mind, one faith, one language, one history, one sexuality, one morality, and one destiny. For all our touting of the democratic notion of cultural and behavioral diversity, in practice any real diversity offends and frightens us because its very existence opens the frontiers that are supposed to keep us safe from all forms of deviance, including our own secret deviancy.

The full recognition of the sheer numbers and variety of outsiders living among us may have been a new aspect of social consciousness in America in the 1960s, but such divergency had been acknowledged in America and Europe many years before the publication of Becker's landmark book, *Outsiders: Studies in the Sociology of Deviance.*

In fact, the civil rights movement became a political issue in the United States in the 1920s, with the Woman Suffrage movement, resulting in the nineteenth amendment to the U.S. Constitution. Under the NAACP and the National Urban League, Martin Luther King, Jr., and others, were instrumental in securing legislation, notably the Civil Rights Acts of 1964 and 1968 and the Voting Rights Act of 1965, prohibiting discrimination in public accommodations, schools, employment, and voting.

Fifty years earlier, in the works of the French poets Baudelaire, Rimbaud, and Mallarmé a new kind of "outsider sensibility" provided language and thought with a style so radical that it could be called a "linguistic heresy." This new language was a celebration of alienation invented by Baudelaire, perfected by Mallarmé, and given its most explosive expression by Rimbaud.

> We might say that it [was a linguistic concept that derives from] a belief in the relationship which necessarily exists between a poem and witchcraft or magic or *sortilege*, as the French call it. A poem comes into being due to a process which, like alchemy, is magical and therefore *foreign* to the rules of logic and even to the rules of instinct. (Fowlie)

I don't think it is coincidental that Baudelaire was homosexual (at least both Marcel Proust and André Gide said he was gay) and that Rimbaud was probably the most open and radical gay male of his day. It is very possible that whatever we now mean when we speak both of "gay culture" and "gay sensibility" had their origins in the time of Rimbaud, at about the same time the term "homosexuality" was invented.*

This culture and sensibility were integral aspects of a distinctly nineteenth-century *sensibility*, perfected by a long line of bohemians and eccentrics, radical politicos, and sexual mavericks. But the nineteenth-century connotation of sensibility was very different from our current use of the term. In the world of bohemians, sensibility was something new—probably something unprecedented in prior periods of Western history. This bohemian sensibility was the visible result of the breakdown of social congruity that severed the bond between person and culture, between tradition and idiosyncracy. In the wake of this breach, bohemians singled themselves out as those willing to abandon the dissolving unity of the old culture in order to invent a delib-

---

*It is by now clear that I use the terms "homosexuality" and "gay" in relation to sexual orientation not only from the time of their inventions—probably the early twentieth century for "gay" and mid-nineteenth century for "homosexuality"—but I also use these same terms to describe far earlier periods of Western civilization and also to describe non-Western peoples, for whom such words have had no significance matching our twentieth-century definitions of the same words. I do this for the sake of simplicity, realizing that by using the terms transculturally and transhistoriclaly I am implying just the opposite of what I believe. I do not believe that "homosexuality" or "heterosexuality" are fixed and globally defined orientations. I believe that sexual orientation has had an ever-changing history that brings into question the possibility of the continuity of any particular form of sexuality. Like many other commentators, I believe that sexuality has had a history, and, as such, sexuality has had a constantly changing social context.

erate new persona. It is still not clear, however, whether bohemians were kicked out of mainstream society or whether they left willingly.

In this context of sensibility, sensibility becomes something like *persona*, an invented "voice," a spiritual and intellectual kind of expression impossible in the bounded tribal world, except among those societies where bizarre, exceptional, and contrary persons are figures of reverence and fear. The kind of sensibility I'm talking about here is not a form of copycat *fashion*. By fashion I mean the mainstreaming and trivialization of sensibility—an affectation attempting to fill the void left by the absence of both culture and persona. In other words, sensibility is an invention. It is created without regard for the group or the marketplace. In contrast, fashion is artifice—a manufactured and marketed facade of individualism without real individuality, a fabrication that stands in for real creativity, a commodified convention that tries to come off as a unique invention, while, in fact, it is a flag for others to follow.

It seems to me that the immense power of modern marketing and advertising has made genuine, individuated sensibility exceptionally rare. Admittedly, I am uncomfortable with the collision of fashion and sensibility that was a vivid aspect of both mainstream and gay culture during the 1980s and 1990s. As I see it, sensibility has been mitigated by imitations of celebrity and by the pop media that profess to deliver titillating eccentricity while they are actually selling a formulated and effortless avant-garde for the youthful masses. For these reasons, what personally concerns me here is the process by which commodification has impacted and transformed the bohemian sensibility of the nineteen and early twentieth centuries into today's fashion.

It is because of the shattering of social cohesion in the West that we can discuss sensibility, fashion, and culture as isolated issues, rather than aspects of a seamless social *gestalt*. And because I will be speaking of a particular kind of sensibility and of a particular attitude about culture, I should make some distinctions.

By sensibility, I mean to suggest an idiosyncratic and intimate "voice" that is invented as its creator's only access to the world of others—the voice that attempts to penetrate the wall that bounds both persons and societies. Whereas the voice of people in congruent societies is, to a very great extent, a legacy of the distinctive and transhistorical tradition of the group, idiosyncratic sensibility comes into existence when there is a breach in that traditional legacy. Individualized sensibility appears when there is a breach in the cohesiveness of self and culture. That breach often results in one of two possible mechanisms. It necessitates either the imitation of personhood through the manipulation of fashion or the invention of personhood through an exploration of idiosyncracy, a process of self-discovery that results in a personal "voice"—in an individuated sensibility. Such an individuated sensibility can be shared by a marginal group or it can define the isolation of just one person.

When social congruity fails, the relationship of culture to traditional sensibility is broken. For instance, the abduction of Africans during the years of the slave trade was such a shattering of cultural congruity. But, remarkably, African Americans reinvented themselves and created a distinctive sensibility blended from the resonance of the cultures of Africa as well as the experience of being estranged in a strange land. In this way, if cultural continuity is broken, some people are capable of re-inventing themselves. The alternative to such re-invention is assimilation or *normalization*—a process by which people attempt to claim an identity that provides a substitution for a lost or hidden identity.

In the days of the *belle epoch*, sensibility was charismatic and audacious. It was far more than a look or a commodified faddishness. The bohemian subcultures had their camp-followers and groupies, but the bohemian world began with mavericks who invented themselves, instead of simply imitating the conformities or idiosyncracies of others. I am hammering at this point because I sometimes fear that one of the sad results of *normalizing the metaphor of transgression* has been the decline of sensibility and the triumph of fashion.

In their day, Baudelaire, Mallarmé, and Rimbaud were not fashionable. They were the spearhead of French symbolist poetry, a form so innovative and alien to the naive realism of their conservative European predecessors (and many of their successors) that it revolutionized the fatuous meaning of "stylishness" in every quarter of society, including the millions of people who have never read a line of their unprecedented work. It was their linguistic "alienation" and their *foreignness* of mind that became the most notable emblem of global modernism. That foreignness also designates their invention of the self-contemplating "stranger"—*artists who peer at themselves and, through themselves, are somehow able to see the world*. Whatever the psychological context of the "self" in other times and other places, it was with the French symbolists that narcissism became, in the truest sense, a central facet in both the culture of modernity and the culture of homosexuality. The one could not exist without the other.

The divided Freudian *self* was presumably discovered inwardly, through the coded language of the "subconscious." Many artists have sought inspiration in the underworld of mind. But the Symbolists found a different source of influence: in the transparency of the world in which they saw their own reflections. The Symbolist messages were not concealed in the oblivion of some imaginary animal memory. For the Symbolists the messages were hidden behind the illusion of a "real" world—the deceptive and occult Hindu realm of *maya*—behind which they found the reality long obscured in the West by its fetish for naturalism. What they sought and believed they found was "an undifferentiated spiritual reality" (Coomaraswamy). The influences of Eastern mysticism were very much at work in the Parisian Latin Quarter of the mid-nineteenth century. That spiritualism became a subtle and pervasive aspect of the revolution in sensibility.

In the hands of bohemians, sensibility was turned into paradox. It became a fashion that was unfashionable, a surrealistic oxymoron. It also became a magnificent transgression that broke the connection between conformity and fashion. It altered the conventional definitions of individuality at the same time that it disrupted the definitions of respectability. In Paris and, later, in Berlin, personal sensibility was no longer a matter of "taste"—that essential passport into the world of middle-class gentility. Instead, sensibility became a metaphor of a quite different ritual of passage, a renewal of the hero's mythic voyage from the ordinary world into an unnamed and nameless new community— located on the Left Bank of the Seine in Paris toward the end of the nineteenth century. That "community" would appear and disappear, moving around Europe and America, popping up in pre-war Berlin, in pre-Bolshevik Russia, in World War II Zurich, in post–World War II Harlem and Greenwich Village. It would have many different aliases, but it would always remain essentially the same. Everyone was welcome into a subculture inhabited by those whom filmmaker Marcel Carne called "the children of paradise." It was in that world that both bohemianism and modern Euro-American "gay sensibility" was born.

Mallarmé was entranced by ideas about the occult that Villiers de L'Isle-Adam introduced to him. Central to Mallarmé's poetic imagination was the Heraclitean paradox that "difference is also not difference"—that "the way up and the way down" are the same. Such aphorisms were absurd, but it was their absurdity that made them attractive to dissidents. Any statement or image with unintelligible meaning became the basis of a new poetic truth in the arts. *Absurdity* and *irrationality* became an access to the meanings long obscured by reason. There was for bohemians great irony in meaninglessness. Irony had become a substitute for meaning in a world in which many intellectuals and artists felt that meaning was no longer meaningful.

Poets of the Romantic era had found their pictorial inspiration in fields of daffodils and the images of painted Hellenic pottery. But there had always been another subversive Western tradition, from the time of the metaphysical poetry of John Donne and mythopoetics of William Blake. That same alternative tradition can be found in the incomprehensible luminosity of paintings of Turner and the surreal density of the "Black Paintings" of Goya.* Apparently, for many artists there is no difference in difference. And there is no way up. Many artists during the nineteenth century undertook a metaphoric "way down" into poetry.[1]

In his *Lettre du voyant*, Rimbaud celebrated the elder Baudelaire as the "King of Seers," praising him for opening a breach in the barriers

---

*In attitudes about imaginative activities such as the arts, and despite hundreds of contrary examples in the imagery of Asian, tribal, and many Western societies, there is in the West a persistent inclination to associate non-realist imagination with psychosis and disease rather than celebrating it as a result of a visionary gift. For instance, it is still acceptable to "explain" El Greco's elongation of his painted figures as the result of some kind of optical disorder. Another example of the pathologizing of art is the blurred distinction between Van Gogh's brilliant visual imagination and his dementia. Even at Spain's Prado Museum, during the two-hundred-fiftieth anniversary of the birth of Goya, it was offhandedly suggested that his series of bizarre and troubling etchings called 'Disasters of War' and his extraordinary 'Black Paintings' were the result not of a luminous and visionary mind, but the result, presumably, of some kind of "still unidentified disease." Unquestionably, there is art that is a reflection of people whose "reason" is compromised, like the creators of the *arte brut* celebrated by Jean Dubuffet and the art made by the inmates of the *Hauses der Kunstler* at the famous Austrian psychiatric institution Gugging. But putting aside such very interesting instances of irrational art created by people considered by society to be totally dysfunctional, it remains that the completely arbitrary and relatively recent focus in the West (and all of its colonies) on so-called realism in art is so closely associated with "normalcy" in art—even associated with the physiology of sensory accuracy—that more than a few critics and scholars have regularly attempted to explain away the visionary and irrational achievements of some of our most revolutionary artists by claiming that their work is the result of a mysterious pathology—some enigmatic affliction resulting in a "deformity" of the heralded but narrow realistic expectations of imagery in the Western arts.

of familiar emotion and pointing downward and upward to a place where, "an abyss away," there were shadows of longings and feelings that gentrified society preferred not to recognize.

Rimbaud's imaginary voyage was a downward spiral—virtually a descent into hell, entitled *Une Saison en enfer*. For Baudelaire, the underbelly of evil would become an inspiration, *Les Fleurs du mal*. But Mallarmé turned the mirror inward, transforming the image of himself into a window through which only the perfect sky could be seen, somewhere beyond the delusive *maya*—those imperfect shapes of the world. For Mallarmé, perfection was discovered in a vacant glass—an image of Narcissus idealized, of the disengaged self at the heart of modernity. This narcissistic concept of otherness, of foreignness, and alienation, still constitutes the most active metaphor of transgression in the modern era, and its metaphoric manifestation can be observed nowhere as clearly as in the twentieth-century Western *idea* of homosexuality.

The era of Baudelaire, Mallarmé, and Rimbaud was a time for acting out social and artistic difference. It was also a time for the exploration of everything forbidden in the middle-class world. Baudelaire, Mallarmé, and Rimbaud invented an alchemy of personal sensibility that brought about one of the fundamental assumptions of marginal people in the twentieth century: a staggeringly disruptive vision of *the foreignness of ourselves*.

Before the Symbolist poets, Narcissus had never been one of us. He had always been the "other" who would not look at us or recognize us. He had been disparaged as an enigma and a menace because he appeared to have abandoned the world and to have made a world of himself. Narcissus was reinvented, and gradually he would come to stand as a metaphor of the homosexual.

The myth of Narcissus gazing at his own reflection in a pond became the metaphor of a disengagement and *foreignness* born of the magical ability of Baudelaire, Mallarmé, and Rimbaud to look into the mirror and see the world beyond the world—the "otherness" so crucial to the idea of modernism. In their rarified otherworldliness they discovered an astounding new worldliness.

Unlike Narcissus, who would not look away from his own reflection, and therefore would not see us, the French poets saw us clearly by looking through the transparency of themselves. From the outside they could see us as we cannot be seen from the inside. In order to tell us what they saw from their unique, alienated perspective, they had to destroy both tradition and traditional language, and they had to recreate a new series of metaphors in which people would be able to catch a glimpse of a reality previously inaccessible to them.

Baudelaire, Mallarmé, and Rimbaud described that new set of metaphors as a *sorcellerie evocatoire*—a magical operation—or an *alchimie du verbe*. In one instance, they destroyed both the identity we find in language and the language we find in identity.

Language defines us. Language is the invisible prison built by culture. For those who are shut out by the words used by others to define them, the destruction of language is, as Rimbaud proclaimed, a breach in the barriers of familiar emotion that leads to a place where, "an abyss away," there were longings and feelings that most of us prefer not to recognize. In the poetry of the Symbolists, transgression became both a metaphor and a radical sensibility. Transgression became a breach in the walls that confine people within their bounded cultures. The Symbolists and their radical ideas occurred because nothing else was possible during the cultural turmoil of their time.

For those whose identities are disputed or denigrated, the use of language is an inescapable harassment. No matter how much we manipulate the impact of words like "nigger" and "queer" and "bitch," the long dark memory that lives in those pejorative words keeps us prisoners of slander. The poets of the nineteenth-century Latin Quarter wanted to invent a new language, free of old insinuations and judgments. They wanted to emancipate words from morality, from sentimentality and clichés.

The Symbolists' distortions of grammar (Rimbaud: "Je est un autre" [I is another]), their misplaced references (Baudelaire: "Hypocrite lecteur—mon semblable—mon frere!" [Hipocrite reader—my alias—my twin!]), the legacy of their brilliant bending of meaning through irony and contrariness (Cocteau: "Je suis un mensonage qui dit la verité" [I am a lie that tells the truth.])—these were the inventions of a new language, the creations of an *alchimie du verbe*, with a striking resemblance to the type of theatrical language devised by modern homosexuals to deal with their history of discrimination—the play on gender, the sarcastic pun, the perfect barb, the clownish and bitter self-aggrandizement, the glib use of mockery to disguise humiliation, the exaggerated masculinity, or the flamboyant play on effeminacy. It is a deadly slapstick. It is an orchestration of absurdity as an expression of retaliation for endless abuse or neglect—for invisibility or scandalous visibility.

A decade after Baudelaire, an Irish fop turned sensibility into high style by perfecting both gesture and attitude as an expression of delightfully empty artifact. He once said, "It is not difficult to walk down Piccadilly carrying a lily; what is difficult is to make people think I did." For Oscar Wilde a pose was everything. Decades later, Madonna would attempt to emulate Wilde's penchant for poses and attitudes. But a woman pretending to be a man pretending to be a woman missed the ultimate tragic nature of Oscar Wilde. His wit was both combative and compensative, intent on indulging personal calamity with an endless string of bitter and terse retorts—a glib and, at the same time, intensely anxious defensiveness. But for all of his verbal outrageousness, Wilde remained a faddish clown anxious for public acknowledgment, the "naughty delight" of a self-absorbed and bourgeois society, often endured and seldom adored, and, finally, despised when he was publicly tried and imprisoned.

Wilde may not have invented gay sensibility, but he certainly codified its tone of bitchiness that is so familiar in Europe and America in the twentieth century:

"Consistency is the last refuge of the unimaginative," he quipped.

"Bad art is a great deal worse than no art at all."

"I can resist everything except temptation," he mused. "Nothing succeeds like excess."

But there is also a telling bitterness associated with Wilde's twisted efforts to deal with human emotion. One night he awakened from a dream and cried out to his friend Reggie Turner, "I dreamed I was dining with the dead."

Turner responded without losing a beat: "I'm sure you were the life of the party." In the age of AIDS, there is something mordant, even bittersweet, about Reggie Turner's Wildean retort. But in modern gay sensibility there is always the paradox of senselessness and deadliness, a fragile attempt to minimize losses, to turn the embarrassing moment into a grand gesture, to change adversity into sardonic absurdity—*somehow* to survive.

Style without substance is a wrecking ball. And yet it is also completely defenseless against the inescapable realities of disease. When Sterling, the interior decoarator of Paul Rudnick's play *Jeffrey*, is faced with the demise of his young lover, he proclaims listlessly that for all its flamboyance and bravado, even *style has its limitations*. He admits that he could not save his friend with raw silk, tassels, and tiebacks.

Style can often defeat adversity with a haughty glance. It can dismiss calamity and turn tragedy into absurdity. But it can't snub death. Yet that was precisely the kind of camp style that worked so well for Dadaism. It made a laughingstock of academic art: "DADA doubts everything. Dada is an armadillo. Everything is Data too. Beware of Dada. Anti-dadaism is a disease: selfkleptomania, man's normal condition, is DADA. But the real dadas are against DADA."[2]

For a while, style without substance also worked, at least compensatively, for homosexuality. But there comes a moment when affectation ceases to be a metaphor of transgression and becomes a corroboration, if not a validation, of homophobia, even for the homophobia of homosexuals. Oscar Wilde, like a great many lesbians and gay men of his time, made no secret of his self-contempt. One of his final works, *De Profundis*, brims with self-loathing. But, all things considered, Oscar Wilde was an original. He was one of the first in a long line of gadflies who proved that the mouth is mightier than the sword. He made wine out of sour grapes. And he taught many of us how to deal with adversity; how to twist a phrase into a showstopping defense against cruelty.

The cunning style popularized by Oscar Wilde was centered on a unique use of language to express the indescribable "alienation" of his life; a defense against what he knew people were thinking. An early warning system, cautioning offenders not say what they had on their minds, not to attempt to duel with words unless they could match Wilde's devilish verbal skills.

Wilde was a poor relation of Arthur Rimbaud, at best a second cousin. But he understood the relationship between language, emotion, and personality. Language creates the boundaries of whatever it is we mean when we speak of "ourselves." What we think and say is largely predetermined by the language we speak. If our language cannot support our description of our unique experience, no matter how intense that experience, then we must either change the language or we must change the experience so it fits the available language.[3] When we say that "there are no words" for something, we are admitting that we must relinquish something we want to express because our language does not allow us to say it. The uniqueness of modernists like Rimbaud was their insistence on changing the language, rather than relinquishing or trivializing what they wished to communicate. They liberated themselves from the perils of language and, in so doing, liberated themselves from the confines of a social reality that diminished them.

There are a great many cultural commentators who believe, as I do, that the results of the modernist deconstruction of language, along with the fundamental revision of all other forms of human expression, have been catastrophic for the Judeo-Christian tradition. Countless literary and visual arts critics, philosophers, and historians have written intriguing tracts on the decimation of Western tradition.* For more than a century, they have vividly explored the decline of the West. They have observed that the syntax of faith has been garbled. They have confided that the authority of divine law has been dismantled. They have convincingly noted that the specific interpretations of positive law have been ineffectually debated. And they have relentlessly questioned the existence of anything as reassuring as cosmic purpose.

It is in the history of the modern arts that these tremendous shifts in attitude are most visible. Take only the shift from the mechanistic ballet of Petipa (*Swan Lake*) to the modern dance of Martha Graham and Merce Cunningham, from the aristocratic lyricism of the landscapes by Jean-Honoré Fragonard to the startling abstractions of Vasily Kandinsky and Jackson Pollack, from the naturalistic prose of Emile Zola to the temporal and spatial ambiguities of novels by James Joyce and Virginia Woolf, from the rationality of the plays by Clifford Odets (*Golden Boy*) to the irrationality of playwrights like Samuel Becket, Harold Pinter, and Edward Albee. These are not merely shifts in fashion and artistic convention, they are major shifts in paradigms, of a "voice" I call *sensibility*.

This revision of all forms of communication is not simply an artistic preoccupation. As we have seen, it has also taken place in philosophy and science, fields in which new terms, new analogies, and new metaphors attempt to make the models of the postquantum and post-Darwinian era accessible to us, resulting not only in a different world but also in a world of difference. Terms, acronyms, and equa-

*Friedrich Nietzsche, Oswald Spengler, F. S. C. Northrup, Arnold Toynbee, Herbert Muller, Wallace Fowlie, Susan Sontag, Joseph Frank, Mark Schorer, Harry Levin, Edmund Wilson, John Aldridge, Philip Rahv, Macolm Cowley, Herbert Read, Clive Bell, Ernst Cassirer, Suzanne K. Langer, David Daiches, Dore Ashton, Robert Hughes, Michel Foucault, Hannah Arendt, Mikel Dufrenne, and untold others.

tions like "DNA," "Kinship System," "Naked Singularity," and "$E=h\nu$" are not simply novel denotations; they are, ultimately, connotations of entirely new mind sets. To define them, we must redefine the entire mentality and worldview of the West.

Given the enormity of cultural shifts during the decades since 1850, it is not surprising that marginal voices, once unheard, have found in the turbulence of change an opportunity to call into question their neglected status in the dominant world. Sadly, but fortuitously, the destruction of the old worldview also requires us to redefine the moral codes that demonized "deviants." The redefinition of sexual orientation is particularly imperative, though it is agonizingly resistant. The unwillingness of people to comprehend homosexuality in terms of the reckless openness of the current paradigm is perplexing, particularly because homosexuals were a central part of a process that dismantled the Judeo-Christian ethical ethos and brought about the new worldview. They were in the front lines with the bohemians, philosophers, and scientists who broke the shackles of the conformity that bounded the West.

George Steiner contends that two major historical events splintered the foundations of Western tradition and precipitated the crisis of modernity: "One epitomized in Mallarmé's 'disjunction of language from external reference,' and the other in Rimbaud's 'deconstruction of self'—Je est un autre (I is another)."

In other words, language can no longer depend on a consistent relationship between what is said and what is meant. The relationship between objects in "reality" and the names of objects "in our minds" has become disjoined. Again, in one instance, a revolution in ideas and expression destroyed both the identity we find in language and the language we find in identity.

This splintering of Western tradition, with its invention of "the foreignness of ourselves," has been the most active metaphor of transgression since the advent of the modern era. At its creative core were the artists, political radicals, and homosexuals of the late 1800s. These provocateurs recognized their "alienation" from the rest of the world, and that recognition gave them a great advantage. They could look over the "event horizon" long before astrophysics discovered that they could not see beyond the boundaries of a black hole, whose event horizon is the point at which light cannot escape the implosion of a collapsing star. Just as Dostoevsky envisioned the "unconscious" before Freud named it, so artists and radicals and homosexuals saw from the vantage of their social separateness events yet to come. Such outsiders are the perpetual subversives of the world, a "dew line," to use McLuhan's famous phrase, that sounds the alarm the rest of us cannot hear—a "distant early warning" of revolutions already taking place at the very edge of our culture. The advantage of the outsider is analogous to the advantage of the Hubble telescope; it is somewhere beyond the clouds that obstruct our vision of other worlds.

Because of its enforced remoteness from mainstream culture, and because of its inability to do more than fake the expectations of the "home culture," the astronomical social displacement of the homosexual has made an immense impact on both those who defined homosexuality and those who have been defined as homosexuals. It is possible to make a credible case, as many cultural commentators have done, that homosexuality has been at the very core of Western culture and creative sensibility at least from the time of Rimbaud: revolutionizing virtually everything about social reality and becoming the catalyst of both modernism and postmodernism. In the process of changing the world, it seems to many observers, homosexuality itself has been profoundly changed.

The influence of homosexuality on Western culture began with the formation of bohemian ghettos. Ghettos are by no means a modern phenomenon. The term is Italian in origin, and may come from the term *borghetto*, meaning "borough," but it had a sinister significance from its first use, designating a neighborhood where Jewish segregation was compulsory. The use of the term and the use of ghettos began in the fourteenth century in Italy, Spain, and Portugal. Jews have been the most brutalized outsiders for three thousand years and were the victims Europe's first ghettos. But ghettoization is not always compulsory. Many outsiders have voluntarily created their own safe havens or ghettos in nations with ethnically diverse populations, where outsiders do not feel particularly comfortable or welcome. During successive waves of immigration into the United States and after the abolition of slavery, various groups created their own neighborhoods: for instance, the Jews and Irish on the Lower East Side of New York City, the African Americans of South Philadelphia and Harlem, the Hispanics of El Pueblo de Los Angeles, the Asians of the many China towns and Japan towns in major U.S. cities. Often such ghettos produce cultures within cultures, with distinctions of language or ethnicity, religion or culture. Though the boundaries of ghettos are often self-imposed, they are nonetheless guarded from within and from without with a good deal of passion. The stranger is often looked on as an intruder, while the ghetto dweller who wanders into the outer world is seen as an alien. Some basic notion of "identity" is the passport into a ghetto— and often that identity is validated only after a good deal of scrutiny. There have been turf wars when one ghetto has overlapped the territory of another.

One of the most fascinating type of ghettos started to evolve during the late Renaissance, when artists became free agents and professionals, attempting to live by their talents, with little support from the church or from wealthy patrons. To a very great extent, when people in the arts left the church and the court, they found their way either into the private households of the rich middle class or into the squalid districts of the poor, where they discovered little resistance to their eccentricities as well as cheap shelter, independence, and an unconstrained moral atmosphere. Such independent artists were not "bohemians," but they set the agenda that would eventually produce a distinctive and segregated community of students, intellectuals, politicos, and people in the arts. That community would also be home to a great many homosexuals.

The derivation of the term "bohemianism, as it applies to intellectuals and artists, comes from the lifestyle of gypsies, built on the belief that before they first appeared in 1427 at the gates of Paris (and were refused entry), gypsies had been nomadic inhabitants of Bohemia. Thackery officially introduced the outcast connotation of the term "bohemian" into English in his 1848 novel *Vanity Fair*.

As an expression of both "alienation" as well as artistic and intellectual independence, the word "bohemian" first came into popular use in France in the late nineteenth century, during the Belle Epoch or "Banquet Years."

La belle epoque (1885–1914) was the era when the banquet became a social ritual, a place to exhibit fashion, talk art, and conspicuously enjoy the pleasures of the good life of the upper middle-class. Roger Shattuck wrote the definitive study of the period, in which he remarks that "in the arts, 1885 is the point from which we must reckon the meaning of the word 'modern.' "

At that point, bohemianism connoted the instability and eccentricities of people who congregated in the Latin Quarter of Paris. The appellation designated the outsider, the radical, the libertine, and the artist. Like the word "queer," the word "bohemian" was derisive and belittling, but it was eventually appropriated and transformed into an acceptable term by those against whom it was used as slander. According to Shattuck, the current use of the word goes back "to a group of young Latin Quarter poets, *chansonniers*, and painters, calling themselves the Hydropathies, who had begun meeting regularly in the 1870s to recite, to sing, and to issue a magazine." Art historian Arnold Hauser has observed that there were two distinctive kinds of bohemians created in the age of impressionism in the 1870s: the modern artist estranged from society who took refuge from Western civilization in distant, exotic lands (most notably Paul Gauguin), and those who took refuge in the Parisian artistic ghetto called the Latin Quarter. According to Hauser,

> Both were the product of the same feeling, the same "discomfort with culture," the only difference being that the first chose "internal emigration" while the others chose real flight.... Both had their source in romantic unreality and individualism, but they were [subsequently] transformed into a form of unique artistic experience attributable above all to Baudelaire.

At the heart of bohemianism is a contempt for bourgeois life and morality and mercenary values. Also at the heart of bohemianism is sensibility, which was quickly appropriated by the middle class and turned into commodity and fashion:

> Bohemianism was originally no more than a demonstration against the bourgeois way of life. It consisted of young artists and students, who were mostly the sons of well-to-do people, and in whom the opposition to the prevailing society was usually a product of mere youthful exuberance and contrariness.... They undertook their excursions into the world of outlaws and outcasts, just as one undertakes a journey into an exotic land; they knew nothing of the misery of the later bohemians, and they were free to return to bourgeois society at any time. (Hauser)

The bohemians of the succeeding generation were less inclined to go slumming as they were to attempt what hippies later attempted: to become part of the life of the "common people," to create a new class of "artistic proletariat," composed of nonconformists whose lives were eccentric, insecure, and perilous. Bohemians abandoned bourgeois society. They took tremendous personal risks. And they had nothing but contempt for middle-class religious morality and artistic naivete. And yet, for all the political naturalism and populism of the bohemians, nineteenth-century Romanticism essential to the celebration of the maverick remained very much at the heart of bohemianism. Baudelaire stood at the margin that separated the two bohemians: the romantic salon types and the proletariat types. He invented bohemianism, but never took the irreversible leap into political activism or personal anarchy. Rimbaud, on the other hand, was the most radical of the bohemians: a vagabond, a sociopath, and a sexual outlaw.

Baudelaire and Rimbaud were the leaders of "a group of desperadoes, who not only broke with bourgeois society, but with the whole of European civilization" (Hauser). It is difficult to appreciate, from our perspective, how much "gay culture" and Western modernism owes to the bohemians of the nineteenth century, or how their influence created an intrinsic relationship between homosexuality and modernity. Bohemians spent their lives in cafes, music halls, brothels, and in the streets. They welcomed and mingled with hustlers, addicts, thieves, prostitutes, vagabonds, street musicians, circus folk, and entertainers. They embraced all those who were denigrated and dismissed by the middle class. Bohemianism became a way of life. Eventually, its influences began to be felt in many major cities. Bohemianism came to America in the early twentieth century. Harlem and Coney Island were among its first strongholds. Then an important artistic ghetto began to emerge in an area north of the original Wall Street heartland of Manhattan, in an Italian working-class district known as the Ninth Ward. By the 1910s and 1920s, this district, renamed Greenwich Village, had become the most famous bohemian community in the United States.

The cultural commentator George Chauncey has written a fascinating study of gay life in the early days of New York City: "In many respects the Village was a prototypical furnished-room district, for it offered cheap rooms to unmarried men and women who wished to develop social lives unencumbered by family obligations, and to engage in work likely to be more creative than remunerative."

The Village was a special kind of ghetto. Unlike many marginal people, bohemians have always exiled themselves. And, rather than being a specific and insular linguistic, ethnic, or religious group, bohemians have always represented a broad cross section of cultures, ethnicities, religions, and nationalities. The one trait bohemians had in common was a profound disdain for the bourgeoisie.

Although there are a great many types of ghettos, and there has been a long and often brutal history of ghettoization, it is the artistic ghetto of bohemians that has become the most active metaphor of the outsider and the source of a great many radical sensibilities and strategies that have deeply influenced world culture. It was in the bohemian ghetto that modern homosexuality found a permissive environment in which it began to forge its sensibility and style. It is virtually impossible to speak of twentieth-century homosexuality without discussing both modernism and bohemianism.

As Chauncey has noted, at the turn of the century, many Villagers were unmarried. They believed in "free-love" and they had broken with many social mores, including ideas about gender behavior and attitudes about class and race. Such rebellion was an essential aspect of sensibility:

> Indeed, the unconventional behavior of many bohemian men—ranging from their long hair, colorful dress, and interest in art to their decided lack of interest in the manly pursuits of getting married and making money—often led outsiders to consider all of them queer. Although not everyone thought their queer tastes extended to sexual matters, the bohemian men of the Village were often regarded as unmanly as well as un-American, and in some contexts calling men "artistic" became code for calling them homosexual. (Chauncey)

In discussing the sensibility of outsiders, Howard Becker stresses that many deviant groups are forced into an "psychological exile," staying very much to themselves and creating stable and long-lasting communities and lifestyles. In Becker's words,

> Like all stable groups, they develop a distinctive way of life . . . where people who engage in deviant activities have the opportunity to interact with one another, they are likely to develop a culture built around the problems rising out of the differences between their definition of what they do and the definition held by other members of society. They develop perspectives on themselves and

their deviant activities and on their relations with other members of society.

This kind of identity politics (the aggrandizement of marginality) is clearly a defensive reaction to social rejection, but it is also the only alternative that many rejected people have as the basis for self-respect. As Becker points out, all forms of separatism tend to elevate the confidence of a subculture at the same time that it tends to soothe the abrasiveness of rejection from mainstream society. Bohemians transformed their social role as outcasts into what might be called both a separatist and supremacist community. Something very similar took place at a later time in the world of Afrocentrism and in the attitudes of radical feminism. In the migration of outcasts into their own worlds, individual sensibility and group culture coalesce into some of the concepts that are the underpinning of identity politics, a subject to which I will return in the chapter on transgression as culture.

When Becker speaks of the "outsider," he is essentially speaking about groups of outsiders; not idiosyncratic individuals who may or may not have some kind of subcultural support system. The response to rejection by an individual and by a group may differ considerably, simply because the individual (i.e., Franz Kafka) must reinvent himself in isolation. The group acts and interacts with its leaders, producing a community. As Becker points out, the members of a spurned group often devise a clear distinction between themselves (as outsiders) and the rest of the world (as insiders). Even among musicians, as Becker demonstrates, the "us" and "them" dichotomy persists—they see themselves as "hip" and others as "squares," and, in so doing, they tend to elevate themselves above those who castigate them. Outsiders also create a coded vernacular and a private body language and unique fashions of dress and grooming. They often produce a communal attitude about morality, money, and sensibility.

Current historical evidence suggests that before the 1850s homosexuals didn't have localized communities. They were spread throughout large and small neighborhoods. Statements from pre–Stonewall Revolt lesbians and gay men persistently profess that they thought they were the only persons of their kind in the world until they found their way into various urban localities. Undoubtedly, there were always furtive mechanisms allowing lesbians and gay men to identify one another and to meet and socialize, but there are no clear indicators of a historic community and, beyond similarities of sexual orientation, there is no clear basis for cultural bonding, like ethnicity, religion, nationality, or language. In the artistic ghettos, however, the basis of commonality was neither linguistic or ethnic. It was a commonality based on difference. Not only did the moral, sexual, and political liberalism of artistic communities allow lesbians and gay men to become integrated into close-knit neighborhoods, but that integration also provided opportunities to create a distinctive lifestyle, including a unique jargon, a reinvented form of domestic relationships, exclusive venues that offered sexual and amorous opportunities, like the bars, cabarets, clubs, baths, and cafes where homosexuals could gather with some degree of freedom, despite sporadic police repression, particularly during election campaigns.

Artistic ghettos, like the Village, also provided a rare opportunity for gays and straights to mingle openly and form often strong and lifelong friendships and artistic relationships. In the 1910s, Carl Van Vechten (like many at the time, a gay man married to a woman) was a prime mover in organizing the famous salons of heiress Mable Dodge Luhan, on lower Fifth Avenue, before Luhan discovered Santa Fe, New Mexico, and went "native." Her salons were renowned for their gathering of vastly different people: anarchists, libertines, artists, straights, gays, and a good many Freudian theorists. Eugene O'Neill mingled with the noted gay painters Marsden Hartley and Charles Demuth, who were part of a mixed crowd of theater and art people both in the Village and in the gay enclave at the tip of Cape Cod called Provincetown.

The lure of the Village to people who are alienated from the mainstream has not lapsed. In the 1940s and 1950s, gays and straights shared gathering places like the San Remo, a writers' bar at the corner of MacDougal and Bleecker Streets in the middle of an Italian section of the Village. As Brad Gooch recounts in his biography of Frank O'Hara, the San Remo had a celebrated clientele: Tennessee Williams, John Cage, Paul Goodman, Dylan Thomas, Allen Ginsberg, William Burroughs, Judith Malin and Julian Beck, Miles Davis, Merce Cunningham, Dorothy Day, and James Agee. The painters tended to favor the Cedar Tavern on University Place and Eighth Street. According to Gooch, "The Cedar was more straight and macho than gay, more art-oriented than literary."

A great many male and female artists, writers, poets, political activists, and intellectuals of the period were ostensibly open to sexual experimentation, and few were homophobic despite occasional bantering and name-calling, such as the famous outburst of Jackson Pollack. A great many Village men and women had an undifferentiated attitude about sex, professing to be straight but having occasional homosexual affairs. All of this was an aspect of the bohemian lifestyle from which evolved a distinctive and idiosyncratic idea about *sensibility as a form of transgression.*

What is important about the bohemianism of the Latin Quarter and the Village, as well as the subsequent burgeoning of a gay subculture in many other urban centers, is the probability that much of what has become known as "gay style," "gay culture," and "gay sensibility" was forged in the liberal and collective atmosphere of artistic ghettos. No doubt, there were subversive and sexually deviant subcultures during many prior periods of Western history, but it is very difficult to establish direct lines of correspondence between what may have been meant by the term "homoeroticism" in the time of Walt Whitman and what is clearly known as "gay sensibility" in the era of the twentieth-century poet Tom Gunn. But what is clear, at least for the moment, is that the artistic communities of Paris, Berlin, and New York City allowed and promoted a gay presence that would have been unthinkable in most European and American communities during the first half of the twentieth century, when *all* forms of deviation and nonconformity were regarded as transgressions. The art communities, however, devised a new mythology of foreignness, and that new mythology became the metaphor of the outsider, idealized instead of denigrated. It seems likely that it was at this point that the modern sensibility of Western homosexuals emerged. What it may or may not have been in earlier periods, there seems to be little or no agreement among historians and activists. I suspect that there have been many different gay "sensibilities" during the long and complex history of Western homosexuality. It is possible that differences in attitudes among gays may have been so great that some aspects of prior gay lifestyle would be unrecognizable to today's homosexuals in Europe and America, much as aspects of mainstream gay sensibility have no existence among many non-Western peoples. The particular sensibility that emerged among bohemian ghettos in the Belle Epoch, however, is the sensibility that marks almost every aspect of twentieth-century culture, yet that sensibility may have been just one of countless manifestations of how lesbians and gay men responded to both themselves and others during other periods of history. Even the social subversions of Arthur Rimbaud or the outrageous posturing of Oscar Wilde may have been exceptionally rebellious episodes in an otherwise conformist and highly assimilated gay identity. Researchers have some idea about the public attitudes toward sexual deviance in the past, but they really don't know very much about the intimate workings of homosexuals in the Western world until recent decades.

In retrospect, it seems evident that the defining characteristics of modern homosexuality began in the nineteenth century as a radically new kind of style and sensibility. Though we are usually inclined to think of "style" as a tenuous and superficial term, it is probable that for radicals of the last two centuries, style has been something far more complex and far more substantial—an intrinsic aspect of sensibility. Bohemians completely changed the context of "style" into a personal and group sensibility by inventing a social model distinct from the attitudes of the fashion-conscious merchant class. The bourgeoisie abhorred and rejected bohemians, while, in turn, bohemians abhorred and rejected the bourgeoisie. The middle class also detested homosexuals. Bohemians shared with homosexuals an exile from the world ruled by the middle class, of which bohemians claimed to want no part and of which homosexuals were not allowed to have a part. To a very great extent, bohemianism and the subculture of homosexuality were as much a contentious response to middle-class ostracization and rejection as an expression of unique identities that were alien to middle-class values. The radical social sensibility of the last two hundred years has been primarily the reaction of outsiders to their rejection by the bourgeoisie. As such, bohemianism and gay sensibility are the result of a response to adversity rather than an expression of an ethnic or religious identity. Bohemians and homosexuals retaliated for the exile imposed on them with great imagination and passion. Even the term "middle class" (not unlike the derogatory gay reference to straights as "breeders") became something of a caricature. To their consternation, members of the middle class found themselves publicly lampooned and ridiculed by bohemians as "squares" and "fossils." The bourgeoisie began to react to their maligned predicament with amazing cunning, depicting those they had rejected from society not as free-thinkers or undesirables, but as elitists and purveyors of a quixotic and unrealistic sensibility—a useless "artistic" mentality in the parlance of the Belle

Epoch and, in today's language, a "touchy-feely" mentality lacking pragmatism, order, and rationality.

Underlying all these machinations is the fact that the coalition of gays and bohemians changed the world. It is impossible to speak of modern Western culture without also speaking of homosexuality. George Steiner, with no intention of flattery, has observed that "Since about 1890, homosexuality has played a vital part in Western culture." He goes on to assert that whereas heterosexuality is the very essence of classic realism, a radical type of homosexual mentality is the essence of modernity: in its narcissism, solipsism, and self-referentiality. "Homosexuality," Steiner continues, "could be construed as a creative rejection of philosophic and conventional realms, of *mundanity* and extroversion of classic and nineteenth-century feeling." Furthermore, homosexuality, Steiner insists, helped lead to "that exercise in solipsism, that remorseless mockery of Philistine common sense and bourgeois realism that is modern art."

Steiner blames Rimbaud for much of this erosion of classicism, for Rimbaud idealized the mythology of the outsider—visionary, saboteur, deviant, desperado. Rimbaud, like Baudelaire, celebrated every "evil" cataloged and disdained by the middle class; every eccentricity and every deviation. He reversed the entire structure of the mythology of transgression, redefining it as a defiant expression of idiosyncratic sensibility. As such, transgression became the metaphor of bohemian activism and cultural heroism—a revolution of the senses, and the reinvention and celebration of the long vilified body. In the West we might reject this new sensibility as wanton hedonism, but in a larger context it was more precisely the deregulation of Puritanism.

During the same eras when painters were turning their backs on well-made landscapes, when poets were turning their backs on the limitations of language, thousands of homosexuals willfully, openly, and knowingly turned their backs on the dictates of the heterosexual norm. Rebellion and nonconformity have been the crucial avocations of modernity, and homosexuals were in the forefront of that insurrection. The dominant metaphor of twentieth-century culture is found in that insurrection. It is a metaphor built on a mythology of transgression. And, as such, modernity necessarily embraces the mythology of homosexuality. From that vivid mythology has evolved what is familiar today as "gay culture."

Jonathan Dollimore has observed that "sexually exiled from the repressiveness of the home culture, homosexuals have searched instead for fulfilment in the realm of the foreign. . . . Not necessarily as a second best." Such an astute observation underscores what I have been saying about the transgressive metaphor of "the foreign" and the way in which the artistic ghetto served homosexuals in very much the same way that the nineteenth-century underground railroad served escaped slaves, whose passage north to freedom was facilitated by a group of radical abolitionists who hid, protected, and ferried the slaves from place to place during their perilous escapes from the south. Bohemian ghettos were the underground railroad of nineteenth-and twentieth-century homosexuals.

Admittedly, the correlation of "foreignness" and "bohemianism" with homosexual sensibility can easily become a cliché. It would be both an indulgence and the solemnizing of yet another fiction about homosexuals to suggest that all or even most lesbians and gay men were or are eccentrics, liberals, specialists in rarified or even traditional art forms, intellectuals, hedonists, or even reasonably outspoken or plainspoken about their sexual orientation. Today, probably more than ever, gay sensibility is in transition, slowly and arduously moving from the outside into the mainstream. There is no question that the diversity of homosexuality has become progressively apparent because of a degree of openness in public forums and in the media and because of the unprecedented collective spirit of massive gay rallies, celebrations, and demonstrations. There is also no question that everyone, gay and straight, has been profoundly changed by the AIDS pandemic. The very word "gay" has been fundamentally altered by its association with illness and death.

The tragic relationship between sexual exorcism and religious taboo has produced a response to AIDS in both the gay and straight communities that is so entangled in issues of blame, guilt, and innocence that it recapitulates the entire history of the Western preoccupation with disease as divine retribution. Though the ideas of Augustine had little currency in the 1980s, when young gay men began to die of a mysterious ailment, the bizarre Augustinian legacy had somehow survived in a dark corner of Western consciousness. If, as Augustine had proclaimed, original sin is carried silently in semen from generation to generation, bringing damnation and death, how could people not be touched by the irrational suspicion that the HIV virus, which is transmitted through blood and semen, was not a terrifying vindication of religious dogma?

In the age of AIDS, it is litte wonder that many gay men have tried to submerge their terror in what may seem like escapism and social triviality. How can anyone dictate how people, especially young people, should respond to an overpowering sense of doom? Many of us remain today so stunned by the continuing devastation and loss of friends that we are inclined to forget that until 1954 thousands of children were crippled and killed by another virus—poliomyelitis. That disease, however, was not demonized. When it was discovered that polio entered the body through the nerve endings of the nose, particularly in public swimming pools, no one considered blaming children for swimming, and no one condemned public pools as carriers of deadly disease. Swimming did not become an act so evil that it deserved the retribution of God. Yet our distorted notions about sexuality and the long traces of a mythology that disparages the body somehow imply that people with HIV deserve an immense burden of guilt. It is still a commonplace for people to regard AIDS as the consequence of an unpardonable sin. In a curious way, gay men are dying of Augustine's curse—a powerful myth of life and death about which the dying know little or nothing. Attitudes about AIDS are still blighted by the suspicion that God is speaking to us through *just one* of millions upon millions of organisms with which we share the earth.

Disease and death have radically changed the gay community, though it is still unclear what will result from those changes.

Leo Bersani has observed that the current gay agenda is contradictory and confusing. He is not happy with the changes he sees all around him. It seems to Bersani that gay strategy has less concern for aggressively establishing a gay sensibility and a gay identity in full view of a bigoted society as much as it seems to be a matter of attempting to achieve a new kind of respectable invisibility. According to Bersani,

What it means just to be gay has become surprisingly problematic. Never before in the history of minority groups struggling for recognition and equal treatment has there been an analogous attempt, on the part of any such group, to make itself unidentifiable even as it demands to be recognized. . . . If the gay presence is threatened by absence, it is not only because of the secret (or not so secret) intentions of those who are fascinated by gays, or even as a result of the devastating work of AIDS, but also because gays have been de-gaying themselves in the very process of making themselves visible. But the habit of invisibility has been so strong that even in coming out we have managed to hide ourselves. So, once again, we melt in—either into those other groups whose oppressed state we yearn to share or into mainstream America.

Until recently, the impact of homosexual attitudes on mainstream culture was largely unrecognized, particularly in the pop world that was presumably dominated by heterosexuals and heterosexual attitudes. But today there can be no doubt that the major trends of modernism as well as the fads, fashions, and mannerisms of straight youth have been largely invented by gays. What straights didn't appropriate from gays, gays appropriated from straights. It is unclear if discos, body piercing, punk and grunge music, raves, Ecstasy, poppers, as well as leather-and-chain dress originated among heterosexuals or homosexuals. Yet one thing seems clear—the cultural lines once used to define sexual orientations have become so blurred that many people, like Leo Bersani, have reason to be genuinely concerned about the future of homosexuality. Has the mainstream been homosexualized or has homosexuality been assimilated and normalized? Ultimately, does it really matter what has taken place in the 1980s and 1990s in the breach that once separated gays and straights? If heterosexuals enjoy aping gay fashion, is there any real damage done? Is there some kind of peril when lesbians and gay men willingly merge with mainstream society, or when they want to be perceived as conventional suburbanites—lipstick lesbians and clean-cut, suited professionals, or buffed and brawny gay hunks?

In the gay press there are ongoing debates about the controversial issues surrounding assimilation. Essayists regularly deal with the emergence of a gay interest in sports. As sports historian Michael Messner sees it, "the problem of masculinity in the gay community" is a paradox similar to the views of another sports historian, Brian Pronger who has written about the "homosexual athlete as a paradox. . . . Given the involvement of sports with masculinity and the recent explosive growth of gay sporting leagues." Essayist Mark Simpson has raised "important questions about bodybuilding, tattoos, pornography, cruising, advertising [images], and team sports."

The issues involved in most of these debates have centered on a concern for the glorification during the 1980s and 1990s of male violence, vapid homoeroticism, and an unbridled kind of heterosexual imitation presumably driven by self-contempt. Gay columnist Frank Browning expresses undeniable hostility in his attitudes about changes in gay sensibility:

> No longer salivating in solitary locker room guilt over the halfback's perfect and apparently untouchable buns, the remade sissy-faggot found out how to make his own buns, pecs, lats, and abs. The very body whose forbidden desires and responses had for so many years been the source of shame itself provided the raw material of psychic transformation. With a few hours a week in the gym, every gay man could become the couturier of his own flesh, stitching and tucking himself into movie-star beauty.

In the activist gay press, the perfected male body and the lesbian wearing lipstick have become unpolitical, an imitation of the heterosexual mentality that is responsible for gay repression. Many gay activists have borrowed Susan Brownmiller's critique of sadomasochism in her still unanswered question: "Does homosexual sadomasochism have its own, peculiarly male, dynamic, or is it an aberration masquerading as the newest issue?"

There are also a great many disputes in the gay community about other aspects of current lifestyles. Transvestitism is often targeted by some lesbians and gay men as a stereotypical behavior with which they don't want to be identified. At the same time, essayists like Homi Bhabha argue that sexual mimicry may be a powerful strategy used against colonial subjection—an appropriation of dominant gender roles and a way of menacing colonial influences through mockery. Such gender mimicry becomes, in Bhabha's memorable phrase, "at once resemblance and menace," a political act that mediates social dominance through extravagant theatricality and impersonation. In Judith Butler's words, "In imitating gender, drag implicitly reveals the imitative structure of gender itself. . . . [Thus] gay is *not* to straight as copy is to original, but, rather, as copy is to copy."

Another writer, Richard Dyer, argues that gay machismo does much social mischief by taking signs of masculinity and "eroticizing them in a blatantly homosexual context."

Conversely, Leo Bersani is very skeptical about the subversive claims for gay machismo, regarding it not as a mockery and repudiation of straight machismo, but as an obsessive respect for it.

Another writer, William Mann, has expressed a nostalgia for prior forms of gay sensibility that is shared by many mature gay men. He, like many, is deeply dissatisfied by the new male style among youthful gays:

> Big, buff, young, white. So perfect that their sexiness—the quality that promotes them and that they promote—becomes muted. Fifteen years ago, there was no such politesse. The image of a gay man was overtly sexual: the Village People, in all their assorted sexual stereotypes; the Castro clone, with his over-emphasized basket and buns; the phallic supermen of Tom of Finland. It was a radical revolution from the limp-wristed, sweatered pansies of the '50s and the androgynous flower children of the '60s. Gay men had arrived in the '70s with a sexual vengeance.

Coming from a completely different point of view is the writing of Bruce Bawer, who believes that the most publicly threatening homosexuals are the ones who act like "everybody else"—those who are *not* part of a highly visible and vocal subculture. According to Bawer, "It's not nonconformist gays but ordinary gays that many people find threatening." From Bawer's point of view, there is considerable error in the "charges heard frequently these days that some 'assimilationist' or 'straight-acting' gays are endeavoring to secure equal rights for themselves by selling out 'gay-acting' or 'nonconformist' gay people— including drag queens and leathermen—with whom straight America is uncomfortable. . . . What [really] makes many straight people uncomfortable is any image of gay life and love that seems too ordinary, too familiar."

These debates will not be resolved in the foreseeable future because they seem to be both a conflict of different sensibilities among the members of different generations, very much like the well-publicized conflicts of mainstream straight society during the 1960s and 1970s. For people who grew up in the gay world of the 1960s and 1970s, what seems to be lost is the transgressive sensibility of Rimbaud that was an intrinsic part of their ideas about gay culture.

The current debates about separatism and assimilation, about conformity and nonconformity, are not uncommon in the politically expedient activisms of marginal groups. Yet, they are debates that anger or sadden many gays, because they put into question both the unanimity and the transcendency of what has been often regarded as the crux of gay sensibility.

For many, the word "assimilation" has always been a red flag because it is built on some of the least scrutinized and most chauvinistic attitudes of America—the notion that we live in a "Land of Opportunity" where all people, no matter their diversity, can freely join the mainstream of a vast and generous society. From the beginning of America, however, some groups, such as orthodox Jews, traditional Asians, and Native Americans have been uncomfortable about the advantages and disadvantages of assimilation—questioning what is gained and what is lost when a distinctive people attempt to join the American mainstream. The idea of assimilation is troublesome because it has for so many centuries been the motive of colonialism and evangelism, which profess that the best thing the members of a dominant society can do for all the people they encounter is to make them imitations of themselves. The rationale of assimilation has been so effectively promoted that many outsiders have accepted it, seeing it as a salvation rather than as a sacrifice. It is in this context of assimilation that many lesbians and gay men find themselves deeply concerned about the future of gay sensibility.

When I was a teenager growing up in the San Fernando Valley home of my adoptive family, I was attracted to a small gay community in the Silver Lake district of Los Angeles not because of any awareness of the sexual opportunities that community offered, but because of my fascination for the extraordinary people who composed the group—adventurous young and older men and women who talked about ideas and about books, music, and the visual arts. They were people who made up a fragile and small artistic nucleus in Los Angeles at the time. Growing up in a community in which everyone seemed able to laugh and flirt with one another at the same time that they talked earnestly and at length about ideas and the arts gave my youth an impetus I could not have easily found elsewhere in Los Angeles or any other city other than New York, which was a magnet to all outsiders. Unquestionably, that Silver Lake enclave, with its special kind of gay sensibility, is obsolete. All of us who have survived the deaths of those who lived in that fragile pre-Stonewall world know that something has vanished. Personally, I lament the passing of that lifestyle almost as much as I mourn the loss to AIDS of all the gay friends of my youthful days of self-discovery and cultural adventures.

For people who grew up before the AIDS pandemic, it is virtually impossible to grasp how young gay men and women deal with their burgeoning sexuality. Whatever the reasons, the mainstreaming of gay sensibility has drastically changed many people's ideas about gay identity. On the other hand, there is no question that a multitude of closeted people have been encouraged by gay activism and gay visibility to affirm their sexuality identities and come together. These "new" homosexuals may have lost some of the advantages others once found in alienation, but they have also been greatly, if imperfectly, liberated from the unthinkably difficult silence of exile.

Yet it was that terrible exile that was in many ways the driving force and the motive of at least one form of gay sensibility in its most decisive and influential manifestation. The centuries-old alienation and homophobia are not gone. But at least there is a new and larger sense of community and a growing recognition of political identity. The emergence of thousand of gays into the mainstream has had and will continue to have an enormous impact on homosexual sensibility. The founding of an openly gay political and social community has revealed the immense diversity among homosexuals, not only refuting many of the gay stereotypes but also bringing into question even the relevance of an idea like the transcendency of "gay sensibility."

Unquestionably, for the great majority of gay people there is an advantage in assimilation rather than alienation. There will be less pain, less self-denial, less self-contempt. But there will also be fewer people who exist at a distance from the unquestioned conventions of the mainstream. There will also be fewer people who are sufficiently detached from arbitrary conventions to be capable of seeing beyond the sentries of conformity, and, perhaps, to be lured into the transgressions that take us beyond the familiar world into other, unknown and unnamed worlds.

If the majority of gays are no longer in the ranks of bohemians and if they are no longer enthralled by the rebellion of an avant-garde, it may be, as many cultural commentators contend, because the avant-garde no longer exists. If homosexuality is no longer defined as a driving force in radical world culture, perhaps it is because world culture has changed so drastically that we no longer recognize it as culture. Even the nature of nonconformity seems to have changed.*

What seems clear is that the lesbians and the gay men of the 1980s brought about the queering of American sensibility and, remarkably, they became visible icons and entrepreneurs of pop culture. If the avant-garde of an earlier era was implemented by homosexuals, it is unquestionable that today's pop culture is dominated by a gay presence. Perhaps that is a role no less remarkable than the gay contribution, one hundred years ago, in the construction of modernity. Perhaps the evolution of a mainstream lifestyle among young lesbians and gay men is every bit as significant as the invention in the 1920s of the rebellious bohemian attitudes that jump started twentieth-century modernism.

Nonetheless, many nagging questions remain. Outsiders have the clear air that allows them to look forward, but they also have the unique ability to see the history of themselves because they stand somewhere outside mainstream history. In the course of the mainstreaming of gay sensibility, are we becoming invisible in a new and fearsome way? In being "accepted" are we in danger of losing ourselves? What becomes of the insurrective imagination of the outsider? Do the strategies of normalization and assimilation deprive us of a hard-won, if separate, social reality? What, then, becomes of the pearl born of the afflictions of the oyster? Do we lose the deviant, the iconoclast, and the artist all in the same instant? Does the painfully acquired metaphor of the adventurous outsider now turn into a new conformity, a behavioral form of "busing"? Does the empowering of sexual émigrés become just another way of getting into politics or living quietly in the suburbs?

From the evidence of the perilous interaction of various ethnic groups, it has become abundantly clear that social exile can as read-

---

*Jonathan Larson's musical *Rent* may be as false a reflection of East Village outcastes in the 1990s as *Hair* was a feigned representation of Manhattan's hippies in the 1960s. But *Rent* suggests that nonconformity is still a vivid cultural phenomenon despite the fact that it is a bohemianism of a new variety. In the *New York Times*, Anthony Tommasini underscores the transformation of bohemianism while he also celebrates its persistent embrace of aliens and outsiders: "The tolerant, playful moments in which the gay and straight characters of *Rent* support one another, the way the bohemians form a tense solidarity with the homeless—such themes reflect the struggling community life that Mr. Larson exulted in" (March 17, 1996).

ily induce separatism as it can induce group identity and collectivism. In the unique case of the bohemians, the need to reject those who had rejected them produced a powerful inclination to embrace any and all people who were also excluded from the middle-class world. The acceptance of outcasts was and still is an essential part of whatever we mean by the expression "the bohemian mystique." It was such an all-embracing bohemian subculture that facilitated the founding of "gay sensibility" and the evolution of what is now known as "gay culture."

The fact that homosexuals in the days before the 1969 Stonewall Revolt could not be themselves without censure, rejection, and discrimination was the cause of a great deal of personal confusion, conflict, and suffering. No one can suggest that we prolong that suffering. Yet I know from my own life that for many men and women of my generation being gay was not simply a form of castigation. It was often a springboard out of the mundane world of our parents and into other worlds. For a long time to come, being gay will continue to necessitate self-discovery, because there are no universal homosexual rules of conduct, and there are few traditions except the pressure of peers and an endless succession of passing but influential fashions. For generation after generation, one of the ironic consequence of gay disenfranchisement was the unassailable fact that homosexuals were outcasts whether they liked it or not. They had to comprehend and accept either an internal exile or an escape into other worlds. For people who were gay before the Stonewall Revolt, the mirror of conformity was both a rebuke and a sham. What they were forced to see in the looking glass was someone else's image of homosexual identity. Heterosexuality was everywhere in the glass—monolithic and inescapable—in every film, in every magazine, in every advertisement, and in every phrase uttered by politicians, clerics, and teachers. So gay people had to fly or die. They had to invent themselves all by themselves or they simply had to accept the unrelenting social insinuation that they were no one. They had to break the rules or they were broken by the rules.

The life of transgression, like so many daring and challenging experiences, provides to those who learn how to survive adversity a deep and lasting sense of individual identity—an inner voice and, if they are lucky, a life fully lived rather than a life defended. For those who can cope with adversity, it is an extraordinary life forged in an extraordinary fire.

When Jean Cocteau was asked which of his possessions he would save from his burning house, he answered, "J'emporterais le feu" (I would take the fire).

That is a choice few were given in the past. Today, it is a choice that few seem willing to risk. "J'emporterais le feu."

TRANSGRESSION

8

AS CULTURE

The problem of desegregating homosexuality from a private ghetto into a heterosexual world, that depends on homosexuality remaining invisible, encapsulates the problem faced everywhere in popular culture today by this frail phenomenon we call masculinity—the problem of looking, that is, how to prevent the "deflation" of "manly visions" by the proximity of homosexuality.

Mark Simpson, Male Impersonation

You can leave your hat on.

Randy Newman, I Know What Love Is

Culture is a way of looking. When individuals succeed in externalizing their personal experiences through the creation of images, sounds, phrases, structures, and movement, the result is culture. In this context, culture is the collective aspect of individuated styles of expression. What sensibility is to the individual, culture is to the community—a distinctive voice. Because of the fragmentation of Western society, culture is not always cogent in the anthropological sense of the term "culture"—an entire way of life of a particular human society, transmitted from generation to generation. For me, Albert Camus perfectly defines the meaning of culture at the end of the twentieth century when he observes that culture is "the cry of men in face of their destiny."

It is Camus's dark statement about modern humankind's confrontation with destiny that provides a basis for a discussion of an idea as transient and elusive as "gay culture." If, in the twentieth century, destiny is represented by the dominion of the majority, then it becomes clear that the invention of a homosexual culture is a necessary response of gays to the rigid and monolithic assumption in the West that normal human beings are heterosexual. At the same time that this heterocentric assumption eliminates the need to denote and define a "heterosexual culture," it also produces the outcry of lesbians and gay men who are confronted by a fate that is built on someone else's notion of destiny.

Heterocentrism vanquishes all alternative possibilities of sexuality. It is this dominion that marks a perilous cultural problem—a way of seeing rather than a way of being—that constantly confronts homosexuals.

A major social difference between homosexuals and heterosexuals is the freedom with which straights have been able to broadcast themselves without limitation and the way, in contrast, that gays have had little opportunity to be a visible and vocal part of community life. As we have seen in the discussion of bohemianism, the straight designation of lesbians and gay as "other" necessitated the invention of an "other culture." Yet, judging from people whom we might regard as "homosexuals" in drastically different societies from our own, this crisis in gay identity is not an intrinsic and inevitable aspect of homosexuality. It is, instead, the result of heterosexual society's way of *looking* at itself in contrast to the way it looks at people who are gay.

Though the psychological differences between heterosexuals and homosexuals are rather few—a matter of the object of desire rather than a matter of the quality and constitution of desire—the unyielding domination of heterocentrism has led inevitably to the necessity for homosexuals to invent themselves and in the process to invent a cultural context of their own—a way of seeing themselves in order to be themselves.

Again, these statements are intended to reinforce the proposition that culture is essentially a way of looking at the world. And since culture is what I want to deal with in this chapter, I will begin by talking about the *arbitrary social process called looking*—about what looking achieves and how the highly variable processes of looking affect people's lives.

Because we can speak of culture as distinct from sensibility, this itself is an indication of the social fragmentation that deprives Western people of tradition and a sense of history and continuity. When I speak of the impact of homosexuals on nineteenth-and twentieth-century culture, I am speaking not of a transhistorical human legacy but, rather, of culture in its most localized sense. What I mean by culture is the modern, Western process by which an exceptional person's sensibility becomes visible in the arts and humanities and is then embraced by society as the creation of an individual and not as the creation of the group. This individuation of culture has elevated the idea of originality to a position it has never enjoyed among traditional and tribal peoples. In the primal world, culture is largely collective and anonymous. In our world, culture is rarely anonymous, and, if it is anonymous, it usually fails to achieve a prominence in the *collective* consciousness because our culture is so stratified in terms of class, ethnicity, and gender.

If we think of culture as the expression of a group rather than as the creation of an individual, it seems to me that there is unquestionably a coherent culture in America that can legitimately be called "black culture." In the same sense, there appears to be a coherent "gay culture." But culture is defined by time and place. How today's black culture relates to the long history of the vastly diverse cultures of historic Africa is not clear to anyone, not even to Afrocentrists. In the same way, no one is satisfied that there is indisputable evidence that gay culture as we know it today is a process with a continuous and consistent history. In other words, despite the political expediency of doing otherwise, it is virtually impossible to claim that a lesbian living in America today has much in common with the classical Greek poet Sappho, or that a gay male of this century can claim any decisive kinship to Plato, Alexander the Greet, or Michelangelo, simply on the basis of sexual orientation.

In art there are no no limits and no final truths. Because of its great malleability, art readily serves the variety of attitudes that come together to make up diverse cultures. Art has always been a matter of how a particular group *looks* at the world. It was Goethe who first noticed a curious lack of any mention of the color blue in the early literature of the Greeks. Since Goethe's essay of 1810, scholars have recognized a peculiar absence of color language in the poetry of the ancient Greeks. For instance, Homer and other early poets lacked terms for "blue" and "green":

> To them, blue was not a color in our sense, but the quality of darkness, whether describing hair, clouds, or earth. . . . The "life world" of Homer on the shores of Troy was profoundly different

from our own . . . Study of other language groups, for example, Chinese or American Indian languages, supports the interpretation that cultures *see* the world, down to its very textures and colors, in ways significantly different from our own. (Zajonc)

The "problem of *looking*" has been at the center of every insurrection, because reality is largely defined in terms of what we choose to see and what we choose *not* to see. The boundaries of transgression are not merely territorial; they are essentially epistemological—a conceptual bias designating the limits of how little we can know because of how much we refuse to know.

The artists of any society can either affirm a traditional way of looking at the world or they can introduce alternative realities—new ways of looking that, at least sometimes, redefine their particular cultures. In the case of Egypt, for instance, such redefinitions were largely absent for a period of over three thousand years. In the West of the twentieth century, such redefinitions have occurred almost on an annual basis. In one case, stability defined Egypt. In the modern world of the West there has been a proclivity for change since the Renaissance and Reformation.

The same is true of the orthodoxy or iconoclasm of leaders in the fields of religion, science, and history. When people modify the conventional way of looking at the world because of interactions between dissimilar groups, their achievements are usually a form of acculturation—slight variations on orthodox themes. But when a person replaces the traditional picture with quite a different vision of the world, that is a genuine revolution in culture.

Because it deals with all forms of *looking*, art is an especially accurate barometer of a society's cultural dynamics. If art remains conventional, with slight improvisations on age-old artistic techniques and themes, then art affirms the orthodox reality of a particular society. But when an alien or idiosyncratic reality is depicted in the arts, then culture itself becomes transgressive. That is precisely what took place in Western culture when Baudelaire, Mallarmé, and Rimbaud reshaped culture by their assaults on language and meaning. They changed our Western way of looking. And, in doing this, they changed our way of thinking. They successfully challenged orthodoxy, and, remarkably, their private visions became not only the basis of a personal sensibility, but also produced a major shift in the philosophical outlook of the West.

From a social rather than artistic point of view, two of the major indicators of radical changes that define modern Western culture were the direct result of the abolition of slavery and the redefined view of the rights of women. From its beginnings, feminism has caused a "crisis of masculinity," just as the rejection of the human use of other human beings as beasts of burden caused a "crisis of race."

The widespread appearance of overt homoeroticism in the culture of the 1980s has created another radical predicament, a "crisis of looking," a process more subtle than the revolutions of race or gender, but equally iconoclastic and influential. Everywhere in popular culture there is now a steady desanctifying of the ancient male enigma, which kept men in the position of the observer rather than the observed. The issue of who looks at whom has been fundamentally changed by women and gays. This process has gradually redefined both "masculinity" and "femininity." And, in most cases, this redefinition has blurred gender differences.

Magazines, billboards, motion pictures, television, and every other media once dominated by a male heterocentric mandate, have methodically stripped the male of his traditionally concealed masculinity, much touted and heroized but rarely explained or put on display. As we have seen, men of the West and Middle East and Orient have consistently built cultures in which their bodies are off limits. Physical competition among men was held to a minimum, except for the competitions of the corporation and the sports arena. Women were expected to judge men by their social status, their wealth, their "personalities," and, at times, by their lineage. As a result, except in the fields of entertainment, the most handsome men had very little advantage over the homeliest of men. And, on the whole, men tended to dislike and belittle handsome men. The heterocentric social tactic of males was built on the premise that, no matter their lack of physical beauty, any man had a reason and a right to approach any woman, even if she were disinterested or far more attractive than the man pursuing her. In contrast, the status of women, with rare exception, was based almost entirely on their physical beauty, and the definition of female beauty was significant only to the extent that a man could claim to control or possess it. Making women objects—something to *look* at—served men in a convoluted manner. By making women things to look at, men were able to divert attention from themselves, making themselves invisible, particularly in the nineteenth and twentieth centuries when it became an accepted tradition for men to dress in uniforms or suits so they faded into one another in the background, in a curiously orchestrated fashion that promoted physical non-competitiveness among men who were actually merciless economic competitors. The responsibility of being "seen" was entirely that of women. For a man to be called "beautiful" was an insult, a questioning of his masculinity. On the other hand, when a beautiful woman was with a man, she was a sign not of the man's good looks or sexual prowess, but of his social power.

Homosexual culture not only questioned but also succeeded in overthrowing this heterocentric constraint among men. In the past, when the male body was visible in certain sports and entertainments, it was required by gender etiquette for men not to talk about other men's bodies. It was also required that women speak about men's bodies only in coded messages: with casual remarks about a man's "smile," his "big chest and broad shoulders," his "self-assurance and manliness." No one but a queer was supposed to talk about the attractiveness of a man's pecs, buns, abs, or groin.

The gradual subversion of this heterocentric mandate by homosexual culture is visible everywhere in Western culture. For generations, the "strongman" at the circus was an obese dolt in tights and crotch-concealing bloomers. But, in the 1890s a young man named Friedrich Muller changed forever the perception of the muscular male body. He was apparently straight, but his most avid audience was unapologetically gay. With some help from Florenz Ziegfeld and the stage-name "Eugen Sandow," the muscular young man became one of the world's most famous and wealthy men solely on the basis of his body—an achievement most heterosexual men would consider offensive. What Sandow achieved was to shift the cultural perception of a male from an icon of great wealth and social power to one of classical beauty. As Kenneth Dutton remarked in his social history of the human body, "Sandow's posing, virtually in the nude, introduced a revolutionary concept: that of the live display of a male body in the public arena, as an object to be admired solely by virtue of its advanced muscular development. The social significance of this new element—that of live public display—can hardly be overestimated."

Sandow the Great unwittingly achieved a major cultural revolution that gays would later use as a launching pad for their own agendas. He transformed the male body into a public object, without the justi-fication of athletic activity or demonstrations of the circus strongman's strength. And this remarkable transformation, ironically, came almost at the same time the sexual category of "homosexuality" was invented. Such a curious coincidence allows us to wonder if the social attitudes that made a homoerotic, theatrical success like Sandow may have also provoked the homophobia of self-conscious male heterosexuals, who sought a psychological mechanism to distance themselves from any male whose attraction to handsome men was suspected of an erotic motive.

What is essential to the career of Sandow is that it was his physical (bodily and not facial) beauty that became the focus of his entire ce-lebrity. With Sandow, the male became an object, if only in theatrical terms. Many men admired him, but many also carefully distanced themselves from his idealized physique. His attractiveness could be cat-egorized as harmless because Sandow's body was part of "show busi-ness," which has always been a conspicuous profession viewed by the majority of men as something far less than serious, manly business. It was also important to straight men that Sandow was not handsome, but rather commonplace in all respects except his perfected physique. In other words, he wasn't a "pretty boy"—which was and still is the competitive term used by men to demean the good looks of both straight and gay men.

Perhaps with the example of Sandow, it becomes clear how much the process of *looking* defines a culture.

The potential homoeroticism of Sandow's public exhibitions was mollified by a heterosexual device put to great use by Charles Atlas and a number of other promoters—the creation of a very lucrative physical training field, long before the invention of home exercise equipment. In the tradition of the circus strongman, and despite San-dow's classical muscularity, the successful commodified male physique exemplified strength not beauty, because strength was considered to be commanding and manly, while beauty was looked on as passive and effeminate. The advertisements of Charles Atlas sloganized the familiar story of the ninety-pound weakling who is embarrassed in front of his girlfriend at the beach when a brute kicks sand in his face, only to be

turned through a program of physical exercise into a he-man who returns triumphantly to punch out his competitor and reclaim his lady
love.

Though the German physical health movement of the nineteenth
century played an important role in the rise of bodybuilding, the invention of photography had the greatest influence on attitudes about
the male physique. Pictorialist photographers used their cameras to
simulate classical paintings, which often depicted the idealized classical
male and female nude. At heart, this arty photography was often homoerotic, but few men were aware that these shadows on paper would
begin a revolution of looking that would culminate in the outrage over
the explicit photographs of Robert Mapplethorpe.

If Sandow innocently launched a subversion of Western masculinity, it was sixty years later, in the 1920s and 1930s, that a theater and
dance photographer named Edwin T. Townsend reapproached the
male nude with a homoeroticism and aestheticism clearly related to his
homosexual sensibility. Using highly sophisticated lighting, rich sepia
photo finishes, and an ardent artistic lyricism, Townsend and his famous model Tony Sansone (1905–1987) completely revised the perception of the male body, turning the heterosexual way of looking into
a decidedly homoerotic kind of culture. This modest revolution in male
physique photography was a clear indicator of the extent of the queering of mainstream culture, a process that has gained enormous momentum ever since the 1920s.

The images of Sansone had been intended to be completely nude,
despite laws that required airbrushing and other techniques used to
modify the photographs for publication. Whereas other male nudes
were photographed in positions that tactfully concealed their genitals,
many of Townsend's photographs of Sansone were unashamedly
erotic, with full-frontal nudes. To quote Dutton again,

Never before had the image of bodybuilders been handled with
such voluptuousness, or come so close to an overtly erotic treatment. . . . Sansone marked an important new development in twentieth-century male iconography. Both before and after him,
attractive facial features have been seen as at most incidental to
success in the world of men's bodybuilding: it is above all the body
that counts. What Sansone incarnated was not the "heroic" bodybuilding convention but the alternative "erotic/aesthetic" conven-

tion—that in which the subject of representation is chosen for his capacity to elicit desire as much as (or more than) admiration. . . . Sansone's importance can be linked with his popularizing a more lithe and athletic male physique than that displayed by Sandow and his other bodybuilder-strongman predecessors. . . . All of these factors combined to make Sansone the most important figure since Eugen Sandow in the history of the developed male body. If Sandow was a Hercules of chiseled white marble, Sansone was a seductive and swarthy Pan. The first was the progenitor of bodybuilding; the second became the prototype of the male pin-up.

The nude male images in "women's" magazines like *Playgirl*, hunk calendars, and the enormous success of males who strip for women, like the Chippendales, are the most obvious result of the photography of Townsend and the modeling of the ex-dancer/actor Tony Sansone. The more profound implication of Townsend's pictures was their infusion into a resistant heterocentric culture of a decidedly homosexual and cultural point of view. Despite countless refutations, it is clear that the eroticism of the male nude in modern popular culture is a heterosexual imitation of gay pornography. The response to the exhibition of male physical perfection, as Dutton observes, has produced a vocal heterosexual male resentment of attractive and well-built men: "There is evidence to suggest that the public visibility of 'ideal' male physiques has led many men to feel increasingly uncomfortable about the look of their own bodies."

I should add that it would be an oversimplification to suggest that this discomfort is felt only by straight males. The same discomfort may be part of the motive for the political resentment of "buffed and beautiful fags" expressed by a number of gay activists.

By 1951, the process of erotizing the male body had become a conspicuous and undeniable cultural reality when Marlon Brando took off his shirt in the film version of *A Streetcar Named Desire*, and suddenly it was not simply the naked male chest but provocative male sexuality that was validated on the American movie screen. After Brando, the male body has never been able to go back into hiding.

There is, of course, far more to the transgressions of culture than male nudity, but the history of the socialization of the male nude provides a particularly vivid picture of the gay cultural attitudes that influenced the whole spectrum of mainstream culture and also led to vast physical transformations of the stereotypes and fashions of gay men themselves. As a result of this process of homoeroticism, by the 1980s the male body had become an object with high visibility, on billboards, in magazine advertising, on soap operas, in films, on stage, in magazines, and in the visual arts. As Mark Simpson observes, the "problem of *looking*" has become a major dilemma, particularly in the American male psyche.

In Europe, by comparison, men devised a paradox about their bodies as early as the 1930s—making it possible for them to be sexless in the atmosphere of business and conspicuously sexual on the beach and at poolside. Yet this widespread sexual exhibitionism was not recognized or discussed in Europe, and certainly never among straight men. The carefully arranged genitalia in translucent bikinis on European beaches remained largely, if not entirely, an unmentionable, no matter how obvious it was that men were arranging themselves in order to achieve the maximum visual impact. Yet, during this European vogue for conspicuous silhouettes and protrusions, American males on beaches did their very best to hide any hint of their sexuality behind layers of jockstraps and baggy bathing suits. So, even at poolside, the exposed male American male body was a "physique," but not a *body* with its inherent sexuality.

Ironically, all these issues of the male body became the unspoken basis of consternation and phobia during the 1990s controversy about lifting the ban on gays in the military:

> Thus the public does not wish to have to look at the queer in uniform and the soldier does not wish to have to look at the queer *out* of uniform. The soldier's fear that he will become the object of an unashamedly queer gaze in the shower is not just the fear that he will suddenly know his own nakedness, but also that he will know the nakedness of his buddies—that he "won't know where to look." The barracks' showers will have become as (homo)sexualized as the billboards, TV, and cinema screens. (Simpson)

Clearly, this revised consciousness about *looking* is a result of the transgressive homosexual culture, which willfully breaks the boundaries of male invisibility and radically changes the way we *look* at one another, or the way we do *not look* at things that are visible but that remain intentionally *unseen*.

It should be remembered that in America, until as late as the 1910s, it was considered indecent to look at one's own body; so it was not unusual for women to take baths in bathing attire.

For many gay activists, the homoeroticism that fully surfaced in the 1980s was not an innovation but a recapitulation of an enduring and transcultural homosexual culture. Such a scheme is politically compelling, but it has to overcome a good many hurdles before its rhetoric can become credible. Gay culture must somehow produce a clearly defined "self" before either a heterosexual or a homosexual ancestor can be claimed.

> Despite our every intuition and deeply felt conviction to the contrary, there is no evidence that consciousness is some entity deep inside the brain that corresponds to the experience of "self," that there is some kernel of awareness that runs the show. . . . After more than a century of looking for it, brain researchers have long since concluded that there is no conceivable place for such a *self* to be located in the physical brain, and that it simply doesn't exist. (Lemonick)

Rodolfo Llinas reaffirms the skepticism of the philosophers of the Enlightenment, and particularly the solipsistic views of David Hume. What the brain does, whether asleep or awake, Llinas notes, is to make images. But these are purely mental constructions, even when they are based on external information. For example, says Llinas, "light is nothing but electromagnetic radiation. Colors clearly don't exist outside our brains, nor does sound. Is there a sound if a tree drops in the forest and no one hears it? No. Sound is the relationship between external vibration and the brain. If there is no brain, there can be no sound."

The politics of sexuality must be seen in the context of the most current and most skeptical thinking about "self," "identity," and "consciousness." To speak of something as utilitarian as "human nature" is quite a reach; but to speak of a conviction about the existence of something clearly and singularly defined as homosexuality is a very risky supposition. Obviously, the same must be said of presumptions about heterosexuality. On the other hand, the conviction of a great many people that they are straight or gay by birth may be as much of a delusion as the conviction that we possess a definable "self." Homosexuality is too often defined as little more than *anything* that is *not* heterosexual, even though no one is certain just what the term "heterosexuality" involves or signifies. Even Freud—and many other specialists who have favored gender polarities (males and females in dimorphic heterosexual unions)—admitted that heterosexuality is "a problem that needs elucidating and is not a self-evident fact" (Freud, 1905).

The recent explorations into gay culture have sometimes become a search for justifications instead of a search for meanings. When George Stambolian, of Wellesley College, interviewed the theater historian Eric Bentley, his first questions were: "Is there a distinctly homosexual imagination? A distinctly homosexual sensibility? Can a homosexual have a nonhomosexual imagination? Does an artist's homosexuality come through in ways other than a definitely homosexual sensibility or matter?"

Bentley answered: "There is no single and constant form of the imagination or sensibility that is well defined by the word 'homosexual,' but, on the other hand, it does seem possible to apply the word with some degree of cogency to a certain type of imagination and sensibility within a certain period and within a certain geographic limit."[1]

Stambolian and his co-editor, Elaine Marks, were not looking for a confirmation of a monolithic homosexual culture. What seems to have interested them was the transgressive nature of gay culture, which appears to be its most consistent and visible characteristic.

> The finest achievement of the French writers derives from their profound understanding of the value of homosexuality as a transgression. Homosexuality tends to move through definitions and across lines of conceptual demarcation. Because it perpetually questions the social order and is always in question itself, homosexuality is *other*. The French have perceived in this otherness a privileged instrument for analysis, a question to raise questions.

But theater historian Eric Bentley cautions, in speaking of homosexual transgression, that we must remind ourselves that we are speaking about a time limited to, at most, the past 150 years. In other times and other places, the modern French attitude about transgression itself would be called into question. The "difference," which is a privileged instrument of analysis, is constantly changing into a different kind of difference. Perhaps that is our greatest confusion about gay culture.

We cannot understand that *difference itself* is constantly changing, that difference, like transgression, is dynamic. Difference is not stable. Conformity is stable. What seems to me to be the most important aspect of the transgressive culture of homosexuality is its ability to respond to the inevitable experience that difference itself is constantly different. It is precisely the constantly shifting and changing inclination of gays to use wit and black humor as a bridge into and out of the society that rejects them, to play with gender roles, and to manipulate mainstream reality, that optimizes the *model of difference* that allows the French to perceive in homosexuals an otherness that is a privileged instrument for analysis, a question to raise questions.

It seems to me that many of the lesbians and gay men who resent the current mainstreaming of homosexuality are disappointed by the *lapse of difference*, which they believe to be the one and only enduring characteristic of gay history. It is possible that some of this nostalgia is a remorse for the loss of contrariness and outrageousness, which is certainly a justified basis for regret, especially for those whose lives were kept afloat by their defiance of the norms that attempted to disparage and annihilate them. In my own experience, however, most of the sense of loss among gays, who grew up in the 1960s and 1970s, is based on the fear that a certain kind of metaphysical difference that once defined them as individuals is no longer part of gay sensibility. What many gay people seem to fear is the extinguishing of difference by the allure of conformity.

Let's presume for a moment that American black culture is held together by a common ethnic heritage and a common experience of social injustice and brutality. In a like manner, let's assume that homosexual culture is held together less by a commonality of social rejection than by a crucial awareness of difference itself—a difference often born, at least in pre-Stonewall years, of the suspicion that being sexually different made a person the one and only "queer" ever to exist. Many young people who had no gay role models were intimidated and often destroyed by their difference; while many other young people grew to understand that their difference was a powerful tool in their construction of individuality. What seems most fundamentally to define homosexual culture is this remarkable ability to manipulate difference to the advantage of those who are dismissed and denigrated for their difference.

Admittedly, from the standpoint of cultural history, it is unclear if the manipulation or the celebration of difference has really been the core mentality of the various cultures created by or acted out by the kind of people whose sexual orientation is now called homosexuality. It is also unclear if the historical identity of homosexuality is a very blurred identity because of social timidity or if this blurring of specific references to recognizably gay behavior in historical documents is the result of the fact that sexual identities were entirely submerged in a variety of different mainstream mentalities that simply didn't have the context of sexuality so prominent in the West and, particularly, in America today.

Is there such a thing as a transcultural and transhistorical gay culture?

This is a question ceaselessly asked by researchers, but it is rarely answered to everyone's satisfaction. There is an immense amount of research that has been carried out in recent years in an effort to locate and define both localized and transcendent evidence of how gender identity and sexual orientation have been conceived in various places and various period of history. This research very much deserved our attention, though it is somewhat of a digression from the central theme of transgression. Though we began our explorations of cultural history with the presumption that we would doubtlessly find familiar attitudes as well as a continuity of individual behaviors and public reactions among gay people, the great majority of researchers and writers have been amazed and disappointed again and again to discover that their expectations are not borne out by other cultures or by history.

If homosexuality is about difference—the clear and wide margin between a person and a mainstream group—then homosexuality might be defined as the challenge to find empowerment in and through alienation. But for many people, difference and alienation are very disruptive and painful experiences. Since the beginnings of the gay liberation movement, the enormous and often distressing challenge to create an identity out of crucial social and sexual difference has been gradually replaced by the far less distressing process of building an identity within a presumably well-defined homosexual culture. Politically, the power of a group identity is essential if gays are to achieve the kind of voice in society that African Americans achieved largely because of the congruity of the black church and the charisma of religious leaders like Martin Luther King, Jr. Since homosexuality lacks the congruity of both a church and an ethnicity, gay activists are inclined to opt for the congruity of a unique, transhistorical culture overflowing with legendary heroes. These heroes include long lists of exceptional people from many different cultures and periods of history—Sappho, Aristotle, Caius Julius Caesar, da Vinci, Michelangelo, Tchaikovsky, Benjamin Britten, Gertrude Stein, Willa Cather, and so many more villains and luminaries that a complete list of them would be very extensive. The opportunity of joining ranks with such a catalog of heroes is very appealing for those who have been excluded from the mainstream and ruthlessly slandered as degenerates and outsiders. Naturally, the visibility of gay luminaries is very comforting for gay people. To be counted among such celebrities is empowering—a hint of a forgotten path leading back to a lost homeland. The perception of a historical continuity peopled by exceptional human beings enforces a sense of unity within a privileged but ostracized group. I sometimes worry, however, about the possibility that something unique and precious is lost when outsiders relinquish the risky business of finding their own identities and, instead, meld with an idealized group identity, especially if that transhistorical and transcultural gay identity turns out to be less than congruent and less than transcendent.

The cultural commentator Robert Hughes has cautioned, with more than a bit of cynicism, that the newer a group's political cause the longer its claim to a historical identity. It is in light of Hughes's caution that I want to spend some time summarizing the work of a few exceptional cultural historians who have dealt with the subject of congruity and disjunction in the history of homosexual culture.

At the outset of his landmark study of homosexual desire in Shakespeare's England, Bruce Smith makes his constructionist view of sexuality clear. He points out that *sex is one of the constants in human experience,* whereas *sexuality is one of the variables:*

> Sexual desire animates human beings in all times and all places, in the form that desire assumes, the objects to which desire is directed, change from culture to culture, from era to era. . . . To distinguish "homosexual" men from "heterosexual" men is, then, a distinctively twentieth-century way of constructing sexuality. It takes sexual desire as a point of departure for personal identity. It presupposes a sexual essence in the desiring subject.

Without questioning that Shakespeare's work is deeply homoerotic and that Shakespeare himself was probably on intimate terms with men, Smith resists the typical projection of many twentieth-century politicos by refusing to see Shakespeare, and many of his contemporaries, as "homosexuals." He insists,

> On one particular point of knowledge we need to be absolutely clear: in the sixteenth and seventeenth centuries, sexuality was not, as it is for us, the starting place for anyone's self-definition. Just because sexuality has become an obsessive concern in our own culture does not mean that it has always been so. In early modern England, as in many non-Western cultures today, sexual activity occupied a radically different position than it does for us relative to all the other activities a person pursues, to other social ties, to other ways of thinking about things in general. No one in Shakespeare's day would have labeled himself a "homosexual." The term itself is a clinical, scientific coinage. . . . The structures of knowledge that impinged on what we would now call "homosexuality" did not ask a man who had sexual relations with another man to think of himself as fundamentally differ from his peers. Just the opposite was true. Prevailing ideas asked him to castigate himself for falling into the general depravity to which all mankind is subject. For sixteenth- and seventeenth-century speakers of English the words "sodomy" and "buggery" sent the mind spinning toward heterodoxies of all sorts: sorcery, religious heresy, and treason. . . . No one in England during the sixteenth or seventeenth centuries would have thought of himself as "gay" or "homosexual" for the simple reason that these categories of self-definition did not exist. But that does not mean . . . that there were no men in early modern England whose sexual desires were turned primarily toward other men.

This same conclusion about the blurring of sexual identities is reached again and again by people in a variety of fields, despite the implication that many of them were hoping to find evidence of a transhistorical gay heritage. For instance, in one of the first surveys of the relationship of homosexuality to the Western visual arts since 1890, Emmanuel Cooper celebrates the homosexual capacity for manipulating difference as a crucial cultural function, but he is not certain that "homosexuals" existed in the worlds he explores:

The concept of what constitutes 'the homosexual' has altered greatly over the last five hundred years and this has influenced the expression of homosexual desire. For instance, in Renaissance Italy the homosexual as we think of him/her today did not exist. Expressions of love (as those found in Michelangelo's poetry for other men) and sexual acts between men were well known, and, if made public, condemned. Leonardo da Vinci and Botticelli were accused publicly of such acts. Yet they were thought of as committing certain immoral acts rather than specifically as "homosexuals."

The historical and cultural issue is not whether men desired men or women desired women; the issue is *the social context of that desire.* What is probably exceptional about the culture of twentieth-century homosexuality is its ability to retain an essential sense of identity while it willingly undertakes radical changes from one place to another and from one time to another. It is a chameleon identity, a chimera that slips from its mooring in one era only to reappear in another era as a new amalgam of disparate parts. Gay culture is marked, if by anything, by a refusal to be something specific. It is difference built on difference. That is its power and that is also its mystique.

A political imperative is hard to buck, but I find that I cannot approach the subject of transgression without noticing that the idealized cultural unity of the "gay community" is a relatively recent construction, and it may be built on the forfeiture of social and personal differences that once defined lesbians and gay men. The gay community may very well be the nexus of a future gay. But, if so, gay culture will be *a difference that is not different.* For over one hundred years, transgression defined gay culture as the highly personal process by which individual homosexuals invented themselves in defiance of mainstream norms. But now I must wonder if the embrace of a gay cultural unity is not also an embrace of conformity. And if that conformity is built on a group identity that is by its very nature constantly changing, do we not lose ourselves in the very process of trying to find a homosexual identity?

The great majority of historians insist that sexual identities were undifferentiated in the earlier epochs of the West. A person sinned against God or nature or law, but there were no particularized categories defining the person who committed sins. The offending act was a sin and only a sin, regardless of whether it involved a beast, a male, a female, a close relative, or someone else's spouse. It was variously called "sodomy," "buggery," and "unnatural vice," but such terms rarely implied a specific act with a particular object. From a social point of view, the embarrassment a sinner experienced was the shame of committing any sin, and it had very little to do with the particular type of sin committed. For instance, it was *sin*—and not homosexuality—that was the documented basis of the condemnation of Leonardo and Botticelli. But the sin was not so great that the Church of Rome felt obliged to submit either artist to public humiliation. To the contrary, it was not until the publication of official records from the archives of Florence in 1896, almost four hundred years after Leonardo's death, that documentary evidence became available attesting that Leonardo da Vinci had been accused of sinful (presumably "homosexual") behavior in 1476. As Cooper and other modern da Vinci biographers, like Serge Bramly and A. Richard Turner, have pointed out, this deliberate suppression of documents related to Leonardo's accusation was a clear attempt to protect his reputation as an "asexual" artist, "married to his art," and quite beyond the temptations of the flesh. It is in this Renaissance context of ambiguous sin that we must understand Renaissance "homosexuality." It was simply one example of the homosexual cultural affinity for transformation and difference, for the evasion of strict categorical definitions of any kind of social or sexual identity.

There are countless examples of a conflict between the twentieth-century perception of a work of art and the perception of the culture and period in which it was created. For instance, in the work of Albrecht Dürer, such as his wood engraving entitled *Bathhouse*, there is for the modern gay viewer an unquestionable homoeroticism. The same may be said of the famous bronze *David* of Donatello. In Botticelli's *Madonna of the Magnificat* the gestures and glances of the male figures, who give far more attention to one another than to the Christ Child, resonate with homoeroticism. Hardly any urbane observer has missed the fact that the female nudes sculptured by Michelangelo have the unmistakable bodies of burly men—with breasts that seem haphazardly appended as an afterthought. Caravaggio was "particularly attracted to young men and it is reported that his sudden departure from Messina in 1609 was a result of his paying too much attention to schoolboys at play. He is also recorded as sharing a 'bardass' [a calamite or young male prostitute] with his friend Onorio Longhi, with whom he lived" (Cooper). But a shared bed and a shared homoeroticism didn't produce a shared homosexual identity. It may, however, have produced some kind of shared attitudes, unnamed and unpunished, but vividly acted out at all levels of society.

The denial of a clear homosexual culture in the time of Caravaggio seems to fly in the face of all our instincts and all the visual evidence. Undisputedly, there is in the images of males in the works of Caravaggio an amazing seductiveness not only in the subject matter but also in the sensual colors, fleshy textures, and extravagance of his sensibility. His notorious image of Cupid in *Amore Vincitore* reveals the familiar and natural face of a peasant boy, not an idealized cherub. From the perspective of other eras, paintings such as *Amore Vincitore* as well as *Bacchus* and *The Lute Player* have an undeniable homoeroticism, but it is difficult to speculate about the response these paintings aroused in the people of Caravaggio's day, much as it is impossible to trace, even through the complex trail of Elizabethan documents, the precise response of audiences to the works and performing traditions of Shakespeare. It is tempting to see these apparently homoerotic expressions in the arts as part of a transhistorical gay culture that is evident to twentieth-century homosexuals. But it is likely that we experience gay sexual orientation today quite differently from the way people experienced an undifferentiated sexuality in the past. The artistic trail that fascinates us and that we want to see as a winding and long road leading inevitably back to a gay homeland may be far more the result of hindsight than the intended messages left for us by artists of the past.

In the time of Shakespeare, women were prohibited from appearing on the stage; so the actors who originated roles such as Juliet and Lady Macbeth and Desdemona were boys. At about the same time, the castrati of the church choir were finding their way onto Europe's stages in secular roles so renowned that the "male soprano or alto" became a pop star in his day. Even Goethe was swept up by the acclaim for the castrati:

A double pleasure is given in that these persons are not women, but only represent women. The young men have studied the properties of the sex in its being and behavior; they know them thoroughly and reproduce them like an artist; they represent not themselves, but a nature absolutely foreign to them.

Today we may roll our eyes at Goethe's naiveté, but our presumptions about his view of the castrated male sopranos and altos of his time may be far less valid than his own response. About two hundred years before Goethe, at Shakespeare's Globe Theater, the paradox of gender was played out again and again as a theatrical convention, that was *not*, as Smith points out, "a man falling in love with a woman dressed as a boy," but, far more perplexingly, "a man falling in love with a boy actor dressed as a woman dressed as a boy."

What did Shakespeare's audience make of such things? They responded without objection or they took the position of the Puritans, who strongly opposed women's parts being played by boys, but for reasons that may surprise us today. The Puritans ranted that in Deuteronomy 22:5 it was expressly forbidden for a man to dress up as a woman, for it "were to alter the order of nature created by God."

The Puritans did not mention, however, that the Bible also expressly forbids people to eat pork.

Homosexuality doesn't seem to be an issue in the complaint of the Puritans. For them, cross-dressing was a transgression of a very literal biblical prohibition and not deviant sexual behaviors. That violation of scripture, apparently, was what perturbed them. The remarkably humorless Puritans felt they were God's fashion police, demanding that men wear trousers—not frocks.

There have been countless debates about the motives and contextual significance of cross-dressing in plays, operas, and ballets during the Renaissance, Baroque, and Rococo periods, but no agreement on the matter seems to be forthcoming. The twentieth-century exploration of the Elizabethan custom has provided two entirely different points of view about homosexual culture. As Bruce Smith explains, the allure and significance of boy actors playing female characters were *either* their presence strictly as the illusion of the women they were pretending to be (and thus a heterosexual appeal to members of the audience) *or* the performance by boy as boys (suggesting a homosexual appeal).

The problem with this kind of self-conscious, twentieth-century cataloging of sexuality is that it takes for granted a heterocentric model and bolsters rather than questions the orthodoxy of the dimorphism of masculine and feminine behaviors that is so prominent in our own world, but may have been far less prominent in the past.

When we look toward remote lands and peoples of radically different cultural histories, we find that "homosexual culture" is even more evasive. For instance, at the time of Shakespeare, the theater in Japan already had a long history of transvestitism that was intimately associated with the Japanese attitudes about women. That attitude was shared with the Elizabethans: a prohibition of females on the stage. The oldest, most continually performed theater works of the world began with Noh drama, in which only men performed. It is still a highly stylized and ascetic form of theater established by the genius of two men: Kwanami Kiyotsugu (1333–1384) and his son Seami Motokiyo (1363–1444). The shogun Ashikaga Yoshimitsu became infatuated with the beauty of the young actor Seami, then a boy of twelve. "The Shogun's relations with this boy seem from the first to have been very intimate . . . a boy-favorite" (Waley). It was in the talents of this youth that Noh found its greatest exemplar as well as its greatest creative genius. But we find nowhere in Japanese historical documents any decisive characterizations of boy-favorites or cross-dressing actors as anything remotely akin to our notion of homosexuality.

Noh was exceptionally subtle and restrained. It was not to the taste of the rising middle class in the seventeenth-century Edo period of Japan. So a more colorful and animated form of Japanese theater took shape in the form of Kabuki, attaining great popularity in Japan during approximately the same period that Shakespeare opened his Globe Theater in London. This new Japanese theater was an entertainment originally performed by women. In fact, it is said to have been invented by a woman. But after 1629, females were officially banned by the government because it was thought that women of the theater used their public appearances to promote careers as prostitutes.

As Ian Buruma points out, with this banning of women from the theater "grew what is perhaps the highest art of female impersonation in the world: the *onnagata*." But it is not clear if we can realistically call this culture of female impersonation an aspect of gay culture. And yet the onnagata represented not only the most cultivated form of cross-dressing in world history, but it has also remained fantastically popular, especially among Japanese women. Buruma reinforces this point with statistics: "According to a pole in a woman's magazine the two 'sexiest stars' were Tamasaburo, a remarkable Kabuki actor specializing in female roles, and Sawada Kenji, a pop singer who likes to perform in semi-drag."

In Japanese culture, cross-dressing has had a very ancient and revered history. Sexual ambiguity is a central aspect of Japanese Shintoism, which was for many centuries the official state religion. When the Sun Goddess met her unruly brother Susanoo, she dressed as a male. Many of her male disciples still engage in cross-dressing, wearing female garments in the presence of the Goddess. Such sexual ambivalence is also important in Buddhist tradition. But despite its fascination, none of this historical information brings us any closer to grasping the essential similarities and differences between various concepts of homosexual culture. As Buruma has pointed out, art in Japan is artifice. The Japanese love nature so much they cannot leave it alone, and yet they attempt to produce an artificiality that is strikingly natural, like their famous gardens. "In other words, no real woman can ever be as beautiful as a woman played by a man, so no woman is quite as stunning as a skillful female impersonator." This aesthetification of nature and gender goes to the heart of the Japanese mind. The onnagata, like the female geisha, whom the Japanese consider to be "a female work of art," are based on the principle of depersonalization. "People do not pretend that the ideal has anything to do with reality. They enjoy seeing Lady Macbeth played by a famous [male] Kabuki star, precisely because it is more artificial, thus more skillful, in a word, more beautiful" (Buruma). For the Japanese, there is no such thing as "*natural* beauty."

It is possible that Shakespeare's audience shared this love of artifice and the skill of performers to transform themselves into *anything*—including members of the opposite sex. In the search for meaning in Elizabethan homoeroticism, we must make educated guesses because the sensibility and the mentality of those Shakespearean productions are entirely lost, while both the sensibility and the mentality of the Kabuki theater have persisted as an unbroken tradition for almost four hundred years (except for a short time just after World War II, when the U.S. occupational commanders attempted to suppress Kabuki as a potentially inflammatory form of nationalism*). It is impossible to say the same about the consistency of tradition in any other theatrical genre, including the works of Shakespeare. Yet even in the clear continuity of Japanese performing arts, the questions of gender identity remain unconscious or intentionally undisclosed—perhaps as an expression of the national mentality I have found among close friends in

---

*It is tempting to speculate about General MacArthur's homophobic motives for banning Kabuki, and it is also interesting to note that a major advisor to MacArthur was both an admirer of Kabuki and a gay man. It was that advisor who succeeded in getting MacArthur to lift the ban on Kabuki performances.

Tokyo who avoid talking to me frankly about the social and artistic ramifications of the sexual orientation of writer Yukio Mishima.

In the West, a transgressive mentality about gender behavior arose in the same era during that "homosexuality" was invented. The mid-nineteenth-century attitude about sexuality and the body in Europe and America was a mirror image of what had taken place during the British occupation of India: The mentality of India's people was so vastly changed from the tenth century, when the intensely erotic facade of the Devi Jagadambi Temple at Khajuraho was built, that in the 1950s, famed Bengali film director Satyajit Ray had to fight the censors in order to show a man kissing a woman in an extreme long-shot in one of the films of his masterful *Apu Trilogy*.

History and mythology have often been sanitized to suit the day. In 1842, Charles Anthon's famous *Classical Dictionary*, a basic re-search tool of its day, proudly announced that "everything offensive" in classical history had been expurgated. Now, Ganymede was not carried away by an eagle so he could become the favorite of Zeus; instead, he was "carried off to Olympus by an eagle to be cupbearer of Jove." Greek and Roman homoeroticism had vanished from the annals of history.

Walt Whitman created a highly rarified homoerotic poetic imagery at the same time that painters Thomas Eakins and Henry Scott Tuke began to create their visual interpretations of "the Greek way of life," as it was euphemistically called. What this "Greek way of life" came down to was an idealization of classical attitudes about the outdoors and the comradeship of young men. As Cooper points out,

> The problem of defining the sexuality of these artists remains. Though none can be seen as homosexual in the modern sense of the word, all expressed at some time powerful homoerotic qualities in their work. Some, such as Eakins, were married; others had relationships with women. All had significant friendships with men.

In the twentieth century, even with the emergence of openly gay visual artists like David Hockney, Robert Mapplethorpe, Della Grace, Rosey Martin, Francis Bacon, Andy Warhol, Judy Pinto, Minor White, George Platt Lynes, Paul Cadmus, Leonor Fini, Marsden Hartley,

Charles Demuth, Audrey Beardsley, and Gustav Moreau, among countless others, it is still difficult to see any evidence of a "gay culture" at work in their paintings except in terms of the occasional homoerotic subject matter. The nude often plays a key role in such "homosexual art," but matters of sensibility and attitude are as disparate as the film-making of homosexual directors like Visconti, Pasolini, and Eisenstein, even in the manner in which they photographed male bodies in their films. On the other hand, there is considerable stylistic similarity be-tween the film *Othello* by a heterosexual filmmaker like Orsen Welles and the *Battleship Potemkin* by a homosexual filmmaker like Sergei Eisenstein.

What possible relationship can be claimed between the renowned (and gay) Wagnerian tenor Lawrence Melchoir and the equally re-nowned (and gay) lyric tenor Peter Pears? And given both the homo-phobia of the world of jazz musicians and the very small gay audience for jazz, how do we attempt to explain a gay jazz star like vibraphonist Gary Burton? "This has certainly been an issue for me," Burton told *The Advocate*. "One of the real ironies for me of finally coming out . . . is the fact that the gay community I was so happy to finally connect with is so uninterested in what I do. . . . The gay community is among the least informed about this music."

In *The Queen's Throat*, his 1993 study of opera in relation to homosexuality, Wayne Koestenbaum fails to explain the attraction of certain operas to certain gay males. He also fails to explain how it was possible for a thoroughly heterosexual composer like Puccini to have composed music that is for many gay opera fans the ultimate emotional experience. Koestenbaum doesn't really deal with opera as a medium of musical expression. He talks about opera's greatest "gay hits," but never touches on what these particular scenes and arias communicate to a particular kind of gay male. He doesn't tell us how the special conventions of opera—the larger than life atmosphere and the artifi-cially exaggerated sentimentalities and tragic gestures—manage to transcend bourgeois realism. He doesn't explain that opera can be such an emotionally flamboyant experience that it somehow heightens and validates the tragic intensity of our own lives. It has always mystified me that a rather decorative and melodious aria by Bellini, Verdi, Puc-cini, or Donizetti sung by Maria Callas has presumably greater power for gay men than the wrenching lesbian lament sung by Tatiana Troy-anos, as Countess Gerschwitz, in the final scene of Alban Berg's *Lulu*.

The consensus among music critics is that the gay audience was not highly visible at performances of distinctly unpopular operas such as Alban Berg's *Wozzeck* and *Lulu*, Béla Bartók's *Bluebeard Castle*, and the epic operas of Richard Wagner. And despite a great many gay composers and performers who are modernists, the gay audience has not been particularly drawn to a group of brilliantly deconstructed "operas," such as the Robert Wilson/Philip Glass *Einstein on the Beach* and Meredith Monk's *Atlas*.

London Times literary critic Michael Tanner points out that the "underlying thesis of [Koestenbaum's] book is that opera, like homosexuality, is transgressive, a flouting of borderlines. But he gets no further than that, and I'm not sure that is any distance at all. Wagner, in many ways the most transgressive, invasive, taboo-ignoring composer of operas, is also one whose gay clientele is no larger than Shakespeare's, I suspect."

What interests me and what apparently interests composer Ned Rorem is the way in which music by gay composers has been politicized. Rorem has never made any secret of his sexual orientation, and he has also never made any secret of his impatience with critics and writers who define him as "a homosexual composer." In discussing a concert of the New York City Gay Men's Chorus, which featured music by Barber, Bernstein, Copland, Gershwin, Porter, and Rorem, the composer expressed justifiable testiness. "Perhaps pink triangles could be placed by appropriate names in the program (although I never knew that Gershwin was homosexual)," Rorem said. "What has Bernstein's and Copland's (and, yes, Gershwin's) Jewishness to do with their music?" Rorem asks if their gayness is more relevant than their Jewishness. A critic might look for Jewish implications in the clearly Hebraic themes of Ernest Bloch's music or for Japanese influences in the music of Toru Takemitsu, but it would be considered something of an ethnic offense to dote on the Jewish implications of a jazz-influenced sonata or a "cowboy ballet" by New York–born Aaron Copland.

At one time, it was widely assumed that modern gay composers were romanticists, composing clever, lyrical, but thoroughly soft and sentimental music. In fact, when critics characterized the music of Benjamin Britten as "clever" and "sentimental," what they were really doing was insinuating his homosexuality. As Rorem told Lawrence Mass during an interview, "Yes, somebody could write about gay music, but they'd have to be able to define it first. . . . Still, I'm not saying it can't or shouldn't be done." And, indeed, it is being done. But the problem Rorem raises persists: No one has been able to define the particular cultural attitudes that influence music composed by homosexual composers, despite the fact that there are a good many experts looking into the matter. Joke Dame teaches feminist musicology at Utrecht University. In her essay "Unveiled Voices," she suggests that by implication music may have gender insofar as the human voice may be a clear and consistent expression of gender. But that supposition begins to falter when we consider castrati and counter-tenors (Dame thought counter-tenor Alfred Deller was a female when she first heard a recording of his voice) or jazz singers like Michael Franks (whom I thought was a female when I first heard his recording of "Dragonfly Summer") or the falsetto style perfected by male gospel and rhythm and blues singers or the falsetto vocalizations of Alpine yodelers. Dame concludes,

> One is inclined to say that voice has gender. After all, in most cases we do hear correctly whether a voice comes from a female or a male body. Nonetheless, pop music provides a crafty example of gender-disguised singing. Equally in Western art music and non-Western music there are examples that might give rise to doubts as to the "genderedness" of the [human] voice.

The abstract nature of music may be the basis of difficulties in characterizing its references to gender. The theater, on the other hand, is like the visual arts, with attitudes and persons taken from life models. Despite New York critic Stanley Kauffman's infamous attack on "three homosexual playwrights" (obviously Tennessee Williams, Edward Albee, and William Inge) and his accusation that they were "homosexualizing the American theater," it is virtually impossible to find parallel sensibilities in the plays of these three playwrights.[2] Even when their subject matter verges on gay points of view, it is still impossible to find commonality between the language, the attitudes, and the theatrical mannerisms that are unmistakably at the heart of an Albee play or an Inge or a Williams play. *A Streetcar Named Desire* and *Suddenly Last Summer* are of an entirely different mentality from Inge's *Picnic* or Albee's *Who's Afraid of Virginia Woolf* and *Three Tall Women*. Being homosexual, even being gay men during, more or less, the same period of time, appears to have had slight influence on the creative personalities of the works of Williams, Albee, and Inge. Their dissimilarities contest Kauffman's homophobic assumption that social suppression had forced gay writers to devise an elaborate and conspiratorial technique of using female characters to perform as their theatrical doubles. Critic Kauffman insisted that the female characters written by Williams, Inge, and Albee were not really women, but gay men in cunning theatrical drag. Kauffman's accusation, however, overlooks the equally compelling question of gender and point of view in the writings of heterosexual playwrights and novelists who create works centered on members of the opposite sex—for instance, O'Neill's Anna Christie, Tolstoy's Anna Karenina, Edith Wharton's Ethan Frome, Flaubert's Bovary, and Leslie Silko's Tayo. Are these male and female characters that were created by heterosexuals any different from Blanche in *Streetcar*, Martha in *Who's Afraid of Virginia Woolf?*, Harper Pitt in *Angels in America*, Margo Channing in *All About Eve*, or Terence McNally's flamboyant portrayal of Maria Callas in *The Master Class*? Can all of these bravura novelistic and theatrical characters be reduced, despite their tremendous impact, to male voices in the guise of women or female voices in the guise of men?

There is much that can be said about the role of gender in literature, but a good deal of the current discussion is so focused on the politics of gender that we sometimes forget that the writer's craft is one of projection. What is projected in terms of gender may have political consequences, but the process of creation, even in a writer as socially self-conscious as Emile Zola, rises to greatness only when it rises above its iconoclastic intentions. As Thomas Mann observed in his remarks about the much-touted naturalist novel *Nana*, Zola's avowed naturalism inevitably turned into myth through the author's intense immersion in the typical.

The gender disguises of literature are universal, and homosexuality has no exclusive claim to the art of psychological cross-dressing. Federico García Lorca's Yerma is a vehicle for the playwright's own voice. Cora is one of several "voices" through which William Faulkner speaks in *As I Lay Dying*. And certainly Molly Bloom in James Joyce's *Ulysses* is one of the most remarkable and daring examples of gender ventriloquism.

The source and socialization of gender behaviors are still the subjects of a great debate. Constructionism wants to divorce sexuality from nature and interpret it, instead, as a cultural construction, while essentialism wants to turn culture back into a function of nature. Neil Miller and Bruce Bawer, two writers who come from very different political points of view, have the same problems I have with the idea of a transcendent gay culture that emphases uniformity rather than emphasizing difference. Miller tells us that when he visited Egypt, he found a country in which "male homosexual behavior was widespread but gay and lesbian identity as we know it was missing. . . . There was no one in Cairo who would describe himself as gay." Miller found out that Egypt was not a society in which gay men and women "were in the closet exactly; rather, it was one in which any notion of sexual categories such as gay and straight was absent." When Miller explained to people engaged in same-sex behavior that he was writing a book about gay and lesbian life around the world, they looked at him blankly, clearly having no idea what he was saying. Miller's experiences in modern travel were duplicated in his travel through history:

> As I traveled farther back into the past—even as recently as the mid-to late-nineteenth century—finding gay antecedents proved problematic. There was Walt Whitman, writing passionate letters to young soldiers during the Civil War. There were middle- and upper-class women living in the same-sex partnerships referred to as Boston marriages. There were women who passed as men. Were all or at least some of these people gay? Almost certainly, in the sense that they had sexual and romantic relations with members of their own sex. But in looking back one hundred and twenty-five years, I found little evidence of gay men and lesbians who saw their sexuality as a primary aspect of their identity or of communities bonded by shared sexual orientation.

Miller's experience reminds me of what happened to Malcolm X when he went to Africa, expecting to find a monolithic culture and sensibility with clear relationships to African-American identity. He was dumbfounded to see peoples who rarely reflected his notion of Africanism and who had a difficult time understanding why Malcolm considered himself an African. Likewise, according to Miller,

> As contemporary gay men and lesbians search for links with other cultures and for our spiritual ancestors, we often come up empty-handed. We find that gay and lesbian identity as we know it today is a small ship tossing on a vast ocean of same-sex behavior. Our

attempt to create a community based on shared sexual orientation is a unique historical and cultural experiment, and a very young one at that. . . . As we attempt to create an international gay and lesbian movement, it is important to realize that other cultures may not share our sense of homosexuality as an identity. . . . The writing of our history cannot be determined by political convenience.

Bruce Bawer has mixed feelings about the source of canonical gay taste. For every one he shares, he says, there are ten he doesn't share. He tell us that he never cared for *Dynasty*, and he isn't a big opera fan, which he equates as two examples of homo-taste, along with idolized stars such as Streisand, Garland, and Madonna:

> In any event, I don't think such tastes are a direct consequence of my homosexuality. Would Alexander the Great have loved *Auntie Mame*? Would Richard the Lion-Hearted have become addicted to *Ab Fab*? When a ten-year-old gay kid finds himself drawn to such phenomena, I suspect, it's not because of a genetic link between sexual orientation and cultural tastes but because of some complex conjunction between his as-yet-unarticulated awareness of his own differentness and society's signals to him about emotional orientation, sexual identity, and gender roles. (Bawer, 1995)

Whatever those social signals may be, they seem to coalesce with a temperament to produce an entirely disproportionate contribution to Western art, architecture, music, and literature far exceeding the numbers statisticians would expect from debatably 1 to 15 percent of the populations of Europe and America. If Sergei Diaghilev had been the only homosexual in the first half of the twentieth century, just his impresarial contribution to music, dance, and the visual arts would have placed gays at the cutting edge of modernism. Single-handedly, he combined the most dynamic artistic forces of Russia and France, discovering and publicly introducing a remarkably vast number of the leading artists between 1910 and 1929—commissioning major works from Ravel, Debussy, Stravinsky, Milhaud, Picasso, Chagall, Bakst, Leger, Cocteau, Rouault, Nijinsky, Fokine, Massine, Balanchine, and, in so doing, unquestionably changed the course of twentieth-century culture.

As Bawer (1995) has suggested, "Western civilization, far from being threatened by homosexuality, is to a staggeringly disproportionate degree the creation of gay men and women." Given the protestations of those who believe homosexuality is an enemy of civilization, the statistical evidence that homosexuality has been indispensable to Western culture is a fact not to be minimized. And, doubtlessly, it is the reason that a belief in a transcendent gay culture and the bonding of disparate people into a gay community is such a political imperative. And yet, such transcendency of identity and culture seems to allude us, unless we can agree that difference and transgression constitute the single most enduring aspect of whatever it is we mean when we speak of a culture produced by lesbians and gay men.

If the gay matrix of so-called high culture is difficult to establish, there is absolutely no question that popular culture in the twentieth century is largely invented and driven by homosexual attitudes and social models. There have always been at least two forms of pop culture: a sanitized and authorized white, middle-class culture as apposed to a subversive and deviant culture. Jazz was always part of the subversive pop underground, to such an extent that the terms "jazz" and "pop" are often used as designations of two completely separate kinds of music. So-called race music was heard in black ghettos and on black radio stations until Motown and Atlantic Records managed, incredibly, to bring it into the mainstream during the 1950s and 1960s. Before that cultural transformation, the rhythm and blues of African Americans entered the white middle-class world only as polite, sanitized, and bloodless "cover versions" by singers like Pat Boone and Dinah Shaw. Eventually, however, the "deviant" black culture overwhelmed the sanitized culture, and the subversification of "white pop" has steadily continued since the 1960s.

At the same time that rhythm and blues began to surface in mainstream culture, the musical influence of gay musicians was transformed from a little-known voice of the underground into an unrelenting and powerful force in pop culture. Much as Cab Calloway, Hoggy Carmichael, and many other straight musicians insinuated references to drugs and sex in their lyrics, gays began increasingly to allude to their sexuality in their songs. One of the typically sentimental tunes of the era was "Lush Life" by the gay songwriter Billy Strayhorn, who went on to become one of Duke Ellington's major collaborators. "*I used to visit all the very gay places,*" the classic Strayhorn tune begins, and then draws a vivid if remorseful picture of the 1940s gay bar scene and its "five-o'clock-tails." The suave and swanky lyrics of Cole Porter were also part of a gay insinuation in pop music, though Porter was essentially a songwriter for the carriage crowd. Jerry Stoller, of the famed rhythm and blues team of Stoller and Leiber, wrote a poignant song about the death of Ramon Novarro, in which there are references to the fact that the silent movie idol had been killed by two hustlers, using as a weapon the black lead dildo given to Novarro by Valentino. The gay inferences of Stoller songs were subtle by comparison to the music of The Village People, whose tunes were among the top disco hits of the 1970s, with coded references to San Francisco's huge gay population and to "macho men" as well as their deathless homage to the YMCA, which for decades had been a meeting place for gay men before the era of backroom bars and the baths.

By the mid-1970s, the gay dance club had become the "Harlem of homosexuals," attracting a huge following of slumming straights. It was the era of music by Paul Jabara, a singer-actor who got his break in the Broadway musical *Hair* and went on to become a hugely self-destructive genius of the New York pop music world. His songs for Donna Sommers launched his career as a songwriter. And his tunes for The Weather Girls and a number of other pop singers revolutionized the attitude, intensity, sexuality, and energy of pop music, ushering in a kind of drugged hysteria in dance clubs that had never existed before or since in the world of white Americans. Jabara brought about a curious union of black female performers and gay attitudes about sexuality that had never been achieved with such great success. As Jabara told me in New York a few years before his death, "It's only through the get-down and dirty frankness of black women that I can vent all my energy as a gay man."

Jabara's songs greatly pre-date the lesbian chic of Madonna, and were full of unabashedly gay energy: with lines in the tune "Success" about the notorious New York gay sex club called The Anvil and frank references to "the boys in the back room bars," as well as naming the dance club that started the phenomenal gay dance rage, Studio 54, a New York venue that was to drugs and dancing what Max's Kansas City was to rock 'n' roll and the bizarre art world populated by Patti Smith, Robert Mapplethorpe, and Andy Warhol.

A great many straights didn't understand exactly what was going on, but the energy of the explosive gay pop movement was so impressive that it invaded almost every part of the heterosexual world. The influence of the music was quickly followed by a great many other gay fashions in dance styles, social drugs, designer clothes and leather paraphernalia, and slang. What straights men didn't get from gays, they eventually appropriated from the African-American fashion associated with hip-hop, gangs, and rap: baseball caps turned backward, loose rumpled shirts, and baggy pants worn very low on the hips.

Today, the gay dance clubs are much quieter. The bars are far less crowded. The people at gay summer resorts are younger than before. And through all of this torpidness there is a haunted awareness that a great many gay men have disappeared. When someone notices the emptiness of favorite gay bars and asks where all the great looking guys have gone, the typically Wildean response in Los Angeles is "Forest Lawn." Cynicism has always been one of the lifesaving responses of gay people to adversity. In a time of plague, survival depends on levity. But beneath the cynicism is a long and silent melancholy. In such a grim and angry moment people are brought to tears by some of W. H. Auden's most poignant lines:

Let aeroplanes circle moaning overhead
Scribbling on the sky the message He Is Dead.[3]

AIDS evokes an inevitable sense of mortality that sends homosexuals in search of a history—a means of seeing into the past since it is so difficult to imagine the future.

If difference no longer defines homosexuality, then it is unclear to me how we can structure a definition. But if homosexuality is about difference—existing in the clear and wide margin between a person and a mainstream group—then homosexuality is an identity that attempts to find empowerment in alienation. I suspect, however, that young homosexuals have forfeited something of their "otherness" in the process of trying to turn themselves into somebody who is neither alienated nor different.

Depending on their politics, some people may view the mainstreaming of homosexuality as a positive social achievement, but I have very mixed feelings about it, because I believe that gay culture has a basis, if in nothing else, in the transgressive play of difference. In the loss of this transgressive capacity to turn alienation into an adventure, I see the transformation of difference into a self-defeating process of naturalization. It is this normalization of homosexuality that turns outcasts into clones of those who made them outsiders in the first place. The motives of naturalization and normalization have become progressively stronger all over the globe since the end of World War II. White American hierarchies of beauty and normalcy have been internationalized. Countless women in China and Japan are undergoing surgery to "anglicize" their eyelids. The French, who love to detest all things American, are one of the first European peoples to go crazy over jeans and T-shirts and cowboy boots. The American black community has long supported an industry that produces skin bleaches and hair straighteners. In the Jewish community, before the brutal lessons of the Holocaust, nose jobs and anglicized names were fashionable. And, as we have seen, gay muscles and lesbian lipstick have taken the process of mainstream naturalization to its theatrical extreme.

When people transform themselves and their identities because they are driven by invention and imagination, that is one thing, but if the transformation is an effort to "pass"—a device used to dodge and ditch an identity that fills people with self-contempt, that is a totally different endeavor. In a society in which "the center cannot hold" and "the falcon cannot hear the falconer,"[4] people are compelled to decide whether they are going to be like everyone else or if they are going to accept the enormous challenge of being themselves—which is essentially a matter of prevailing rather than surviving in a world that, as Yeats wrote in "The Second Coming,"

> . . . the ceremony of innocence is drowned
> The best lack all conviction, while the worst
> Are full of passionate intensity.

Homosexuality crosses all lines of ethnicity, nationality, and religion. Its only unique characteristic is its quixotic and mysterious *difference*. By becoming "average" many gay people have failed to become anybody. Somehow the hope to be accepted has been confused with the determination to be compliant. The issue of human socialization is not a matter of defining one's sexuality, but of defining one's self. Until people confront the social sources of their anonymity, they remain locked within the rules that brought about their disenfranchisement. They remain, like Kafka's indecisive and self-loathing characters, standing for a lifetime at the Door of the Law, hoping that someone else will give them permission to enter the realm of their own lives.

When we honor the contributions to culture made by homosexuals, we are honoring the achievements of *individuals*; we are not giving homage to a "lifestyle" or an abstract political group. We are praising the *person* who succeeded in transforming alienation into a voice, in using difference to make a difference. We are celebrating an individual who retained the kind of vision of which only individuals are capable. It was Gore Vidal who observed that there are homosexual acts, but there are no homosexuals.

Joyce Carol Oates hopes that one day there will be "novels by women that are not women's novels; novels by minorities" that are not minority novels. When we recognize a book as being "interesting" because it is by a minority person, the condescension is palpable. As the outstanding translator from the Chinese Amy Ling affirms: "Only if a work is recognized simply for being a good book . . . will we have all gotten somewhere."

Joyce Carol Oates and Amy Ling return us to the theme of transgression that underscores the differences rather than the consistencies discovered by a great many researchers both in Western history and in other societies. Perhaps a new and urgent meaning emerges from a commentary already quoted from George Stambolian and Elaine Marks's book *Homosexualities and French Literature*:

> The finest achievement of the French writers derives from their profound understanding of the value of homosexuality as a transgression. Homosexuality tends to move through definitions and across lines of conceptual demarcation. Because it perpetually questions the social order and is always in question itself, homosexuality is *other*. The French have perceived in this otherness a privileged instrument for analysis, a question to raise questions.

This is an eloquent statement, but we must remember that the "difference" that is a "privileged instrument of analysis" is constantly changing into different kinds of instruments, requiring different kinds of analyses. It is sometimes difficult for us to remember that difference, like transgression, is dynamic. Difference is *not* stable. It is conformity that is motionless and fixed. From my point of view, a self-contempt driven by a furtive alienation has had a striking and punishing impact on difference, turning what was once a consciously unique culture into a new kind of unconscious conformism.

By 1985, homosexuality had become the poor relation of multiculturalism. Idiosyncratic homosexual behavior was viewed politically as aspects of an outdated culture that emphasized diversity and eccentricity rather than the attributes of a narrowly structured group solidarity. At the same time that multiculturalism was supposed to embrace "difference," difference was being extinguished by various schemes of identity politics. Somewhat like the attitude of Afrocentrism (that, as Kwame Anthony Appiah notes, places "racial" identity ahead of all other considerations), the gay liberation movement gradually rejected the triumph of difference as it became deeply and paradoxically involved in both the politics of multiculturalism—which sees sexual diversity as just one aspect of the multiplicity of human possibilities—and the politics of homocentrism—that places the importance of sexual orientation above all other considerations of identity.

The motivation behind a gay political identity must be seen as a way of looking back at the people who completely dominated public forums for generations. Again, it is clear that culture is a way of looking. If gay culture was produced as a response to heterocentrism, it follows that a gay political identity has been invented in an effort to empower gay culture beyond the boundaries of the gay ghetto.

As I have said, if destiny is equated with the domination of a majority, then it becomes clear that the idea of a homosexual culture has been a necessary response of gays to the rigid and monolithic assumption that human beings are heterosexual. Though this heterocentrism effectively eliminates any need to define "heterosexual culture," it produces an urgent need to invent a gay culture.

It is with this harrowing paradox of individual difference in conflict with group identity that lesbians and gay men end the twentieth century.

TRANSGRESSION

9

AS REVELATION

[My wife and I] feel a sense of privilege for being right on the fault line between the past and the future. That fault line is where we have to live—all of us. It's more fun to be there where you take the risk rather than trying to drag people back to the past for safety sake.

Episcopalian Bishop Walter Righter

What other people reproach you for,
cultivate.
It is yourself.   *Jean Cocteau*

There has been a great deal of talk about the "dumbing" of America. There has also been a good deal of discussion about the decline of substance and the triumph of mindless style. And so, for a time, it seemed as if the American intellectual, so influential as a public voice in the 1930s through the 1950s, had vanished into the morass of ignorance, or at least was well on the way to extinction. Specialization, for all its achievements, has tended to bury public discourse and has turned social interaction into a closed set of narrowly defined relationships within various isolated groups, with little affinity for other groups. Alliances are commonly defined in terms of specialization or social identity: built on attitudes about profession, class, ethnicity, religion, or gender.

Now, after almost four decades of a disastrous silence from the kind of intellectuals whose overviews are not entirely bound to special interests, Robert S. Boynton has announced in the *Atlantic Monthly* that the public intellectual has in recent years made a strong comeback in America. Boynton believes that this new intellectual group is composed of a score of African-American scholars and writers, including Shelby Steele, Glenn Loury, Stephen Carter, Stanley Crouch, Henry Louis Gates, Jr., Cornel West, and Toni Morrison. So far, there are no known homosexuals among these new intellectuals, but, in time, there surely will be, because the aim of these public voices is the establishment of a distinction between the importance of unrestrained individualism as opposed to various constraints demanded by various identity groups. According to Boynton,

> Central to this new paradigm is the explicit rejection of identity politics and the victimology that so often lies at the heart of efforts to mobilize the allegiances of racial or ethnic groups. In general, identity politics is based on the belief that social groups have certain essential characteristics that extend to all their members. . . . It can define a group's essence so narrowly that it isolates its members from the rest of society, degenerating into what the sociologist Todd Gitlin describes as "a grim and hermetic bravado celebrating victimization and stylized marginality." The inevitable logic of identity politics, these black intellectuals argue, leads a group to envision itself as necessarily alienated from American culture at large, and to define itself in its very essence as being victimized by the ideas or structures it opposes.

Ironically, it seems that just as African Americans are attempting to discover an individuality that is unbounded by group identity, homosexuals, who long wrestled with their personal isolation, are now attempting to build a sense of political community. Such a process is not only understandable among people long isolated by bigotry and dogma, but the politicalization of lesbians and gay men is a clearly a political imperative. If sexual orientation is the force behind gay liberation, it is no less valid a force than the black church of Martin Luther King, Jr., which unquestionably impelled the civil rights movement. For gay people, sexual orientation serves as the decisive mechanism of collectivism and political activism in exactly the same way that the black church served as the social mechanism that propelled and unified the civil rights movement in the 1960s. And yet all forms of collectivism and activism have their dilemmas—a certain time and a certain place and an equally certain demise—especially if they build their agendas on a collective sense of victimization.

Henry Louis Gates, Jr., sees victimization as a political mannerism—a divisive activity that allows a person (submerged in the "group") to escape the challenge of becoming an individual. Identity politics defines "alienation" in impersonal terms, not as a stressed or rebellious relationship of an individual to society, but as a group's fatalistic vision of itself as hopelessly victimized. Gates is critical of the Black Power and Black Aesthetic movements' attempts to dislodge the hegemonic idea of whiteness and replace it with an equally restrictive concept of blackness. Gates concludes that in the end these group efforts yielded little more than "a gestural politics captivated by fetishes and feel-bad rhetoric."

As Boynton explains, in rejecting the ideological straightjacket of identity politics, the new generation of black intellectuals is asserting the fundamental right of African Americans to emerge from the group and think differently from one another.

What African-American intellectuals have achieved is the kind of discourse greatly needed in the world of homosexuals, where many people are obsessed with efforts to become submerged in a "homosexual group" that is defined by a single, homogenous, and alienated "identity." The social intent of homosexual identity politics is to justify making a hermetic "idea" about homosexuality both the motive and rationale for a battle against heterosexual hegemony. This kind of political purpose, in terms of human rights, is admirable, but it is also dangerous. The impact on the individual, as African-American intellectuals have pointed out, can be highly counterproductive, affirming rather than denouncing stereotypes, upholding a widely advertised and sloganized peer pressure that denies the individual's right to be his or her own person, and turning victimization into a rationalization for all kinds of personal failings and public offenses that have nothing to do with any group's "identity."

A new generation of African Americans is attempting to close the debate about a troubled and delusional group identity. They have jettisoned the old rhetorical questions: "How should *we* act?" and "How should *we* look?" and replaced them with new questions: "How should I act?" and "How should I look?" It is no longer a question of "Are you with us or against us"? Instead of the old obsessions with elaborating schemes of *group* conformity, many black leaders have commenced a discussion of the black *individual,* who must find his or her *own* definition of both blackness and self, who must abandon the confines of the "group" without compromising the hard-earned achievements in civil rights and without slowing the momentum of continued efforts to win true social and political justice. The leaders of this new African-American point of view will no longer stand by while black people are suffocated by the mandates of identity politics and group rhetoric, whether the definition of the "group" is built on biology, sensibility, or culture. They have loudly voiced the position that the problem is not their own "race" but the racism of others.

The message that has been heard in the African-American intellectual community during the 1990s is also finding its outspoken voices in the gay and lesbian community. There are educators, researchers, and activists who are proclaiming that the homosexual ghetto built on homophobia has produced a falsehood about gay identity that must be debunked. Beyond providing an indispensable shelter from heterosexual bigotry, the gay ghetto has, according to many outspoken critics, induced a hermetic group identity that has become stultifying rather than liberating. It has made "gayness" the primary, if not the sole, basis of identity among homosexuals, especially among young homosexuals who accept as role models the countless gay icons manufactured and exploited by the media.

As the debates about identity continue, the lure of assimilation becomes a major issue within all marginal groups. According to at least one side of this discussion is the belief that in order to evade the sense of alienation imposed on homosexuality by the dogma of Western societies, a great many lesbians and gay men have opted for an impositional identity that diminishes rather than multiplies their options. Though it is called a "gay identity," it is largely shaped either by heterosexuals or by a defenisve homosexual response to homophobia and hetercentrism. One often-voiced criticism of gay activism is the observation that people who have been marginalized, who have been turned into outsiders, have only two choices—to be themselves as individuals or to retreat into *alienation as a lifestyle,* becoming victims in a subculture that survives on the rhetoric of victimization.

The creation of a "gay community" was founded not only on political expediency, it was also the result of the effort to reduce the tension among highly diverse lesbians and gay men, attempting to put an end to the inclination of the members of one gay group to rebuff the members of another. The idea of community was supposed to bring to an end the inclination to designate certain groups as outsiders among outsiders. Much as African Americans once debated who and what is "really" black, gays have argued about what is and what is not truly gay. The aim of identity politics is always the same: to homogranize a highly diversified population, to create an identity not out of variety but out of a politically correct conformity. From the beginning of gay liberation the political effort has been aimed at stopping gay people from rejecting other gay people because they do or do not wear leather harnesses or because they do or do not wear sweaters, because they do or do not wear lipstick. The political ethics of the movement were supposed to make it unacceptable for people to judge lesbians and gay men on the basis of whether they were butch or fem. Activists hoped to create a cohesive and accepting community despite all the intermingling of vastly dissimilar persons and attitudes. That agenda has not been very successful. The schisms are still explicit and unpleasant between drag queens, leathermen, pedophiles, transsexuals, bisexuals, fetishists, lipstick lesbians, butch lesbians, and a great many of the mutually exclusive categories of homosexual identities. As a result of these tensions within the ghettoized world of homosexuals, the alienated gay community has steadfastly made aliens of its own, in a curious mimicry of the dominant society's rejection of people who are different.

Gay political and intellectual organizations and publications, which are fully aware of the disparities and antagonisms within the gay community, are required to debate what kind of homosexuals are "acceptable" and which are "unacceptable." For instance, there are the churlish debates about the acceptability or unacceptableness of pedophile groups, such as Men Who Love Boys, which have been sources of enormous conflict within various ethical schemes of the gay world. It is commendable that a group of denigrated people should valiantly attempt to denigrate no one. But such an admirable ethical position often fails among marginal groups that have been taught far more about self-contempt than self-confidence. The tension between self-contempt and self-confidence has greatly fragmented gay political efforts. If we accept the invented definition of homosexuality that has categorized people as child molesters, queers, leather freaks, queens, dykes, she-males, or sadomasochists, it is likely that we will have to continue debating that specific kinds of "homosexual" behaviors are unacceptable and which are acceptable. We will find ourselves in the airless solipsism of a group identity, with its paranoia and single-issue policies, its irrational allegiances and its self-defeating psychology of "victimization"—a suffixation that results from the admirable but contradictory effort to be both inclusive and conformist.

When people accept the dominant society's definition of them as a "outsiders," they are likely to act out the biblical drama of Noah, trying to fit two of every possible fellow-deviant into their identity ark. Or, conversely, they become gay by default, and homosexuality becomes an extension of mainstream culture—the spare tire of the Rolls Royce of heterosexuality. Both of these approaches to marginality are perilous. The debate that results from trying to be inclusive tends to suggest that "normal" homosexuals are attempting to oust "abnormal" homosexuals, spotlighting and confirming straight stereotypes of "abnormal behaviors." The conservative effort to mainstream homosexuality by excluding people whose conduct is considered unacceptable is likely to make being gay not an identity but a tolerated aberration. In both agendas, conservative and progressive, the result too easily provides a highly divisive mechanism allowing homophobes to manipulate both the perceptions and the interactions of the gay community. Though it may sound a bit like political banter, it remains that colonialism has always defined *others* either as aliens or as members of a reluctantly assimilated lower class. When the Department of the Interior was allocating Indian reservations, it required the Shoshone and Arapaho, who had been enemies for generations, to share the same land. This combining of incompatible people into one "group" was a cunning ploy, because when people are busy fighting with one another they have little energy to fight their real adversaries. What the Department of the Interior fully grasped was its Machiavellian power to impose an identity on incompatible people who, somehow, accepted both the idea of their oneness and the experience of their incompatibility as destiny.

The conservative inclination to create an exclusive rather than inclusive gay community attempts to dodge questions about the essential character and identity of gayness. Conversely, the progressive effort to be inclusive rather than exclusive about gay identity tends to raise profound questions about the highly diverse "nature of homosexuality." During the youth movement of the 1960s, we saw this same fragmentation among politicos who wanted to change the system and hippies who simply wanted to get stoned and "do their own thing" because they believed that the system could not be changed. Activists like the members of the Weathermen were so intent on their group identity and their political attack on the Establishment that, for at least a few days in 1969, they championed Charles Manson as "a hero of the People's Revolution," rather than realizing that he was a nutcase.

Long before Manson's crime, the media had been searching for the embodiment of the drugged out, demonic, hippie-devil. The same process is at work in regard to homosexuality, evidenced by the media and fundamentalist focus on the most outrageous or nonconformist participants at Gay Pride activities. In this way, the "group" somehow becomes responsible for the most exploitative characterizations of its "members." Consequently, many progressive members of the gay community are convinced that they *must* identify with every manifestation of "gayness," even if they cannot grasp the validity of certain behaviors any better than the media and fundamentalists. At the same time, conservative members of the gay community attempt to set up standards that exclude those whom they regard as offensive.

The burden of group identities can be unbearable. A Jewish friend told me that his grandmother reacted to news of the Kennedy assassination by mournfully exclaiming, "My God, I hope a Jew didn't do it!"

Why should the ethnicity of an assassin matter? Because in a bigoted society such things matter a great deal.

It is this same sense of group paranoia that overwhelmed the gay and lesbian community when we learned about the crimes of Jeffrey Dahmer. Dahmer became the Charles Manson of homosexuality. The homophobic queer homicidal maniac; the cannibalistic pervert our parents had warned us about. The *us* who is not *us*! And yet, by some people's definition of "gay men," Dahmer had *somehow* become one of us. We had to try to find a place for him in the homosexual ark. Lesbians and gay men found themselves in the unacceptable position of having to explain that when Dahmer committed his heinous series of crimes, he was not acting out his homosexuality any more than Richard Speck was acting out his heterosexuality when he murdered eight nurses in Chicago.

Ultimately heterosexuality did become a central aspect of Speck's trial. His attorneys argued that their client couldn't help his aggressive and murderous crime because he bore an extra Y chromosome, associated with criminality by several sociobiologists. In short, the attorneys claimed that, biologically speaking, Speck was *too* heterosexual. As it turned out, Speck was a "normal" XY male. But the dangerous political implications of the legal manipulation of a sociobiological genetic theory cannot be underestimated.

Despite all the biological strategy of the Speck trial, the media don't describe straight criminals as heterosexuals. They even make a tolerable attempt to avoid mentioning the ethnicity of non-white offenders. Yet they consistently refer to sex offenders who are gay as *homosexuals*.

The treacherous hierarchial view of sexual orientation has forced gay people to decide whether to announce or conceal their sexual orientation. Despite political slogans about the virtues of "coming out," the decision whether or not to be openly gay is exceptionally difficult. No matter how vigorously we have attempted to redefine the term "homosexuality," it still has the built-in pathological context as a distortion of heterosexuality. Homosexuality is not about being someone. It is, on the contrary, about *not* being what one should be, namely, a heterosexual. We speak of ourselves as homosexuals only because our orientation has been given a name that doesn't designate what we are but what we have failed to be.

Probably one of the many reasons some people are reluctant to reveal their homosexuality publicly is because they are uncomfortable with an arbitrary definition of who and what they are and with whom they do or do not share their identity. For instance, the openly gay novelist Djuna Barnes deeply resented being called a lesbian, not, apparently, because of any moral proprieties or because of her social coyness, but because the categorical description of her sexuality seemed to her too loaded with unacceptable preconceptions.

In the *New York Times Book Review*,[1] Miranda Seymour discussed the sexuality of famed author Djuna Barnes: "*Nightwood* led many of Barnes's admirers to suppose she was an evangelist for lesbianism. Given that the novel was devoted to an obsessive love affair between two women, Lady Ottoline Morell could hardly be blamed for writing to praise Barnes's courage in defending same-sex love. Barnes was furious. She had never regarded herself as a lesbian."

What seems clear to many gay people and to even the most avid essentialists is that there is no definitive identity called "homosexuality" except for the one invented by heterosexuals. Willingly or not, the fact that a group of highly diverse people have been defined as "homosexuals" has made it both politically expedient and psychologically useful to attempt to discover a basis of a community among those who have been arbitrarily defined as homosexual.

Every society tries to find itself in history. Europeans see themselves in the achievements of ancient Greece. African Americans identify with primordial Africa, at a time when Lucy and her kin began their first, perilous steps toward humanness. Jews see themselves in the Canaan of Abraham. And homosexuals find themselves in the heroes of all the great civilizations of the past. These historical presumptions about a congruent ancestry are a vital part of all cultures. They are also elements of a group identity that inevitably leads to ethnocentricity. The problem with the historicizing of a particular group's sense of identity is that the group often invents an ancestry based on cultural imagination rather than historical data. Homosexuals, like most distinctively modern populations, cannot truly confirm themselves through the prestige of a legendary past because they can't readily find themselves in history. For anyone who has made a solemn search of history it is clear that whoever we are today is not necessarily who we were in the past.

When Alcibiades spoke in Plato's *Symposium* about his love of Socrates, did he mean what we mean when we speak of love today? When people saw Alcibiades and Socrates strolling down the paved streets of Athens, what did they think and what did they say? We don't know the answers to these questions, any more than we know what the ancient people of the high Andes (whom we arbitrarily call Moche and Chavin) called themselves. We know very little about how the Greeks experienced themselves. How can we possibly speak of Socrates as our kin? We know almost nothing about ancient Greek music; so how can we know anything about a Greek philosopher of almost twenty-five hundred years ago? We don't even know exactly how the Greeks performed their great plays. Specialists have painstakingly studied dancing figures painted on more than a thousand Hellenic vases, but still they don't have any idea exactly how the Greeks danced.[2] So how can we possibly know how they made love?

What we see in the past is too often what we believe we see in the present. In the murals of Pompeii, in the ancestral carvings of the Luba of central Africa, in Japanese prints, in the rock paintings of Australia, we find a constant repetition of a grandiose organ psychoanalysts and anthropologists call "the phallus"—an exaggerated endowment so immense that it suggests a symbolic organ rather than one with any anatomical significance. Whatever the meanings of the images of an exaggeratedly large phallus, it might appear, on the basis of worldwide evidence today, that "a large penis would render a man more manly," Thomas Laqueur remarks in his book *Making Sex*. We know, however, that the ancient Greeks had quite the opposite point of view, that certainly nullifies one of the most proclaimed twentieth-century clichés about the sexual taste of gay men. According to Laqueur,

> A large penis was thought comic in ancient Greek art and drama, appropriate to satyrs, while the preferred size was small and delicate: "little prick" (*posthion*) was among Aristophanes' terms of endearment. Young athletes in Athens tied down the glans with a leather string, apparently for cosmetic reasons, to make the male genitals look small.

This attitude about male genitals is confirmed by countless idealized Hellenic sculptures of athletes. On the other hand, one glance at the male stars of thousands of hours of both straight and gay videos makes it absolutely clear that things have measurably changed.

What these examples of cultural relativism suggest is that few perspectives are truly transcultural and transhistorical, even those that appear to be most fundamentally human. There are a great many lesbians and gay men who are fully aware of the staggering social, philosophical, and sexual differences between the endless variety of people cataloged as homosexuals. At the same time, most lesbians and gay men are also aware that the problem homosexuals face is not a matter of their own diverse sexuality behaviors but the political pressures created by the homophobic attitudes about gay people. The historian of sexuality Jeffrey Weeks has said that sexual identity is a creation built through choices laid out by history. As such, biology simply limits the choices, it doesn't determine them. Weeks has asked some fascinating questions:

> Why has modern culture been so concerned with the details of individuals' sexual behavior, searched out in the way we look, the ways we dress, the ways we wave our hands or cross our feet, our ability or not to whistle, the true secrets of our being? Why does freedom of the individual, the cornerstone of Western values, always stop short of sexual freedom?

By accepting the category of "homosexuality," those who are presumably described by it are caught up in somebody else's debate, and are not engaged in a discussion about their own attitudes about identity.

What do drag queens have in common with leathermen? What relationship exists between transvestites and transsexuals, who seem fundamentally as different as homosexuals are supposed to be different from heterosexuals? A transvestite actor named Holly Woodland told me in an interview in the 1970s that she is a boy who likes pretending to be a woman. The incentive for Holly was "make-believe" and "dressing up." When I asked her if she would prefer to be a female, she was both insulted and amused. "Of course not!" she exclaimed. "What would be the fun in that?"

What is the difference between a straight transvestite and a gay transvestite? Do the clothes make the man or is a person straight or gay simply because of his *motive* for wearing the women's clothes? If we look at transvestitism strictly from a heterocentric point of view, the fascination with dressing up becomes less significant than the dimorphic gender imperative—whether a transvestite likes to have sex with men or with women.

A transsexual is a person who does not want to dress up. The standard rationale of sex-change surgery and therapy is the implication that a man or a woman feels like he or she is living in the wrong body, a claim that may or may not have a great deal to do with the persistent social pressure to naturalize desire. Whatever the motives, transsexuals and gay transvestites claim they are influenced by quite different motives. But, because of the negative mandate of sexual normalization insinuated by heterosexual society, it is extremely difficult to grasp the fundamental motives driving the choice of those who undergo sex-change operations.

Why are men who sleep with other men considered gay, while many men are considered heterosexual when they are part of a large subculture of males who are attracted to "chicks with dicks"—she-males who have female breasts and feminized bodies but retain male genitalia? What sense of sexual identity does a she-male have in common with a straight transvestite, a gay transvestite, a gay hunk, a lipstick lesbian, a leatherman, a diesel dyke, or a child molester who abuses both girls and boys because he is attracted to children without regard for their gender? What does a gay sadomasochist have in common with a straight sadomasochist? Why is sadomasochistic behavior less an issue than the gender of the person with whom the S/M act is performed? What is more fundamental from a behavioral point of view, the motive of sadomasochism or the sex of the person with whom the sadomasochist engages in S/M acts? Why, historically speaking, has a male in female clothing been a form of buffoonery in the West, while a woman in men's clothing usually induces a silent astonishment? Why was the male attire of Dietrich, Garbo, and Hepburn so easily accepted in a field as socially conservative as the Hollywood motion picture industry? How was it possible for Linda Hunt to play a male character brilliantly in the film *The Year of Living Dangerously,* while the only time males play "women" in films is when they are making fools of themselves or portraying drag queens?

There appear to be few substantial answers to these confounding questions despite the fact that all variety of same-sex behaviors are somehow defined as homosexuality and all opposite-sex behaviors are somehow squeezed into the definition of heterosexuality.

The greatest distance between people is not space but culture. It is culture that sets up the boundaries by which we judge others and by which others judge us. What makes Africans distinctive is their culture, not their color or their other superficial physical features. What distinguishes Jews is not their Semitic origins, but their three-thousand-year-old culture, ever-changing but kept alive through a social malleability that made Jews capable of reacting creatively to their ceaseless alienation.

Kinship is the basis of culture, because it is only among kin that distinctions of language, art, and faith are perpetuated. Homosexuality does not constitute a kinship group. It does not share a place of origin or a native language. It doesn't possess a distinctive ethnicity, a nationality, or a religious faith. It doesn't share a common political point of view. Yet it undoubtedly possesses its own modern culture—a ghetto culture born not of sexuality but of the sexual cleansing carried out with great conviction and zeal by heterosexuals.

Long before homosexuals were distinguished on the basis of their sexuality, they were primarily identified by their humanness. James Baldwin said that the word "community simply means our endless connection with, and responsibility for, each other." It is in these terms that we should celebrate the gay community—not as a group but as a coalition of diverse individuals who are *endlessly connected* simply because we must care about one another. This is the cultural and political lesson to be learned from the unique perspective of the outsider—to understand the self-defeating destiny of those who have won everything, but in the wake of their victories have somehow lost themselves.

History is written by victors, not victims. One of the most fascinating aspects of the twentieth century has been the efforts to rewrite history from the viewpoint of those long written out of history. If the story of the Western world is to be rewritten, Phillip Brett urges homosexuals to realize the enormous potential of their role as outsiders rather than politicize their history of victimization:

> For part of the very substance of accepting a gay identity in Western culture in our time is by implication the cultivation of that sense of difference, of not subscribing to the straight world's tendency to project itself onto everything it encounters and to assimilate everything to its own idea of itself, but instead valuing, exploring, and trying to understand different things, different people, and different ideas, in terms that are closer to the way in which *they* perceive *themselves*. It is, in other words, worth the risk.

If there is a value in the experience of alienation, it is the knowledge that adversity can be transformed into a process of self-invention. That psychological process is the most significant potential of the modern homosexual in the West. In the role of outsiders, lesbians and gay men have created an international secret language, outrageously overcompensative attitudes about the sexual majority, equally exaggerated ideas about gay identity, and a unique sense of life that idealizes alienation as the basis of a clandestine camaraderie that enables people to convert pain into passion that gives some small compensation and some sense of significance to the often futile experiences of being outsiders.

Considering the floundering world in which we live, that sense of significance is not a modest achievement. Norman Storm has provided a dismal picture of our late twentieth-century dilemma:

> The modern world that was invented around 1500 is coming to an end. It was then, roughly when America was discovered, that everything we associate with the modern era came to pass: printing, law, the nation-state. Now, all of that is at an end. We are

back to the medieval world of beggars, criminality, plagues, conflagrations, anarchy, and superstitions."

And yet, they say that we are made of stardust.

They say that our very flesh is created, molecule by molecule, from the remnants of some distant star that exploded cataclysmically and sent the components of our lives streaming through the cosmos. In the unthinkable fire of that cataclysmic death of a star we were born. The iron in our blood. The calcium in our bones. These precious particles of our lives are stardust.

When we look at one another we should see something so miraculous that we cannot be distracted by the wall of opinions, concepts, and dogma that always stands between us, forcing us to see something alien—when what we should be seeing is stardust.

Loren Eiseley exquisitely acknowledged the miracle of our lives:

This is what the mind of man is just beginning to achieve . . . a little microcosm, a replica of whatever it is that, from some unimaginable "outside," contains the universe and all the fractured bits of seeing which the world's creatures see. . . . I too am aware of the trunk that stretches loathsomely back of me along the floor. I too am a many-visaged thing that has climbed upward through the glitter of blue glacial nights. . . . I am the unfolding worm, the mud fish, the weird tree of Igdrasil shaping itself endlessly out of darkness toward the light. . . . And yet, if all life were to be swept from the world, leaving only its chemical components, no visitor from another star would be able to establish the reality of such a phantom. . . . Yet this is the same dust which, dead, quiescent, and unmoving, when taken up in the process known as life, hears music and responds to it, weeps bitterly over time and over loss.

The mythology that created our repressed society has long outlived the society it created. Until we are profoundly aware of that regressive mythology and how it is manifested in our lives, we cannot change it. And, until we change our myths, we cannot change our minds and so we cannot change our societies or our destinies. We must continue to repeat all of the atrocities of our interminable self-contempt.

Desire will always bear the history of its oppression. It cannot escape its reputation, because it cannot overcome its mythological past. It cannot disgorge itself from its disgust for itself. It cannot repudiate itself. But it also cannot quell its animal ferocity, because that ferocity is the marvelous and fearsome power that drives the process of life that produced us. Whatever else we may be, beasts or stardust, we are surely a momentary emanation of a natural process, which embraces every possibility of life without pity or malice or moral consternation. We may wish to be angels, but we cannot be angels because angels are the echoes of a fabulous innocence we have never possessed. There was no Eden except the Eden of our minds. And there was no paradise lost, except the paradise of our forsaken animality. All that remains are inimitable beasts who have miraculously dreamed themselves into their extraordinary and infinitesimal existence.

Our dream is always greater than our constraints. Homosexuality outrages many people because it defies their tenacious religious myths about naturalness and normality, about good and evil. Homosexuality haunts and fascinates the public conscience because it is feared as a latent and contagious matter of human choice and because it tells us something about ourselves we do not want to know. Yet, through all of this, homosexuality remains a profound metaphor of the unbounded possibilities of desire, just as homophobia persists as a symbol of the limits of our capacity to cherish one another.

Desire will never be completely contained or vanquished. It is a fire that burns at the very heart of whatever it is we mean when we speak of "life." It prowls through the shadows of all our days, flickering and smoldering. It secretly groans in our languid sleep, when our bodies have dominion over our minds, fanning into life the embers of our long ago, savage childhood. Its memory has left its footprints in our minds. And, if we dare to listen, it speaks to us of delights that know nothing of renunciation and evil. Our bodies remember. Only our minds forget. And we cannot change our minds until we change our mythologies.

Such change is the gift given to us by mythic heroes, who go into an exile of their own choosing, who leave all that is familiar and safe behind, who trick their way beyond the boundaries of their little mythologies so they may have a glimpse of all the possibilities of other ways of looking at the world.

For some, the adventure never begins. They hang behind with the brutes, because it takes enormous courage to step out of the life that others want us to live.

For others the adventure never ends.

And for still others, there is no choice whether or not to accept the call of the quest, because exile is our only homeland.

It is here that the adventure finds its heros—outside in the dark, in the woods where familiar landmarks disappear and the pavement ends, beyond the forbidden mountains, and more distant than all the charted skies. The gate of conformity opens to the hero, leading the way toward a horizon where the light dies in the mouth of darkness. But it is not the darkness that frightens the hero. What is truly terrifying is the realization that the hero's quest must be undertaken *alone*.

No group or family or community can go on the quest for us. No one can give us an identity. It is something we must invent in the darkness within ourselves. There are no boundaries for those who are outsiders. There is only the unbounded world of possibility. Alienation forces us out of our home community. But in exile we can discover a home in ourselves. All at once we know that we must make the choice of whether to create or destroy ourselves.

I don't want to seem to be idealizing alienation or suggesting that social rejection and discrimination make people smart or strong or artistic. But I do hope to repeat the ancient aphorism that tells us that only by being pushed from the nest do we discover the possibility of flight. In the tension of alienation is an impetus that has always brought out the best as well as the worst in human beings. My purpose is to propose that, as a response to sexual bigotry, there have been a great many brilliant achievements made by gay men, lesbians, and by all *others*. Undoubtedly not all outcasts are mythic heros, but the heroism of the mythic journey has always been one of the most exceptional adventures of *Homo sapiens*.

In this sense, alienation is a gift. It is the *only* doorway that exists in closed societies. It is a doorway always left open, a fracture in the barrier that stands between ourselves and ourselves.

This affirmation of the lives of outsiders serves those for whom alienation has always been a castigation rather than a gift. It is the gift of those who stand in an ideal isolation, astronomers of those deepest spaces where they flash their desperate messages across the infinite space that separates all peoples.

And yet "homosexuality" is an invention intended to silence and diminish us, to extinguish the fire that allows us to know one another. Western religion and science have conspired to isolate and denigrate us. Heterosexuality is a concept that attempts to denounce possibilities that it cannot and will not imagine. The categorization of "homosexuality" is supposed to deprive us of our humanness. It is a Machiavellian devise that attempts to send us into hiding. Instead, remarkably, it has sent us on a journey we might never have dared. It forced us to be different so we could learn the unimaginable lessons of difference. Jean Cocteau, that mannered little Frenchman with dainty hands and an effeminate voice, perfectly understood the lessons we learn as aliens. And so he said: "What other people reproach you for—cultivate. It is yourself."

Perhaps that is also the lesson of the stardust that glistens at the core of our existence. Out of the death of a star we have the opportunity to invent ourselves without timidity or apology. Because of a cataclysmic cosmic disaster, we have this one chance to imagine at least the possibility of being whatever it is we mean when we use that most mysterious of all words . . . *myself.*

NOTES

CHAPTER 1

1. See Highwater, *Language of Vision*, chap. 16.

CHAPTER 4

1. "The Barna Report" (January 1992), *Time*, March 19, 1993.
2. *American Sociological Review*, December 1992, according to *Newsweek*, November 29, 1993.
3. See Highwater, "Body as Sin," in *Myth and Sexuality*.
4. William Butler Yeats, "The Second Coming."

CHAPTER 5

1. See Highwater, "Tewa Rain-Power Ceremony," in *Ritual of the Wind*.
2. See Highwater, "Body as Lover," in *Myth and Sexuality*.

CHAPTER 6

1. Alexander Vilenkin, *Discover,* "The Mediocre Universe," February 1996.
2. "Sex as Suicide," *Time*, January 15, 1996.
3. *Discover,* "The End of Self," April 1996.
4. Frank Sulloway, "The Trouble with Sigmund," *Newsweek*, December 18, 1995.
5. *Time*, "Science, God, and Man," December 28, 1992.
6. *The Advocate*, "The Gay Gene," December 26, 1995.
7. *Time*, "Gay Genes: Can Homosexuality Really Be Inherited?" November 13, 1995.
8. "Nature Plus Nurture," *Newsweek*, November 13, 1995.
9. Chandler Burr, "The Destiny of You: Once a Gay Gene Is Found, Can Gene Therapy Be Far Behind?" *The Advocate*, December 26, 1995.

CHAPTER 7

1. See Senior, *The Way Down and Out*.
2. Tzara, *Dada Manifesto on Feeble Love and Bitter Love*.
3. See Highwater, *Language of Vision*.

CHAPTER 8

1. See Stambolian and Marks, *Homosexualities and French Literature*.

2. Stanley Kauffman, "Homosexuality and Its Disguise," *New York Times*, January 23, 1966. The homophobic attack of gay playwrights had begun five years earlier, on November 5, 1961, when *New York Times* drama critic Howard Taubman wrote a feature entitled "Not What It Seems: Homosexual Motif Gets Heterosexual Guise." In the article, Taubman accused the same three acclaimed playwrights of intentionally portraying marriage negatively and portraying women as destroyers and sex maniacs.

3. W. H. Auden "Twelve Songs," from *Number Nine, Stop the Clock* (1936).

4. William Butler Yeats, "The Second Coming."

CHAPTER 9

1. Miranda Seymour, "Djuna: The Life and Work of Djuna Barnes," *New York Times Book Review*, November 26, 1995.

2. See Highwater, *Dance*.

BIBLIOGRAPHY

Abelove, Henry, Michele Aina Barale, and David M. Halperin, eds. *The Lesbian and Gay Studies Reader*. London: Routledge, 1993.

Ackroyd, Peter. *Dressing Up: Transvestism and Drag: The History of an Obsession*. New York: Simon and Schuster, 1979.

Aldridge, John. *After the Lost Generation*. New York: McGraw-Hill, 1951.

Altman, Denis. *Coming Out in the Seventies*. Boston: Alyson, 1981.

——— *Power and Community*. London: Tyalor & Francis, 1994.

Altman, Denis, Carole Vance, Martha Vicnus, Jeffrey Weeks, and others. *Homosexuality, Which Homosexuality?* London: GMP, 1989.

Appiah, Kwame Anthony. *In My Father's House*. New York: Oxford University Press, 1992.

Arbus, Diane. *Arbus*. Millertown: Aperture, 1972.

Arendt, Hannah. *The Life of the Mind*. Vol 1, *Thinking*; Vol 2, *Willing*. New York: Harcourt Brace Jovanovich, 1978.

Auden, W. H. *Complete Poems*. New York: Vintage, 1991.

Bailey, D. Sherwin. *Homosexuality and the Western Christian Tradition*. San Francisco: Shoe String Press, 1955.

Barkow, Jerome H., Leda Cosmides, and John Tooby, eds. *The Adapted Mind*. New York: Oxford University Press, 1992.

Barthes, Rolland. *Sade, Fourier, Loyola*. Berkeley: University of California Press, 1976.

Bataille, Georges. *Erotism: Death and Sensuality*. San Francisco: City Lights Books, 1986.

———. *Literature and Evil*. London: Marion Boyars, 1990.

Bawer, Bruce. *A Place at the Table*. New York: Simon and Schuster, 1994.

———. "Canon Fodder." *The Advocate*, May 14, 1995.

Becker, Howard S. *Outsiders: Studies in the Sociology of Deviance*. New York: Free Press, 1963.

Bentley, Eric. See Stambolian, George and Marks, Elaine

Bersani, Leo. *Homos*. Cambridge, Mass.: Harvard University Press, 1995.

Bhabha, Homi. "Of Mimicry and Man." In *Politics and Ideology*, ed. James Donald and Stuart Hall New York: Open University Press, 1986.

Bingham, Roger. *The Human Quest*. Melnthorpe: Cicerone Press, 1995.

Blei, Franz. See Rahv, Philip

Bodmer, Walter, and Robin McKie. *The Book of Man: The Human Genome Project and the Quest to Discover Our Genetic Heritage*. New York: Scribner, 1994.

Boswell, John. *Christianity, Social Tolerance, and Homosexuality*. Chicago: University of Chicago Press, 1980.

Boynton, Robert S. "The New Intellectuals." *Atlantic Monthly*, February 1995.

Bramly, Serge. *Leonardo: The Artist and the Man*. London: Penguin, 1991.

Brett, Philip, Elizabeth Wood, and Gary C. Thomas, eds. *Queering the Pitch*. London: Routledge, 1994.

Bronski, Michael. *Culture Clash: The Making of Gay Sensibility*. Boston: South End Press, 1984.

Brown, Donald. *Human Universals*, 1991.

Browning, Frank. *The Culture of Desire*. New York: Vintage, 1994.

Brownmiller, Susan. *Against Our Will: Men, Women, and Rape*. New York: Simon and Schuster, 1975.

Bryce, James. See Muller, Herbert

Burton, Gary. " TK." *The Advocate*, May 2, 1995.

Buruma, Ian. *A Japanese Mirror*. London: Penguin, 1984.

Butler, Judith. *Bodies That Matter*. New York: Routledge, 1993.

Byne, William. "The Biological Evidence Challenged." *Scientific American*, May 1994.

Campbell, Joseph. *The Hero with a Thousand Faces*. Princeton: Princeton University Press, 1949.

———. *The Masks of God: Oriental Mythology*. New York: Viking, 1962.

———. *Transformations of Myth Through Time*. New York: Van der Marck Editions, 1990.

———. *Conversation with Joseph Campbell and Jamake Highwater* [video documentary]. New York: Cinema Guild, 1986.

Camus, Albert. *Notebooks, 1935–1942*. New York: Knopf, 1962.

Casson, Lionel. *Mysteries of the Past*. New York: American Heritage, 1977.

Chauncey, George. *Gay New York*. New York: Basic Books, 1994.

"The Church Search." *Time*, April 5, 1993.

Clark, Stephen R. L. "A Map of Everything." *New York Times Book Review*, September 24, 1995.

Conner, Randy P. *Blossom of Bone*. San Francisco: HarperSan Francisco, 1993.

Conrad, Joseph. *Heart of Darkness*. New York: Modern Library, 1902.

Coomaraswamy, Ananda. *The Transformation of Nature in Art*. New York: Dover, 1934.

Cooper, Emmanuel. *The Sexual Perspective*. London: Routledge, 1994.

Core, Philip. *Camp: The Lie That Tells the Truth*. London: Plexus, 1984.

Cronin, Helena. "True Lies." *New York Times Book Review*, July 24, 1994.

Damasio, Antonio R.. *Descartes' Error: Emotion, Reason, and the Human Brain*. New York: Oxford University Press, 1994.

Dame, Joke. "Unveiled Voices." See Brett, Philip

Davies, Paul. *About Time*. New York: Simon and Schuster, 1995.

Davies, Paul, and John Briggin. *The Matter Myth*. New York: Simon and Schuster, 1992.

Dawkins, Richard. *The Selfish Gene*. Oxford: Oxford University Press, 1989.

De la Croix, Horst, and Richard G. Tansey, *Gardner's Art Through the Ages*. New York: Harcourt Brace Jovanovich, 1975.

De Montigny, Dumond. *Memoires historiques sur La Louisiane*. Paris: Luxembourg Memoir, 1753.

De Rougemont, Denis. *Love in the Western World*. New York: Pantheon, 1940.

Degler, Carl N. *In Search of Human Nature: The Decline and Revival of Darwinism in American Social Thought*. New York: Oxford University Press, 1991.

Delbanco, Andrew. *The Death of Satan*. New York: Simon and Schuster, 1995.

Dennet, Danield G. *Darwin's Dangerous Idea*. New York: Simon and Schuster, 1995.

Doig, Federico Kauffmann. *Sexual Behavior in Ancient Peru*. Lima: Kompaktos, 1979.

———. *Manual de arqueología peruana*. Lima: Peisa, 1980.

Dollimore, Jonathan. *Sexual Dissidence*. Oxford: Oxford University Press, 1991.

Douglas, Mary. *Natural Symbols*. New York: Pantheon, 1982.

———. *Purity and Danger*. London: Ark, 1985.

Downing, Christine. *Myths and Mysteries of Same-Sex Love*. New York: Crossroad Press, 1989.

Duberman, Martin. *About Time: Exploring the Gay Past*. New York: Meridian, 1991.

———. *Stonewall*. New York: Plume, 1993.

Duberman, Martin, Martha Vicinus, and George Chauncey, Jr. *Hidden from History*. New York: Meridian, 1989.

Dutton, Kenneth R. *The Perfectible Body: The Western Ideal of Male Physical Development*. New York: Continuum, 1995.

Durham, William. See Degler, Carl

Dyer, Richard. See Simpson, Mark

Eiseley, Loren. *The Star Thrower*. San Diego: Harcourt Brace Jovanovich, 1978.

Ellis, Havelock. *Sexual Inversion*. New York: Harcourt Brace Jovanovich, 1897.

Evans, Arthur. *The God of Ecstasy*. New York: St. Martin's Press, 1988.

Fiedler, Leslie. *Freaks: Myths and Images of the Secret Self*. New York: Anchor Books, 1978.

Ford, Clellan, and Frank A. Beach. See Encarta Encyclopedia, 1994.

Foucault, Michel. *The History of Sexuality*. New York: Pantheon, 1978.

Fowlie, Wallace. *Rimbaud and Jim Morrison*. Durham, N.C.: Duke University Press, 1994.

Freud, Sigmund. *Three Essays on the Theory of Sexuality*. London: Hogarth Press, 1905.

———. *The Letters of Sigmund Freud*. New York: Dover, 1961.

Fromm, Erich. *The Sane Society*. New York: Holt, 1955.

Fry, Roger. *Visions and Design*. London: Chatto and Windus, 1925.

Gates, Henry Louis, Jr. See Boynton Robert

Gimbutas, Marija. *Goddesses and Gods of Old Europe*. San Francisco: HarperSan Francisco, 1974.

Goethe, Johann Wolfgang von. See Brett, Philip.

Gooch, Brad. *City Poet: The Life and Times of Frank O'Hara*. New York: Knopf, 1993.

Gould, Stephen Jay. *Ever Since Darwin*. New York: Norton, 1977.

———. *The Panda's Thumb*. New York: Norton, 1980.

Graves, Robert, with Raphael Patai. *Hebrew Myths: The Book of Genesis*. New York: McGraw-Hill, 1963.

Greenberg, David F. *The Construction of Homosexuality*. Chicago: University of Chicago Press, 1998.

Halberstam, David. "Discovering Sex." *American Heritage*, May–June 1993.

Halperin, David M., John J. Winkler, and Froma I. Zeitlin, eds. *Before Sexuality*. Princeton: Princeton University Press, 1990.

Hauser, Arnold. *The Social History of Art*. Vol. 4. New York: Random House, 1951.

Hayman, Ronald. *Thomas Mann: A Biography*. New York: Scribner, 1995.

Heinrich, Bernd. "What Is Natural?" *Discover*, June 1994.

Heller, Erich. *The Basic Kafka*. New York: Pocket Books, 1979.

Helminiak, Daniel A. *What the Bible Really Says About Homosexuality*. San Francisco: Alamo Square Press, 1994.

Highwater, Jamake. *The Primal Mind*. New York: Harper & Row, 1981.

———. *Ritual of the Wind*. New York: Viking/Van der Marck Editions, 1984.

———. *Myth and Sexuality*. New York: New American Library, 1990.

———. *The Language of Vision*. New York: Grove Press, 1994.

———. *Dance: Rituals of Experience*. New York: Oxford University Press, 1996.

Hocquenghem, Gay. *Homosexual Desire*. Durham, N.C.: Duke University Press, 1972.

Hughes, Robert. "Behold the Stone Age." *Time*, February 13, 1995.

———. *Culture of Complaint*. New York: Oxford University Press, 1993.

Huxley, Aldous. *Time Must Have a Stop*. New York: McGraw-Hill, 1944.

Johnson, George. *Fire in the Mind*. San Francisco: HarperSan Francisco, 1995.

Kafka, Franz. "Before the Law." In *Parables and Paradoxes*. New York: Schocken Books, 1935.

Kaplan, Louise J. *Female Perversions*. New York: Doubleday, 1991.

Katz, Jonathan Ned. *Gay American History*. New York: Crowell, 1976.

———*The Invention of Heterosexuality*. New York: Dutton, 1995.

Kauffman, Stanley. "Homosexuality and Its Guises." *New York Times*, January 23, 1966.

Kevles, Dan. "The Gay Brain." *New Yorker*, April 3, 1995.

Kinsey, Alfred. *Sexual Behavior in the Human Male*. New York: Hall, 1948.

Koestenbaum, Wayne. *The Queen's Throat*. London: Penguin, 1993.

Kristeva, Julia. *Strangers to Ourselves*. New York: Columbia University Press, 1991.

Kuhn, Thomas S. *The Structure of Scientific Revolutions*. Chicago: University of Chicago Press, 1970.

Laing, R. D. *The Politics of Experience*. New York: Penguin, 1963.

Laqueur, Thomas. *Making Sex*. Cambridge, Mass.: Harvard University Press, 1990.

Lauritsen, John, and David Thorstad. *The Early Homosexual Rights Movement*. New York: Times Change Press, 1974.

Lehman, Peter. *Running Scared*. Philadelphia: Temple University Press, 1993.

Lemonick, Michael D. "Glimpses of the Mind." *Time*, July 17, 1995.

LeVay, Simon, and Dean H. Hamer. "Evidence for a Biological Influence in Male Homosexuality." *Scientific American*, May 1994.

Lever, Maurice. *Sade: A Biography*. New York: Harcourt Brace Jovanovich, 1993.

Levine, Laura. "Men in Women's Clothing." *Criticism*, no. 28, 1986.

Llinas, Rudolfo. See Lemonick, Michael D.

Mairowitz, Zane. *Introducing Kafka*. Boston: Totem Books, 1994.

Mann, William J. "Perfect Bound." *Frontier*, January 13, 1995.

Marcel, Anthony. *Discover*, January 1985.

Mass, Larence D. "A Conversation with Ned Rorem." See Brett, Philip

Masters, Brian. *Killing for Company*. New York: Random House, 1993.

Maxwell, Kenneth. *The Sex Imperative: An Evolutionary Tale of Sexual Survival*. New York: Lenum Press, 1994.

Mercatante, Anthony S. *Good and Evil: Mythology and Folklore*. New York: Dutton, 1978.

Merleau-Ponty, Maurice. *Phenomenology of Perception*. New York: Humanities Press, 1962.

Messner, Michael A. *Power at Play: Sports and the Problem of Masculinity*. Boston: Beacon Press, 1992.

Meyer, Moe, ed. *The Politics and Poetics of Camp*. London: Routledge, 1994.

Miller, Henry. *The Books in My Life*. New York: Grove Press, 1951.

Miller, James. *The Passion of Michel Foucault*. New York: Anchor Books, 1993.

Miller, Neil. "Background Search." *The Advocate*, June 13, 1995.

Miller, Stephen G. *Arete*. Chicago: Ares, 1979.

Millett, Kate. *Sexual Politics*. New York: Avon Books, 1969.

Muller, Herbert. *The Uses of the Past*. New York: Oxford University Press, 1957.

"Nature Plus Nurture," *Newsweek*, November 13, 1995.

Nehamas, Alexander. *Nietzsche: Life as Literature*. Cambridge, Mass.: Harvard University Press, 1985.

Osborne, Lawrence. *The Poison Embrace*. New York: Vintage, 1993.

Osborne, Robert E. *Aesthetics and Art Theory*. New York: Dutton, 1970.

Pagels, Elaine. *Adam, Eve, and the Serpent*. New York: Random House, 1988.

Palmer, R. R., and Joel Colton. *A History of the Modern World*. New York: Random House, 1971.

Panofsky, Erwin. *Studies in Iconology*. New York: Harper & Row, 1992.

Pener, Degen. "The Games Men Play." *Out*, June 1994.

Penfield, Wilder. *The Mystery of the Mind*. Princeton: Princeton University Press, 1975.

Pronger, Brian. *The Arena of Masculinity*. New York: St. Martin's Press, 1990.

Rahv, Philip. Introduction to *Selected Stories of Franz Kafka*. New York: Random House, 1948.

Rajchman, John. *Truth and Eros*. New York: Routledge, 1991.

Rawson, Hugh. *Wicked Words*. New York: Crown, 1989.

Roberts, J. M. *History of the World*. New York: Knopf, 1976.

Rorem, Ned. *The Nantucket Diary*. New York: Ecco Press, 1987.

Rutledge, Leigh W. *The Gay Decades*. New York: Plume Books, 1992.

"Science, God, and Man." *Time*, December 28, 1992.

Senior, John. *The Way Down and Out*. See Shattuck, Roger

Seznec, Jean. *The Survival of the Pagan Gods*. Princeton: Princeton University Press, 1972.

Shattuck, Roger. *The Banquet Years: Origins of the Avant-Garde in France*. New York: Vintage, 1968.

Shipman, Pat. *The Evolution of Racism*. New York: Simon and Schuster, 1994.

Silverberg, James. See Degler, Carl

Simpson, Mark. *Male Impersonators*. New York: Routledge, 1994.

Smith, Bruce R. *Homosexual Desire in Shakespears' England*. Chicago: University of Chicago Press, 1991.

Sontag, Susan. *Illness as Metaphor*. New York: Vintage, 1978.

Stambolian, George, and Elaine Marks, eds. *Homosexualities and French Literature*. Ithaca: Cornell University Press, 1979.

Steele, Valerie. *Fetish: Fashion, Sex, and Power*. New York: Oxford University Press, 1996.

Steiner, George. "Eros and Idiom." In *On Difficulty and Other Essays*. New York: Oxford University Press, 1978.

Stent, Gunther S. *Paradoxes of Progress*. San Francisco: Freeman, 1978.

Stevens, Wallace. *Opus Posthumous*. Princeton: Princeton University Press, 1950.

Stewart, Steve. *Gay Hollywood: Film and Video Guide*. Laguna Hills, Calif.: Companion, 1993.

Stoppard, Tom. *Hapgood*. London: Faber & Faber, 1994.

Storm, Norman. "A Plague on the West." *Sunday Times*, (London) April 17, 1994.

Tanner, Michael. "Rigours and Raptures," *Times Literary Supplement*, November 5, 1993.

Tennant, F. R. *The Sources of the Doctrines of the Fall and Original Sin*. New York: Schocken Books, 1968.

Theweleit, Klaus. *Male Fantasies*, Vol 2. *Male Bodies*. Minneapolis: University of Minnesota Press, 1989.

Thorne, Tony. *The Dictionary of Contemporary Slang*. New York: Pantheon, 1990.

Trigg, Roger. See Degler, Carl

Tripp, C. A. *The Homosexual Matrix*. New York: Meridian Books, 1987.

Tyler, Parker. *Screening the Sexes*. New York: Anchor Books, 1972.

Tzara, Tristan. *Dada Manifesto on Feeble Love and Bitter Love*, 1921. See Wilson, Edmund

Waley, Arthur. *The No Plays of Japan*. New York: Grove Press, 1920.

Weber, Eugen. *The Western Traditon*.[Annenburg/CPB television series], 1989.

Weeks, Jeffrey. *Sexuality*. London: Tavistock, 1973.

Weisberger, Edward. *The Spiritual in Art: Abstract Painting, 1890–1985*. Los Angeles: Los Angeles Museum of Art, 1986.

Wertheim, Margaret. *Pythagoras' Trousers*. New York: Random House, 1995.

Whyte, L. L. *The Next Development in Man*. New York: Holt, 1948.

Wilson, Edmund. *Axel's Castle*. New York: Scribner, 1969.

Wilson, Edward O. *Sociobiology*. Cambridge, Mass.: Harvard University Press, 1975.

———. *On Human Nature*. Cambridge, Mass.: Harvard University Press, 1978.

———. "Article," *New York Times Magazine*, October 12, 1975.

Wright, Robert. *The Moral Animal*. New York: Random House, 1994.

Yates, Frances. *Giordano Bruno and the Hermetic Tradition*. Chicago: University of Chicago Press, 1964.

Zajonc, Arthur. *Catching the Light*. New York: Bantam Books, 1993.

Zukav, Gary. *The Dancing Wu Li Masters*. New York: Morrow, 1980.

Zweig, Paul. *The Heresy of Self-Love*. Princeton: Princeton University Press, 1968.

INDEX